Politics of the Russian Language Beyond Russia

Russian Language and Society Series

Series Editor: Lara Ryazanova-Clarke, University of Edinburgh
This series of academic monographs and edited volumes consists of important scholarly accounts of interrelationships between Russian language and society, and aims to foster an opinion-shaping 'linguistic turn' in the international scholarly debate within Russian Studies, and to develop new sociolinguistic and linguo-cultural perspectives on Russian. The series embraces a broad scope of approaches including those advanced in sociolinguistics, rhetoric, critical linguistics, (critical) discourse analysis, linguistic anthropology, politics of language, language policy and related and interdisciplinary areas.

Series Editor
Lara Ryazanova-Clarke is Professor of Russian and Sociolinguistics at the University of Edinburgh.

Editorial Board
Professor Lenore Grenoble (University of Chicago)
Professor John Joseph (University of Edinburgh)
Professor Aneta Pavlenko (University of Oslo)
Professor Vladimir Plungian (Institute of Russian Language/Institute of Linguistics, Russian Academy of Sciences)
Professor Patrick Seriot (Université de Lausanne)
Dr Alexei Yurchak (University of California, Berkeley)

Titles available in the series:
The Russian Language Outside the Nation, ed. Lara Ryazanova-Clarke
Discourses of Regulation and Resistance: Censoring Translation in the Stalin and Khrushchev Era Soviet Union, Samantha Sherry
French and Russian in Imperial Russia: Language Use among the Russian Elite, ed. Derek Offord, Lara Ryazanova-Clarke, Vladislav Rjéoutski and Gesine Argent
French and Russian in Imperial Russia: Language Attitudes and Identity, ed. Derek Offord, Lara Ryazanova-Clarke, Vladislav Rjéoutski and Gesine Argent
Russian Speakers in Post-Soviet Latvia, Ammon Cheskin
Public Debate in Russia: Matters of (Dis)order, Nikolai Vakhtin and Boris Firsov
Language on Display: Writers, Fiction and Linguistic Culture in Post-Soviet Russia, Ingunn Lunde
Politics of the Russian Language Beyond Russia, ed. Christian Noack

Visit the Russian Language and Society website at
www.edinburghuniversitypress.com/series/RLAS

Politics of the Russian Language Beyond Russia

Edited by Christian Noack

Edinburgh University Press is one of the leading university presses in the UK. We publish academic books and journals in our selected subject areas across the humanities and social sciences, combining cutting-edge scholarship with high editorial and production values to produce academic works of lasting importance. For more information visit our website: edinburghuniversitypress.com

© editorial matter and organisation Christian Noack, 2021, 2023
© the chapters their several authors, 2021, 2023

Edinburgh University Press Ltd
The Tun – Holyrood Road
12(2f) Jackson's Entry
Edinburgh EH8 8PJ

First published in hardback by Edinburgh University Press 2021

Typeset in 11/13 Monotype Ehrhardt by
Servis Filmsetting Ltd, Stockport, Cheshire

A CIP record for this book is available from the British Library

ISBN 978 1 4744 6379 9 (hardback)
ISBN 978 1 4744 6380 5 (paperback)
ISBN 978 1 4744 6381 2 (webready PDF)
ISBN 978 1 4744 6384 3 (epub)

The right of Christian Noack to be identified as the editor of this work has been asserted in accordance with the Copyright, Designs and Patents Act 1988, and the Copyright and Related Rights Regulations 2003 (SI No. 2498).

Contents

List of Tables	vii
List of Contributors	viii
Acknowledgements	xii

Introduction: Language and Culture in Russia's Soft Power Toolbox   1
Christian Noack

1. The 'Russian World' and Ukraine   19
   Michał Wawrzonek

2. Russian in Belarus: A Feature of Belarusian Identity or Moscow's 'Trojan Horse'?   45
   Mark Brüggemann

3. Between Emotions and Pragmatism: The Russian Language in Kazakhstan and the 'Russian Factor'   68
   Natalya Kosmarskaya and Igor Savin

4. Speakers of Russian in Ireland: 'What unites us is language, but in all other respects we are different'   92
   Feargus Denman

5. Media Use of Russian Speakers in Germany   120
   Olga Tikhomirova

6. The Role of Russian for Digital Diplomacy in Moldova   138
   Dmitry Yagodin

7. Promoting Russian Higher Education   161
   Sirke Mäkinen

8. Stable or Variable Russian? Standardisation versus
   Pluricentrism   187
   Ekaterina Protassova and Maria Yelenevskaya

9. The Russian World in Perspective: Comparing Russian
   Culture and Language Promotion with British, German and
   French Practices   215
   Christian Noack

Index   241

Tables

5.1 Frequency of media use to get information about politics and current affairs (%) — 133
5.2 In which language do you use the media (%)? — 134
5.3 Perceptions and opinions according to media consumption (% of respondents) — 134
5.4 Attitude towards immigrants and refugees according to media consumption (% of respondents) — 134
5.5 Media used to learn about current affairs (comparison of two groups: Russian-oriented and German-oriented) — 135
5.6 Comparison of attitudes of the two major groups — 135
5.7 Distribution of votes in the 2017 federal elections in Germany — 135

Contributors

Dr Mark Brüggemann studied Slavic Studies and Political Science at the University of Oldenburg (Germany). He defended his PhD there in 2012 on the topic 'The Belarusian and Russian Languages in Their Relationship to Belarusian Society and Nation. Ideological-Programmatic Positions of Political Actors and Intellectuals 1994–2010'. Currently he is a lecturer at the Institute of Slavic Studies at the University of Oldenburg. His research interests comprise language policy, national and ethnic minorities, language and nation-related discourses in Belarus, Poland, Russia and Ukraine.

Dr Feargus Denman is currently a research fellow in Russian and Slavonic Studies and a visiting teaching fellow in European Studies at Trinity College, Dublin. He holds an A.B. (2007) in Social Studies with a Language Citation in Russian from Harvard University. He received his PhD in 2017 with a thesis titled 'Our Languages, Our Language Ideologies, and Russian Language in Ireland: Monolingualism in the Midst of Cultural and Linguistic Diversity' from Dublin (TCD), 2017. His doctoral research examined the conceptualisation of Russian in Ireland between 2000 and 2010 in the historic context of state policy and on the basis of newspaper discourse analysis, sociolinguistic survey results and focus-group discussions.

Dr Natalya Kosmarskaya is a Senior Researcher at the Centre for Central Eurasian Studies, Institute of Oriental Studies, Russian Academy of Sciences (Moscow). Her fields of research are Ethnic and Diaspora Studies, Migration Studies, Urban Studies, and Central Asian Studies. She has over ninety publications on these topics in Russian and in English, among which feature contributions to a number of collected volumes like *Global Russian Cultures*, edited by K. Platt (Madison, 2019), and to academic journals such as *Nationalism and Ethnic Politics*, *Nationalities Papers*, *Europe-Asia Studies*, *Journal of Multicultural and Multilingual Development* and the *Russian Journal of Communication*. Her books (in Russian) include *Children of the Empire in Post-Soviet Central Asia: Mental Shifts and Practices of Adaptation* about Russians in Kyrgyzstan, 1992–2002 (Moscow, 2006) and *Post-Soviet Diasporas: History, Politics, Identity* (2020).

Dr Sirke Mäkinen is a Senior Lecturer in Russian and Eurasian Studies at the Aleksanteri Institute, University of Helsinki, Finland. She is the Head of the Nationwide Expertise in Russian and Eastern European Studies (ExpREES) Master's School. Sirke holds a Doctor of Social Sciences degree (2008) from the University of Tampere, Finland. She is also a lecturer in Political Science, especially International Politics, at the University of Turku, Finland. Sirke has published in journals such as *Geopolitics*, *Europe-Asia Studies*, *International Studies Perspectives*, *Nationalities Papers*, *Journal of Contemporary European Studies* and *Problems of Post-Communism*. Her research interests include international education, foreign policy, geopolitics and qualitative methodology.

Dr Christian Noack is Associate Professor in the chair group of East European Studies at the University of Amsterdam, where he teaches a course on 'Russia's Soft Power'. He participated in the Jean Monnet Network project 'Nemesis: Memory and Securitization in in the European Union and Neighbourhood' (565149-EPP-1-2015-1-RU-EPPJMO-NETWORK), in the framework of which the current book project was developed. Christian's research interests comprise questions of nationalism and religion in Europe, European memory politics, and the history of mobility and tourism in Eastern Europe. He currently leads the HERA funded project 'The European Spa as a European Public Space and a Social Metaphor'.

Dr habil. Ekaterina Protassova is Adjunct Professor in Russian Language at the University of Helsinki. She holds a PhD in Philology and a habilitation in Pedagogy and has over 300 scholarly publications. Ekaterina headed and participated in various international and national projects investigating language pedagogies, child and adult bilingualism, and the role of language and culture in immigrant integration. Her service to the profession includes editorial work for various journals and publishers, and organisation of seminars and conference panels.

Dr Igor Savin is a Senior Researcher at the Centre for Central Eurasian Studies of the Institute of Oriental Studies at the Russian Academy of Sciences (Moscow). His main research areas include ethno-political conflicts and minority issues in Central Asia; labour migration from Central Asia to Russia and Kazakhstan; and the integration of migrants into receiving societies, on which he has authored numerous journal articles, book chapters and three monographs. They comprise contributions to *Local Governance and Minority Empowerment in the CIS*, edited by V. Tishkov and E. Filippova (Budapest, 2003); to *Meskhetian Turks: Between Integration and Resettlement*, edited by T. Trier and A. Khanzhin (Münster, 2007); and, with N. Kosmarskaya, to *The New Russian Nationalism: Imperialism, Ethnicity and Authoritarianism 2000–15*, edited by P. Kolstø and H. Blakkisrud (Edinburgh, 2016).

Olga Tikhomirova, Master of Arts in Linguistics, has worked since September 2018 as a journalist at the German state broadcaster *Deutsche Welle*. She is also a PhD student at the Ruhr University in Bochum, and a cofounder of the Nemtsova Foundation for Freedom. Before coming to Germany, she worked with Boris Nemtsov as the press secretary of the Solidarity movement (2009–12) and as the director of PARNAS party (2012–15). Between January 2016 and August 2018, she directed the Boris Nemtsov Foundation for Freedom, established in Germany after Nemtsov's assassination.

Dr habil. Michał Wawrzonek is Associate Professor at the Institute of Political and Administrative Science of Jesuit University in Cracow. He holds a PhD in Ukrainian Literature and a habilitation in Political Sciences from the Jagiellonian University in Cracow, where he worked until 2017. His research focuses on Russian–Ukrainian and Polish–Ukrainian relations, religion in post-Soviet Ukrainian social and political life, politics in Ukraine and Ukrainian political thought. He has published in, among others, *East European Politics, Societies and Cultures* and the *Journal of Ukrainian Studies*. He edited *Religion and Politics in Ukraine: The Orthodox and Greek Catholic Churches as Elements of Ukraine's Political System* (Newcastle upon Tyne, 2014) and *Orthodoxy Versus Post-Communism? Belarus, Serbia, Ukraine and the Russkiy Mir*, with Nelly Bekus and Mirella Korzeniewska-Wiszniewska (Newcastle upon Tyne, 2016).

Dr Dmitry Yagodin is a postdoctoral researcher at the Aleksantari Institute for Russian and Eurasian Studies of the University of Helsinki. He is interested in comparative media studies, public diplomacy, environmental communication and digital cultures. Much of his work focuses on examples from the post-Soviet space. He is currently studying the use of social media in national and international communication with a grant by the Academy of Finland. He recently also co-edited two books based on large-scale multinational comparisons, *Media and Global Climate Knowledge* (Basingstoke, 2017) and *Journalism and the NSA Revelations* (London, 2017).

Dr Maria Yelenevskaya is affiliated with the Department of Humanities and Arts at the Technion-Israel Institute of Technology. Throughout her pedagogical career she has developed teaching and testing materials for EAP courses, including multimedia modules for computer-assisted language learning. Her research is devoted to language in multilingual and multicultural settings, lingua-cultural aspects of immigration, computer-assisted language learning and linguo-cultural aspects of humour. She has over seventy scholarly publications. She serves on the editorial board of three international scholarly journals and is a board member of Israel Association for the Study of Language and Society.

Acknowledgements

The creation of new Russian cultural foundations in Moscow in the late 2000s intrigued me from the start, and my colleagues Olga Sinitsyna in Moscow and Patty Gray in Ireland, where I was then based, encouraged me to turn this interest into a research project.

The opportunity to realise this project came with a Jean Monnet network grant for which my colleagues Luiza Bialasiewicz and Micha Kemper and I had successfully applied in 2014, together with Victor Apryshchenko and Oxana Karnaukhova from the Southern Federal University in Rostov. The project 'Memory and Securitization in the European Union and Neighbourhood – NEMESIS' ran from 2015 to 2018, and my work on this book has enormously profited from discussion with the colleagues involved in the project. In addition to the above mentioned, my thanks go to Oliver Hinkelbein from Bremen University, Kerry Longhurst from the Collegium Civitas in Warsaw, and Johannes Leitner and Hannes Meissner from the Fachhochschule des BFI Wien.

Together with my colleague Ewa Stańczyk, I also developed a course on 'Russia's soft power' at the University of Amsterdam in the framework of the 'NEMESIS' project, which has been taught in the European Studies BA programme since 2017. I wish to thank Akudo McGhee for helping me to publish this course as an online module, too.

The Jean Monnet grant allowed us also to host two panels on 'Russian Language Policies Abroad' in the framework of the IPSA conference 'Politics of Multilingualism: Possibilities and Changes' in May 2017. Paul Koopman and Tatjana Das have been extremely helpful in the preparation of these panels. Most of the chapters in this book are based on papers presented at this conference. I am particular grateful to Natalya Kosmarskaya, Igor Savin, Sirke Mäkinen and Maria Yelenevskaya, who agreed to enrich the project at a later stage with their invaluable contributions.

Finally, without Michael Williams's patient advice and generous help, editing this volume would simply have been impossible.

INTRODUCTION

Language and Culture in Russia's Soft Power Toolbox

Christian Noack

This book zooms in on language promotion as a mainstay of the Russian Federation's recently reinvigorated cultural diplomacy activities. Russia is currently attempting an economic and political reintegration of the post-Soviet space based on geopolitical discourses of Eurasianism and arguments stipulating the region's civilisational distinctness from the West. In such discourses, the uniqueness of Russian culture and Russian language, as well as the latter's role as an overarching lingua franca serve as important arguments. The authors of this collection sound out how Russia's language promotion takes shape in a number of targeted countries, ranging from former Soviet republics like Ukraine, Belarus, Kazakhstan or Moldova, to Western countries like Germany and the Republic of Ireland. We examine the use and status of the Russian language in these countries, analyse the role of Russian-language media, and discuss whether or not this provides Russia with significant foreign policy leverage. Research for this book was, among others, conducted in the framework of the Jean Monnet network 'Memory and Securitization in the European Union and Neighbourhood' (NEMESIS), Project Number 565149-EPP-1-2015-1-RU-EPPJMO-NETWORK.

The authors take Russia's impressive capacity building in the realm of cultural and public diplomacy as a starting point. Since 2007, nongovernmental foundations like the Russkii Mir[1] Foundation, and a new branch of the Foreign Ministry named the Federal Agency for the Commonwealth of Independent States Affairs, Compatriots Living Abroad, and International Humanitarian Cooperation (or Rossotrudnichestvo for short), have been created with the aim of rebranding Russia internationally. The promotion of the Russian language and of Russian culture abroad is one of the most important tasks for both the Russkii Mir Foundation and for Rossotrudnichestvo. Referring to one's cultural achievements and historical accomplishments, and promoting one's language is of course in no way unique in cultural diplomacy. What is remarkable in the Russian case, though, is the political context in which Russia resumed its cultural diplomacy activities after a hiatus of more than a decade. It coincides with an overall reorientation of foreign policy and with the rise of a debate in the country about the need to apply soft power. At the same time, the renewed cultural diplomacy activities are closely intertwined with other political discourses rising to prominence during the 2000s, namely those of the 'compatriots' (i.e. Russian speakers living beyond Russia's borders, mainly in the former Soviet space) and of the 'Russian World'. Both claim the existence of a larger polyethnic civilisation deeply influenced by Russian culture and language, which transcends the borders of the Russian Federation and is largely congruent with a Eurasian space earlier covered by the Soviet Union and the Russian Empire. Indeed, Russia's foreign policy doctrines since the mid-2000s hardly conceal the Kremlin's intention to play a preeminent role in this area, unofficially called the 'near abroad'.

Scrutinising Russia's language promotion in theory and practice thus means engaging with a core aspect of the Kremlin's geopolitical reorientation, in which both the rise of the term 'soft power' and the focus on the former Soviet space can hardly be overlooked. At the intersection of the two, promotion of language and culture has an important role to play, as Russia sees preserving, and possibly expanding, the role of the Russian language and of Russian culture in this area as a guarantee of political influence.

With the term 'soft power', Joseph Nye famously described the exertion of power by attraction rather than by coercion. Without denying the importance of 'hard power' in the shape of military threats or economic pressure, Nye aimed at a re-evaluation of the importance of 'soft' factors in international relations, such as cultural clout and shared values. With Nye, the authors of this volume consider public and cultural diplomacy as important domains of soft power, in which states actively promote their cultural appeal. In so doing, they are not just striving to enhance mutual understanding between cultures, but trying to influence opinions and actions in other countries and societies to advance certain interests and values (Nye 2004, 2008).

Nye's soft power concept has been severely criticised for its vagueness and its failure to conceptualise the 'power' part of it. This is particularly true for the question of actorness; in Nye's concept, this is mainly allocated to the countries that exert soft power, which for Nye is mainly the US. This generates substantial methodological and source problems. While the intention to 'attract' can be fairly easily traced in policy documents, the actual effect of 'being attracted' is much more difficult to track and measure at the receiving end (Feklyunina 2016; Cheskin 2017). Hence, the authors of the volume analyse Russia's promotion of culture and language beyond the question of political intention (who is targeted?), exploring the actual process of cultural mediation in the target countries (how is the Russian language promoted?) and the perceptions on the receiving side (for whom is the Russian language attractive, and why?).

RUSSIAN SOFT POWER AND THE RETURN OF CULTURAL DIPLOMACY

Putin's self-assured speech at the 2007 Munich security conference and the 2008 war between Georgia and the Russian Federation dominated the Western perception of the Kremlin's turn to a more assertive foreign policy after the mid-2000s. Arguably, the use of military force against pro-Western Georgia made some contemporary observers overlook Russia's attempts during the same period to diversify its foreign policy and revitalise public and cultural diplomacy instruments and policies.

A number of more specific factors facilitated this reorientation. First, economic stabilisation and growth during Putin's first two terms paved the way for conducting a much more self-assured foreign policy, above all in Russia's immediate neighbourhood. Up to this point, the Commonwealth of Independent States had never developed into a functioning institution and the Putin administration itself, in its quest to secure Russia's position as the dominant regional power, had started several inconclusive initiatives aiming at reintegration of the former Soviet space. Only with the creation of the Customs Union in 2010 and the Eurasian Economic Union in 2015 did these attempts acquire a more distinctive shape.

Second, political technologists increasingly influenced the conduct of politics in Russia, applying their skills above all in media communication and the organisation of elections in the service of Putin's 'sovereign democracy'. In this context, Russia perceived Western attempts to promote democratisation through moral and financial support of nascent civil society structures as the soft power facade camouflaging the West's attempts to deploy 'political technologies' that would undermine Russia's position in its own sphere of interests. The successful 'Rose' and 'Orange' revolutions seemed to be just two particularly alarming examples. If Russia's foreign policy was to serve both international and domestic interests efficiently, it needed to acquire the same capacities as its Western competitors to influence public opinion abroad (Saari 2014: 50–1). In that sense, Putin himself has never ceased treating soft power with some ambivalence, seeing it as a tactical ruse but, at the same time, a capacity Russia needed to be able to apply.

Alongside 'hard' power, the Kremlin therefore has sought to mobilise 'soft' or cultural resources in its foreign policy. As a rule, these initiatives emphasise the shared experiences and values across post-Soviet space, as opposed to the ostensibly 'different' development paths of the West, allegedly imposed on states like Georgia or Ukraine. This reading links questions of identity and belonging in Eurasia intrinsically to the influence of the distinctive Russian culture that shaped first the Russian Empire and then the Soviet Union. The idea of a common civilisation or a 'cultural ideational space' (Hudson 2015: 331) in the shape of a 'Russian World' rose to prominence in Russia's recent attempts to recalibrate its foreign policies and to incorporate cultural diplomacy and soft power tools.

Against this backdrop, the Kremlin's take on soft power has oscillated between two positions: adopting international 'best practice', epitomised in the public diplomacy of Western states like the US, UK or Germany (or more recently that of the Chinese competitor in the East) versus creating its own brand of public diplomacy, based on Imperial Russian and/or Soviet traditions (Saari 2014: 56). The two positions are not entirely incompatible, but at least in the political discourse, the 'best practice' concept seems to have won the upper hand and allowed the term 'soft power' to enter the vocabulary of Russia's leading politicians by the second decade of the twenty-first century.

In 2012, for example, Russia's Foreign Minister Sergey Lavrov publicly declared soft power to be 'one of the main components of countries' international influence'. However, he found Russia's progress in the field still wanting: 'We cannot deny that Russia is well behind other countries in this respect.' Notably, he conceived of the 'Russian World' as 'a huge resource that can help strengthen Russia's prestige globally' (quoted in Forsberg and Smith 2016: 131). Introducing the new Concept of the Foreign Policy in the Security Council in 2013, President Putin himself employed the term 'soft power', too, emphasising that the new Concept focused 'on modern foreign policy tools, including economic diplomacy, elements of so-called soft power, and careful integration into the global informational space' (quoted in Simons 2014: 444).

Indeed, the 2013 Concept of the Foreign Policy of the Russian Federation fully reflects this change in attitude. Article 9 stipulates that 'today traditional military and political alliances cannot protect against all the existing transborder challenges and threats'. Article 10 adds:

Economic, legal, scientific, environmental, demographic and IT factors become as important for states in influencing the world politics as the military power. Of increased relevance are issues related to sustainable development, spiritual and intellectual education of population, improving its well-being and promoting investment in human capital. (Concept 2013)

The understanding of twenty-first century policies as being based on a clash of cultures becomes fully evident in Article 13, which states:

For the first time in modern history, global competition takes place on a civilizational level, whereby various values and models of development based on the universal principles of democracy and market economy start to clash and compete against each other. Cultural and civilizational diversity of the world becomes more and more manifest. (Concept 2013)

Article 20 recognises soft power as 'a comprehensive toolkit for achieving foreign policy objectives, building on civil society potential, information, cultural and other methods and technologies alternative to traditional diplomacy'. The same article, however, contains an only slightly veiled critique of Western interventionism, alluding to Colour Revolution scenarios:

[I]ncreasing global competition and the growing crisis potential sometimes creates a risk of destructive and unlawful use of 'soft power' and human rights concepts to exert political pressure on states, interfere in their internal affairs, destabilize their political situation, manipulate public opinion, including under the pretext of financing cultural and human rights projects abroad. (Concept 2013)

What is particularly relevant for the studies collated in this volume is that the document further defines the former Soviet space as the key target area for the Russian Federation's foreign policy. The concept justifies the need for closer regional interaction with the 'common historical background' of the CIS, greatly enhancing the 'capacity for integration in various spheres'. Article 44 prioritises the Eurasian Economic Union as 'a model that would determine the future of the Commonwealth states'. Links between members are seen in Article 45 as being built on 'preserving and increasing common cultural and civilizational heritage which is an essential resource for the CIS as a whole and for each of the Commonwealth's Member States in the context of globalization'. Russia explicitly pledges to provide support for 'compatriots living in the CIS Member States' and to help them negotiate agreements 'on the protection of their educational, linguistic, social, labour, humanitarian and other rights and freedoms' (Concept 2013). Against this backdrop, cultural diplomacy took on the task of proving a deeper, 'civilisation' linkage unifying this area, and principally opposing Western attempts to drag individual states out of this civilisational entity.

THE 'RUSSIAN WORLD' AND ITS MAINSTAYS

Russia's new geopolitical focus was often couched in quite explicit cultural terms. A 2011 opinion piece in the governmental newspaper *Rossiiskaia gazeta* by the chair of the Institute of Contemporary Development, Igor Jurgens, claimed that Russia's soft power rested on three pillars. First, Russia as the patron of Orthodoxy acted both as an *antemurale* against the eastern expansion of Latin Christendom and, simultaneously, as a harbinger of European civilisation in the vast expanses of Eurasia. Second, the Orthodox empire functioned as a defender of 'multi-ethnic alliances of nations' against the expansion of the nation state principle (quoted in Simons 2014: 445). Last but not least, the Soviet Union managed to portray itself as a credible ideological alternative to the liberal-capitalist model of the West.

Most contemporary analysts within and outside Russia concur that Russia at present does not field an alternative ideological profile any more, even if Russia is often described as a stronghold of conservative values. Of the remaining two arguments, Orthodoxy may hold a degree of potential attraction in south-eastern Europe and the Middle East, but it is definitely in the core area of the former empire and the Soviet Union, that is, the Eastern Slavic republics of Belarus and Ukraine, that such arguments are potentially most persuasive. As to the imperial past, it is indeed often presented by the current political elite in Russia as the historical warrant of cultural and ethnic diversity. An outstanding example of this was Putin's speech before the Federal Chamber after the annexation of Crimea on 18 March 2014. 'Crimea', Putin claimed, 'is a unique blend of different peoples' cultures and traditions. This makes it similar to Russia as a whole, where not a single ethnic group has been lost over the centuries' (Putin 2014). Like Putin, apologists of empire argue that such cultural diversity is manageable and defendable only through a strong state bridging the petty egoisms of the nationalities that, according to a broadly shared sentiment in Russia, lie at the core of the disunion that terminated the Soviet experiment. Such views neither take into account that the Union was finally dissolved as a result of a political initiative originating in Russia, nor do they reflect that even within the Russian Federation, it is the Russian people that form the demographic backbone. Not all of the people 'saved' by imperial magnanimity would necessarily subscribe to the view that Russian language and culture, supposedly due to their higher level of development, naturally serve as a common denominator of regional integration, as suggested by the Kremlin's political elite (Rukavishnikov 2011: 79–80).

To be sure, such imperial rhetoric is substantially toned down when practical steps are undertaken towards a reintegration of the Soviet space under Russian leadership. At least on the surface, however, the status and the functioning of the Russian language, and with it of Russian culture, is a highly politicised issue, which any exploration of Russia's current language promotion has to take into account. Whether referring to the function of Russian as the lingua franca of the dissolved Soviet Union implicitly or explicitly, Russian discourse discards institutional multilingualism, such as practised by the EU, as a weakness and suggests at the same time that there is no viable alternative to Russian as the means of internal communication. Putin himself spoke in 2013 of the 'very many advantages' of Russian being the prospective common language of the whole Eurasian Union. Other Russian experts likewise have emphasised the role of a common language for integration, pointing to research that allegedly proves that 'the use of a common language has a positive effect on the intensity of trade and investment relationships' (quoted in Ryazanova-Clarke 2017: 448). As discussed in the chapters by Mark Brüggemann or Natalya Kosmarskaya and Igor Savin in this book, the reactions to such 'rational' Russian designs of 'communicational integration' on the basis of the 'language of the rouble' (Ryazanova-Clarke 2017: 448) have been cautious even in member states of the Eurasian Union such as Belarus or Kazakhstan.

ASYMMETRIC BILINGUALISM, OR WHY THE STATUS OF A LANGUAGE MATTERS

The prominence of Orthodox and Russian cultural heritage in Russia's soft power strategies mirrors the progression of a protracted identity debate in post-Soviet Russia (Shevel 2011: 179–92). After 1991, most of the other former Soviet republics embarked on state-building projects that followed the principle of 'one nation – one language', and thus pursued nationalising linguistic policies. By contrast, Russia, as a multinational state in which the titular nation's share amounted to about 80% in 2010, adhered to Soviet multinational and multilinguistic philosophies. Soviet policies of language had already been based on the ascription of a particular status to the Russian language, which was not so much seen as the expression of a Russian *Volksgeist* but as a vehicle of transnational modernisation. Although many observers identified the survival of imperial heritage as one of the key problems of Russian state building (Hosking 1997), Russia's economic and social instability and the fact that about one-fifth of the population was ethnically non-Russian rendered 'one nation – one language' policies unrealistic.

Moreover, both the imperial and Soviet predecessor states had conceptually distinguished between the state and the nation, describing the former with the term 'rossiiskii' and the latter with 'russkii'. Rhetorically adhering to the theory of polyethnicity and multilingualism, the Soviet Union developed a delicate balance between the preservation and development of minority languages and cultures ('national in form, socialist in content') on the one hand, and advancing Russian language and culture as a proxy for denationalised common 'achievements' of the Soviet peoples on the other. Even in periods that are generally perceived as 'Russifying' in terms of language and culture, like the late 1930s, Stalin's regime consciously avoided the impression that the spread of Russian, necessary as it may have been (e.g. in the Red Army), would proceed at the expense of the status of and proficiency in minority languages (Blitstein 2001). The outcome of this Soviet language policy was the development of an asymmetric bilingualism in the USSR. In the Union republics, but even more so in the national republics and autonomies within the RSFSR, the non-Russian population was as a rule bilingual, whereas only a small percentage of ethnic Russians living in the non-Russian republics or national territories were fluent in the titular languages. Until the late Soviet period, Russian functioned not only as the lingua franca but also as the main means of social ascent (Brubaker 1996; Tolz 1998; Pavlenko 2006).

After 1991, the political elite in the Russian Federation favoured the 'statist' interpretation of a Russian nation and shied away from openly declaring the new state as being exclusively the home of ethnic Russians. This option had two important consequences. In terms of language policy, the new state replicated the Soviet multilinguist rhetoric, but secured in practice the predominance of Russian in those subjects of the Federation where Moscow's weakness during the 1990s had resulted in far too self-assertive language policies by the titular nations, such as in Tatarstan (Wigglesworth-Baker 2016). Therefore, the former Soviet asymmetric bilingualism was hardly ever superseded by a real bilingualism. In terms of territory, however, the new state of the Russian Federation was considerably smaller than its predecessors, and the shrinking of the borders left larger groups of Russian speakers 'stranded' in newly independent states, whose language policies granted Russian a minority language status at best, or no status at all. For these groups of Russian speakers, the experience of being a less favoured linguistic minority replaced the privileges that they had enjoyed under the conditions of Soviet-style asymmetric bilingualism.

In many independent states, except for the two Eastern Slavic republics, Ukraine and Belarus, Russian speakers seemed to face the alternative of linguistic assimilation or re-migration to the Russian Federation (Pavlenko 2006: 88). Such re-migration characterised demographic trends above all in the 1990s, yet it was limited by the extent of the contemporary economic and social crisis in the Russian Federation (Chudinovskikh and Denisenko 2014: 8–10). In this situation, Russian politicians discovered the beached diaspora and claimed that the Federation had legal and moral obligations towards their 'compatriots', as this group was increasingly called in the public discourse.

RUSSIAN SPEAKERS AS 'COMPATRIOTS'

The State Duma passed its first 'Federal Law of the Russian Federation about state policy of the Russian Federation concerning compatriots abroad' while still under Yeltsin in 1999. The law has been substantially amended several times since, most recently in 2013. Initially, the definition of who belonged to these compatriots was based on the citizenship principle, and all former USSR passports holders were in principle eligible for the status of 'compatriot'. At the same time, the subjective will of an individual formed the basis for inclusion into the group of compatriots; it was therefore open to anyone identifying with the fate of the Russian state, Russian culture or the Russian language. In the long run, the re-migration option, which included a simplified process for acquiring Russian citizenship (still nominally pegged to compatriot status in paragraphs 5 and 11 of the 2010 version of the Federal Law), was found unpromising by the compatriots themselves, as it quickly became apparent that Russia intended to address its demographic and structural problems by settling the re-migrants in depopulated and unattractive border regions. The number of compatriots returning to Russia in the 2000s remained insignificant, and the Russian government realised that the preservation of a numerically strong diaspora beyond the borders was politically more advantageous, in particular if these people could be nudged into demonstrating a degree of loyalty to the Russian Federation (Shevel 2011: 196).

With later revisions of the 'Law on the compatriots', above all those in 2010 and 2013, 'essentializing measurements of "compatriotism"' were introduced (Ryazanova-Clarke 2017: 446). The amended law lists some objective criteria according to which individuals are identified as potential compatriots. Paragraph 1 enumerates 'citizens of the Russian Federation who are constantly living outside the territory of the Russian Federation' and 'individuals and their descendants living outside the territory of the Russian Federation that belong, as a rule, to peoples which were historically living on the territory of the Russian Federation', and includes 'persons who are direct descendants of people who once lived on the territory of the Russia Federation and who have made a deliberate choice for spiritual, cultural and legal bond with the Russian Federation',[2] even if they emigrated and acquired foreign citizenship (Federal Law 2010). If there is one factor potentially uniting them, it is knowledge and use of the Russian language, which Russia sets out to perpetuate with its language promotion.

Many observers have pointed out the deliberate vagueness of the concept of 'compatriots' (*sootechestvenniki*) (Shevel 2011: 192–9). On the one hand, it allows politicians in Russia to include the largest possible groups of Russian speakers outside the Federation into a constituency for which Russia claims responsibility, thus creating a 'globally sprawling virtual expanded nation' (Ryazanova-Clarke 2017: 447). On the other hand, the centrality of language and the fact that the status of compatriots is linked to subjective, active and even emotional identification with Russian language and culture suggests the cultivation of a Herderian concept of language as an expression of a national spirit. Therefore, the 2010 amendment of the law does not automatically include descendants of USSR passport holders in the near abroad in the category unless they actively identify as compatriots. This sense of 'belonging' requires active promotion of the Russian language, supported by evidence of 'civic or professional activity to preserve the Russian language . . . [and] culture abroad' (Federal Law 2010). Here the subjective identification becomes instrumental, potentially transforming 'loyalty to the Russian culture and the Russian language . . . into the loyalty to the Russian state' (Ryazanova-Clarke 2017: 447).

In other words, Russian legislation suggests a close interrelationship between language preferences and identity, rather than using a thoroughly ethnic definition of Russianness. This could not but politicise the Russian Federation's language, above all in the near abroad. In extreme cases, such as Ukraine, fears that Russia would use the language issue as a sort of Trojan Horse were not exactly alleviated by repeated threats to furnish compatriots, or even all willing Ukrainians, with Russian passports (Underwood 2019). Against this backdrop, the chapters in this book dealing with the promotion of the Russian language in the so-called near and far abroad examine the potential responsiveness of the target audience members themselves. The chapters by Michał Wawrzonek, Mark Brüggemann, Natalya Kosmarskaya and Igor Savin, Feargus Denman, and Olga Tikhomirova document a quite weak link between the use of language and identity. What is more, Ekaterina Protassova and Maria Yelenevskaya's contribution documents the first signs of a parting of ways between the Russian language(s) spoken in the Russian Federation and elsewhere. Such pluricentrism will in the future possibly weaken the Russian Federation's claim of 'ownership' of the Russian language, which President Lukashenka in Belarus already disputes for political expediency, as Brüggemann shows.

THE POLITICS OF THE RUSSIAN LANGUAGE BEYOND RUSSIA (STRUCTURE AND CONTENT OF THE BOOK)

Recent research has proved the possibility of applying the concept of soft power more productively, shifting the emphasis from 'examining elite outlooks' to 'focus on reception'. Cheskin (2017), Hudson (2015) and Feklyunina (2016) emphasise the constructive nature of (soft) power as negotiated. Soft power is thus created through a continuous renegotiation process of collective identities. We can assess the weight of a state's soft power vis-à-vis another state by investigating the extent to which a discursively constructed collective identity projected by the first state is accepted or rejected by different audiences in the second state (Hudson 2015: 331–2).

In this understanding, soft power emerges as an 'accumulated ideological potential, which then may serve to frame certain policies', and research shifts to the response of the target audiences to the communicated message, as soft power measures 'do not inevitably yield the results intended' (Hudson 2015: 331–2).

This approach informed the nine studies on Russian language promotion abroad collected in this volume. The first three chapters deal with the linguistic situation in Ukraine, Belarus and Kazakhstan, three countries with significant Russian minorities and an even more significant spread of the Russian language among the population as a whole.

The first chapter by Michał Wawrzonek, 'The "Russian World" and

Ukraine', discusses the clashes of Ukrainian and Russian state interests in the field of language policies in this country. The Ukrainian government actively promotes the spread of Ukrainian as part of the state's assertion of its sovereignty in public discourse. By contrast, Russia's foreign policy aims at buttressing the widespread use of Russian in Ukraine, regarding the Russian-speaking population as 'compatriots'. Wawrzonek's research, like that of many other recent studies of the perception of the 'Russian World' in Ukraine (Feklyunina 2016; Cheskin 2017; Ryazanova-Clarke 2017), points out Russia's inflexible and self-assertive approach to the 'imagined' community. He suggests that the 'Russian World' ideology, with its religious overtones, was already incompatible with the very idea of Ukraine being a separate nation and Ukrainian being a language (and not merely a dialect of Russian) before the Maidan and the schism of the Orthodox Church. Russia's aggression since 2014 has obviously further enhanced civic identification with the Ukrainian state and its independence, which proved to be detrimental for the concept of the 'Russian World'.

Mark Brüggemann's chapter, 'Russian in Belarus: A Feature of Belarusian Identity or Moscow's "Trojan Horse"?' explores the coexistence of three linguistic codes in this country: Belarusian, Russian and a Belarusian–Russian mixed speech, *trasianka*. Russian had been the preferred language during the Soviet period, but this shifted to Belarusian during the early years of Belarusian independence. From Lukashenka's ascent to power in 1994 until 2014, bilingualism was the official doctrine in state language policies. The chapter explores how, in the wake of the Ukrainian crisis, the government's position has changed and Belarusian is cautiously employed as an element of distinction from Russia. At the same time, Lukashenka continues to challenge Russia's claim to sole ownership of the Russian language, since historically Belarusians contributed to the latter's development extensively.

In the third chapter, 'Between Emotions and Pragmatism: The Russian Language in Kazakhstan and the "Russian Factor"', Natalya Kosmarskaya and Igor Savin offer both a micro- and a macro-perspective on the linguistic situation in that country. Building on a series of interviews and roundtables with Kazakhstani students and experts, as well as basing themselves on a broad array of earlier studies, the authors deconstruct Russia's claim that the Russian cultural and linguistic space in Central Asia is dependent on Russia's external support. Kosmarskaya and Savin show that the Russian language is used almost equally by ethnic Russians, Kazakhs and other minorities in the country. Neither the symbolic upgrading of the Kazakh language nor Russia's inept attempts at influencing the situation have significantly changed this. The authors suggest that the Russian Federation should readjust its external promotion of language and culture, which has so far been geared almost exclusively to the so-called compatriots, and should take the needs of non-Russian Russian speakers into serious consideration.

Chapters 4 and 5 discuss the use of the Russian language in the 'far abroad'. In his contribution, 'Speakers of Russian in Ireland: "What unites us is language, but in all other respects we are different"', Feargus Denman explores language use and identity issues among Russian speakers in the Republic of Ireland. In the Republic, some 20,000 people speak Russian. A good fifth of this population is Irish-born, while only 9% are Russian nationals. The majority of people who speak Russian in Ireland have arrived since 2000 from the Baltic EU member states and other former Soviet republics. Denman analyses how gaps between the de facto community in conversation and a putatively general community of speakers of Russian within Ireland are negotiated and how the links between them are alternately invoked and challenged.

Like Denman's contribution, Olga Tikhomirova's chapter, 'Media Use of Russian Speakers in Germany', suggests that the language–identity nexus is less tightly knit outside the former Soviet space, whether in countries with small Russophone communities like Ireland or those with more sizeable groups like Germany. In the case of the 3–4 million Russian speakers in Germany, Tikhomirova points to the irony that the larger parts of this group emigrated from the Soviet Union and its successor state precisely because they saw themselves not as Russians, but as Germans or Jews. Nonetheless, German society tends to perceive them as *Deutschrussen*, particularly because of their continuous use of Russian as a first language in oral communication. For the German case it has often been argued that this makes the group particularly perceptive to disinformation spread via Russian-language media. Tikhomirova sketches a more nuanced picture, showing that the Russian speakers are indeed consuming Russian-language media to a substantial degree, but that they prefer entertaining content over informational formats.

Dmitry Yagodin's chapter, 'The Role of Russian for Digital Diplomacy in Moldova', analyses the use of the Russian language in media as well, returning to the former Soviet space. The Republic of Moldova is ridden with political uncertainties, divided by acute language and media policy issues, and plagued by a continuous national identity crisis. Yagodin analyses Moldova's exposure to Russian public diplomacy initiatives, in particular those implemented with the help of social media formats recently growing in popularity and sophistication. By comparing the approaches of two competing actors, the EU and Russia, in their use of social media as foreign policy tools, Yagodin found the effectiveness of Russian-language digital diplomacy rather wanting.

The third part of the book zooms out again and discusses the role and importance of the Russian language abroad in comparative terms. In Chapter 7, Sirke Mäkinen discusses the promotion of Russian higher education abroad. Across the globe, attracting foreign students to one's universities has become an ever more important aspect of cultural diplomacy, partly due to commercial considerations, partly to secure influence on future generations of foreign elites. Which role does the Russian language play in this context? Mäkinen finds surprisingly cynical attitudes towards the use of Russian among Russian educational managers. While acknowledging that offering more courses in English than in Russian would facilitate the internationalisation and commercialisation of the Russian educational system, leading Russian specialists admitted that much of the educational promotion still rests on the assumption of the widespread use of the Russian language. Quotas for compatriots and other student groups from the near abroad suggest that a political agenda, that is, retaining Russia's primacy as an educational great power, prevails over attempts at a broad and commercially successful internationalisation of education.

In Chapter 8, 'Stable or Variable Russian? Standardisation versus Pluricentrism', Ekaterina Protassova and Maria Yelenevskaya discuss the relationship between metropolitan and diasporic Russian. They provide an overview of variations of Russian as it is spoken outside the Russian Federation. The authors record numerous lexicographical and grammatical changes under the influence of the titular languages spoken in the former Soviet republics and other countries with sizeable Russian minorities, such as Israel or Finland. At the same time, both Russian authorities and Russian-language teachers, the main mediators of the language, display a stunningly conservative attitude towards language changes, vigorously rejecting neologisms.

The institutional basis of Russia's soft power has so far rarely been reviewed in comparative perspective. This is addressed in the concluding chapter by Christian Noack, 'The Russian World in Perspective: Comparing Russian Culture and Language Promotion with British, German and French Practices'. Starting from the question of whether Russia's recent cultural diplomacy offensive is based on international best practice or is a revival of Soviet traditions, Noack finds both, embodied in the Russkii Mir Foundation and the state agency Rossotrudnichestvo, respectively. While, for example, French cultural foreign policy resembles Russia's in terms of having a similar structure that combines public and state institutions, Russia's language and culture promotion differs from Western practice in important ways. It is essentially unidirectional, instead of inviting cultural exchange, and it is geared towards defending the status and use of the Russian language, in particular in the near abroad. As discussed above, the suggestions of a close nexus between language use and identity and the narrow focus on 'compatriots' do nothing to increase the attractiveness of Russia's activities. Finally, in terms of practical material in the fields of online teaching and teacher training, the quality and quantity of Russkii Mir's and Rossotrudnichestvo's offers lag significantly behind those of their Western European peers. This inertia, also discussed in the country studies in Chapters 1–3, can only be partly explained by a lack of funding.

What do these findings about Russian language promotion and its perception in the 'near' and 'far' abroad tell us about the 'attractiveness' of Russian soft power politics? Starting from the reception of Nye's concept, we discerned a very instrumental approach towards soft power among Russia's political elite. Foundations like Russkii Mir formally emulate Western models of culture and language promotion. The financial dependence of both Russkii Mir and Rossotrudnichestvo on state funding and the narrow political definition of aims and targets in Russian legislation cast severe doubts on their relative independence. Indeed, chairs and boards of both organisations are occupied by representatives from the inner circle of Russia's political elite.

In terms of the target audiences, we find a strong focus on the former Soviet space. While Russkii Mir and Rossotrudnichestvo claim to promote access to Russian culture and language promotion for anyone abroad, actual Russian language promotion aims primarily at preserving existing cohorts of Russian speakers across the near abroad, who are conceived as quasi-natural agents of Russian influence in these countries. The Kremlin seems to assume that shared historical experiences provide a fertile ground for a positive perception of Russian language and culture. There is an almost unquestioned expectation that the Russian language will play the same integrative functions for the former Soviet space that it had been ascribed in the USSR. Our research has shown that this is hardly the case, even in the linguistically closely related Eastern Slavic states of Ukraine and Belarus. True, across the former Soviet space the command of the Russian language still offers important advantages, in terms of access to the Russian labour market, educational system and the broad informational space of the Runet, for example. The willingness to engage with Russian language promotion is seriously diminished, however, by the ideological loading of culture and language in Russian discourse, of which the compatriot laws and the 'Russian World' ideology are the most visible expressions.

Beyond that, Russia's external cultural promotion preserves a rather traditional understanding of high culture with essentialist and static features, of which the Russian language is the most visible expression. There is little space for popular culture in this culture promotion, and instead of seeing culture as an autonomous free space for negotiation of political possibilities, identification with Russian culture serves rather as a bone of contention in the target societies, in particular in the near abroad. By promoting an understanding of Russian culture in terms of a narrowly codified high culture and by declaring the active use of Russian as an expression of national attachment, Russia's policies almost exclude utilitarian approaches to the learning of the language by non-Russians. Enforcing a civilisational choice between Russia and Europe on independent Ukraine, Moscow's policies clearly floundered, and it did not make bigger inroads anywhere else in the former Soviet space. We found this to be somewhat less the case in other countries with sizeable groups of Russian speakers, like Germany, Israel or Ireland, where a more obvious disjunction between language and identity is at play, for example in the case of Russian-speaking Germans or Jews.

Interestingly, many of the potential mediators, that is, the teachers of Russian language outside the Russian Federation, seem to share the very normative take on the Russian language and readily support Moscow's claim to impart a 'correct' version of the language as codified in the Russian Federation. In the long run, it is rather doubtful that this 'frozen' language, which increasingly differs from spoken language both in Russia and in the 'near abroad', will help spread the use of the Russian language and secure its status as a world language. While the Russian discourse on the promotion of Russian culture and language pays lip service to cultural exchange, Russia's policy in practice focuses on the preservation of the beached diaspora in the former Union republics. For this target group, command of the Russian language is instrumental for access to Russian-language media or the Russian educational system. The political convenience of buttressing this cohort is obvious, yet the actual support often seems rhetorical rather than genuine.

NOTES

1. The Foundation renders its name as *Russkiy Mir* on its website. In this book we use *Russkii Mir* with capital letters for the organisation, the spelling in accordance with the Library of Congress transcription system for Russian names and terms. The concept is referred to as *russkii mir* in small letters.
2. Translations from this document here and below by the author, Christian Noack.

REFERENCES

Blitstein, Peter (2001), 'Nation-building or Russification? Obligatory Russian instruction in the Soviet non-Russian school, 1938–1953', in Ronald Grigor Suny and Terry Martin (eds), *A State of Nations: Empire and Nation-Making in the Age of Lenin and Stalin*, Oxford: Oxford University Press, pp. 253–74.

Brubaker, Rogers (1996), *Nationalism Reframed: Nationhood and the National Question in the New Europe*, Cambridge: Cambridge University Press.

Cheskin, Ammon (2017), 'Russian soft power in Ukraine: A structural perspective', *Communist and Post-Communist Studies* 50, pp. 277–87.

Chudinovskikh, Olga and Mikhail Denisenko (2014), *Population Mobility in the Commonwealth of Independent States: Whither Common Migration Policy?*, CARIM-East Research Report, CMR Working Papers No. 74 (132), Warsaw: Centre of Migration Research, University of Warsaw.

Concept of the Foreign Policy of the Russian Federation (2013), Approved by President of the Russian Federation V. Putin on 12 February 2013, The Ministry of Foreign Affairs of the Russian Federation, <http://www.mid.ru/en/foreign_policy/official_documents/-/asset_publisher/CptICkB6BZ29/content/id/122186> (last accessed 30 January 2018).

Federal Law of the Russian Federation 'About state policy of the Russian Federation concerning compatriots abroad' (2010), Accepted by the State Duma on March 5, 1999 and supplemented on 23 July 2010, <http://pravo.gov.ru/proxy/ips/?docbody=&nd=102059861> (last accessed 27 January 2018).

Feklyunina, Valentina (2016), 'Soft power and identity: Russia, Ukraine and the "Russian world(s)"', *European Journal of International Relations* 22 (4), pp. 773–96.

Forsberg, Tuomas and Hanna Smith (2016), 'Russian cultural statecraft in the Eurasian space', *Problems of Post-Communism* 63 (3), pp. 129–34.

Hosking, Geoffrey (1997), *Russia: People and Empire 1552–1917*, London: HarperCollins.

Hudson, Victoria (2015), '"Forced to friendship"? Russian (mis-)understandings of soft power and the implications for audience attraction in Ukraine', *Politics* 35 (3–4), pp. 330–46.

Nye, Joseph (2004), *Soft Power: The Means to Success in World Politics*, New York: Public Affairs.

Nye Joseph (2008), 'Public diplomacy and soft power', *The ANNALS of the American Academy of Political and Social Science* 616 (1), pp. 94–109.

Pavlenko, Aneta (2006), 'Russia as a lingua franca', *Annual Review of Applied Linguistics* 26, pp. 78–99.

Putin, Vladimir (2014), President of Russia. Address by President of the Russian Federation, 18 March, <http://eng.kremlin.ru/transcripts/6889> (last accessed 25 August 2016).

Rukavishnikov, Vladimir (2011), 'Russia's "soft power" in the Putin epoch', in Roger Kanet (ed.), *Russian Foreign Policy in the 21st Century*, Basingstoke: Palgrave Macmillan, pp. 76–96.

Ryazanova-Clarke, Lara (2017), 'From commodification to weaponization: The Russian language as "pride" and "profit" in Russia's transnational discourses', *International Journal of Bilingual Education and Bilingualism* 20 (4), pp. 443–56.

Saari, Sinikukka (2014), 'Russia's post-Orange Revolution strategies to increase its influence in former Soviet republics: Public diplomacy *po russkii*', *Europe-Asia Studies* 66 (1), pp. 50–66.

Shevel, Oxana (2011), 'Russian nation-building from Yel'tsin to Medvedev: Ethnic, civic or purposefully ambiguous?', *Europe-Asia Studies* 63 (2), pp. 179–202.

Simons, Greg (2014), 'Russian public diplomacy in the 21st century: Structure, means and message', *Public Relations Review* 40 (3), pp. 440–9.

Tolz, Vera (1998), 'Forging the nation: National identity and nation building in post-communist Russia', *Europe-Asia Studies* 50 (6), pp. 993–1022.

Underwood, Alice (2019), 'Citizenship without borders: Russian passports for Ukrainian citizens', *The Russia File*, 3 May, <https://www.wilsoncenter.org/blog-post/citizenship-without-borders-russian-passports-for-ukrainian-citizens> (last accessed 20 May 2020).

Wigglesworth-Baker, Teresa (2016), 'Language policy and post-Soviet identities in Tatarstan', *Nationalities Papers* 44 (1), pp. 20–37.

CHAPTER I

The 'Russian World' and Ukraine

Michał Wawrzonek

INTRODUCTION

The concept of *russkii mir* (the 'Russian World') has several meanings. On the one hand, it is an attempt at conceptualising the identity of Russia and her place in the post-Soviet space, with strong reference to the spread of Russian language and culture. On the other hand, the name stands for a foundation created to realise these very goals through activities abroad. Following its emergence after the collapse of the Soviet Union, the concept of *russkii mir* also became an important element in the public discourse shaping the contemporary political community in Ukraine (Curanović 2012; Szostek 2014; Pikulicka-Wilczewska and Sakwa 2015; Laruelle 2015, 2016; Ballinger 2017; Suslov 2017; Hale et al. 2018). The aim of this chapter is to analyse the importance of the 'Russian World' both as a concept and as an institution, as tools for influencing Ukrainian social space.

Social space is understood here with Bourdieu as awareness in context, that is, as 'the universe of points of view reflecting each other ad infinitum'. Social space is also shaped by the 'coexistence of points of view, in the dual sense of positions in the distribution of capital (economic, informational, social, etc.) and of the corresponding powers'. Because of the roles of language and culture in the concept of *russkii mir*, symbolic capital and symbolic violence will be particularly important. As noted by Bourdieu, points of view, 'in the sense of structured and structuring position-takings on the social space or a particular field, are by nature different and competing' (Bourdieu 2000: 183). Such differences and competing forces cause conflict and competition.

In the case of the Ukrainian social realm, 'conflicts and confrontations of points of view' relate also to the ontological status of that space. In other words, Ukraine's potential to create distinct autonomous structures within the post-Soviet meta-space is at stake, as is the scope and the meaning of that autonomy.

CONCEPTUAL BACKGROUND

Viacheslav Nikonov described the origins of the idea of *russkii mir*, and of the foundation carrying the same name of which he was the first director, as follows:

> What do we mean when we use the collocation *russkii mir*? ... President Putin [in 2007] said 'In this year which has been declared the "Year of the Russian Language", there is every reason to remind us that Russian is the language of a historic brotherhood of people, the language of true international communication. It not only carries a whole stratum of global achievements, it is the living space of the many millions of people that make up the Russian World [*russkii mir*] which is, naturally, much larger than Russia itself.' The collocation *russkii mir* was therefore used for the first time by the head of the Russian state. In that moment, just as he is today, Valerii Tishkov [an anthropologist and former chairman of the State Committee of RSFSR on nationalities] was sitting next to me, and he suggested: 'Well, this is very important, we need to think this through.' (Nikonov 2010: 70)[1]

Using Bourdieu's terms, we could say that the quote above is a 'verdict' or a 'performative utterance', meaning a 'a legitimate exercise of power to say what is and to make exist what it states' (Bourdieu 2000: 187). Nikonov's foundational myth about the origins of the concept of *russkii mir* perfectly illustrates Bourdieu's ideas that

> the state is the site par excellence of the imposition of the *nomos*, the official and effective principle of constructing the world, with, for example, all the acts of consecration and accreditation which ratify, legalize, legitimize, 'regularize' situations or acts of union (marriage, various contracts, etc.) or separation (divorce, breach of contract) which are thus raised from the status of pure contingent fact, unofficial or even disguised (a 'relationship') to the status of official fact, known and recognized by all, published and public. (Bourdieu 2000: 186)

The central role of language in this concept had already emerged clearly during the above-mentioned 2007 roundtable. Valerii Tishkov asserted that,

> guided by the norms of international rights and by concern for the Russian language, Russia shall not cease to raise the question of official bilingualism for several countries of the former Soviet Union (Kazakhstan, Ukraine, Latvia, Moldova, Kyrgyzstan). If the equal status of Russians is not acknowledged, then Russia shall support both forms of internal self-determination of culturally different groups: the ethno-national – through the federalization of several post-Soviet states, where there are more or less homogeneous areas with a Russian population – or that of extra-territorial cultural autonomy. A strategy supporting irredentist variants is possible, yet brings about greater political risks and may be realistically carried out only with regard to Abkhazia and South Ossetia, based on the latter's initiative. (Tishkov 2007 quoted in Moser 2013: 144–5)

Despite the formal claims to its 'multicultural character', the 'Russian World' was primarily conceived as a community of the Russian-speaking peoples. The Russian language is the pivotal element among the 'spiritual resources' of *russkii mir*. In 2010, Aleksei Gromyko suggested that the Russian language constituted the Russian World and that the Russian language should be thought to be 'the main carrier of its historical codes and senses' as well as forming the 'basis of its culture' (Gromyko 2010: 22). President Vladimir Putin himself added that the Russian language preserved 'an entire layer of truly global achievements' (Russkii Mir 2020).

Supposedly a community marked by common language and culture, the Russian World depends nonetheless on state power and state institutions to carve out the social space emerging from the concept and the discourse about it. In the light of the passage quoted above, the concept became meaningful and important in describing the post-Soviet space precisely because it originated with Putin. In such circumstances, the question of whether this description accurately reflected any actual reality or projected an idea upon it was clearly of secondary importance.

According to Nikonov's account, an expert discussion under the title 'The Russian World: What Is It and What Needs to Be Done?' was organised only two weeks after Putin's speech; and merely one month later, the president signed a decree creating the Russkii Mir Foundation (Nikonov 2010: 70).

Using the same 'state-official' key, the advocates of the 'Russian

World' concept described the social importance and aims of their activities. So-called Russian Centres were intended to become the organisational mainstay of the Foundation abroad. There, they were supposed to be set up jointly either with local partners in the target countries, or with Russotrudnichestvo. The latter, the Federal Agency for the Commonwealth of Independent States Affairs, Compatriots Living Abroad, and International Humanitarian Cooperation, had just been created under the auspices of the Ministry of Foreign Affairs.

In the annual reports published by the Foundation, a separate section is always devoted to the growth of the network and the activities of these Russian Centres. The 2008 report recorded the high level of attendance during the opening ceremonies, supposedly confirming the significant social importance of Russian Centres (Russkii Mir 2009: 30). A list followed of representatives of the highest echelons of power in Russia who had attended the openings of new Russkii Mir centres in a given year. The subsequent reports for 2009 and 2010 repeated the same pattern. Only after 2011 were positive reactions of the target audiences mentioned for the first time (Russkii Mir 2012: 6). The report from 2012 is exceptional, in that the focus shifted to the target audiences of the Russian Centres and their positive reactions became the exclusive measure of their social importance (Russkii Mir 2013a: 20). 'High attendance levels' returned in 2013 (Russkii Mir 2014a: 6). With the Ukrainian crisis unfolding in 2013–14, reference to the 'social importance' of the centres was replaced by information about the mounting problems emerging from the 'escalation of the political situation in Ukraine and the surrounding area', or the 'difficult political situation in the world and the openly anti-Russian attitudes of the leaders of several states' (Russkii Mir 2015a: 21; 2017a: 35).

From the beginning, the Russian World was perceived as a civilisational community. In 2009, the then head of the Russian Orthodox Church, Patriarch Kirill, reiterated the basic assumptions of the idea of the *Russkii* community and designated its core area as comprising the territories of Russia, Ukraine and Belarus, but also parts of two other countries, namely Moldova and Kazakhstan (Russkaia Pravoslavnaia Tserkov' 2009; Religiia v Ukraine 2010). Russia was called upon to consolidate the *russkii mir* community by promoting its common values, mental habits, and shared cultural and historical legacy. The Russian language, for its part, was considered to be one of the foundational elements of this community. Hence, Russian speakers in the post-Soviet space were conceived as natural members of the *russkii mir* community.

As Lara Ryazanova-Clarke observes,

the discursive construction of value of the Russian language as a means for material advancement in the Russian transnational situations ('profit') is constantly intertwined with manufacturing the transnational semantics of belonging to Russia (what is termed here the transnational 'pride'). This is often overlaid with the instrumental value-attribution for Russian for establishing and perpetuating power relations, exerting control and, finally, warmongering. (Ryazanova-Clarke 2017: 444)

In other words, the new concept invested the Russian language with considerable symbolic and cultural capital. One of the basic tasks of *russkii mir* is the stabilisation and spread of the patterns of the Russian post-communist model of social life with the aid of this symbolic and cultural capital.

Aleksei Gromyko, distinguished separate categories of political values on which this common civilisation would be based. These would include the sacral character of power (*sakralnost' vlasti*), paternalism and sovereignty (Gromyko 2010: 21). And there is one more social 'virtue' which recurs as an essential element of the *russkii mir* habitus, namely passivity. In this logic, it is of secondary importance whether many people actually know about the contents legitimising the binding ideological order or whether they identify themselves with them. Indeed, as the case of Ukraine shows, those who are interested in the details of this content quickly notice various inconsistencies encoded in it. A case in point is the declarations of Patriarch Kirill, who, just a few months after the annexation of Crimea and during the Russian Army's involvement in the conflict in Eastern Ukraine, assured the Ukrainians that 'any war with people with other views and opinions' was 'absolutely alien' to the mentality of the *russkii mir* (Russkaia Pravoslavnaia Tserkov' 2014).

Because of these findings, we can treat the concept of the 'Russian World' as a tool that legitimises the specific political regime, which in the recent past has become known as 'managed democracy'. According to Sergei Markov, it was a 'natural stage in the development of Russia, from Soviet dictatorship through the anarchy of the Yeltsin years to normal democracy' (Markov 2004). Markov maintains that, until this normal democracy and the rule of law emerge, 'the state must be guided by a firm but gentle hand in the name of development and, finally, of democracy' (Markov 2004).

The crises following the Orange Revolution may be interpreted as a consequence of the failed attempt to establish a political regime in Ukraine according to the model of 'managed democracy'. After the Colour Revolutions, a new term gained currency in the Russian political vocabulary, that of 'sovereign democracy'. It seems that one of its characteristics was *sobornost'*, that is, the attachment to unity. As A. Kazantsev points out,

> this 'culture of unity' (*sobornaia' kul'tura*) rejects partisanship and fragmentation. It aims at demonstrating inner unity by the unanimous acceptance of the decisions taken among the elites behind the scenes. It also principally rejects procedural or legal constraints. (Kazantsev 2008: 3)[2]

The concept of *russkii mir* also connects to another important, yet somewhat independent category, that of the 'compatriots'. President Boris Yeltsin and Andrei Kozyrev, Russia's first foreign minister, introduced the term 'compatriots abroad' into the political lexicon in 1992. Compatriots were defined as 'individuals who live outside the borders of the Russian Federation itself yet feel that they have a historical, cultural, and linguistic linkage with Russia. These people want to preserve these ties no matter the present status of their citizenship' (Zavelev 2016). On the one hand, the concept of the compatriots was useful in realising some of the soft aims of foreign policy. On the other, it attempted the definition and creation of wider community borders, while at the same time centring them on Moscow. Already in 1993, the Russian government had become involved in the process of institutionalising the concept of the compatriots. The State Duma and the Council of Ministers formed special commissions for working with the compatriots (Iakubova et al. 2018: 93).

In 1999, the State Duma adopted the law 'On State Policy of the Russian Federation toward Compatriots Abroad'. Initially, this initiative lacked impact, but under Putin it gained momentum. As mentioned above, only a year after the Russkii Mir Foundation was created, so too was the Rossotrudnichestvo, which was supposed to set up Russian Centres abroad jointly with the Russkii Mir Foundation.

The ambiguity on the question of just who the compatriots really are is perplexing. Oxana Shevel rightly points out that

> such flexibility serves a functional purpose as it allows Russian policymakers broad room to manoeuvre. They can target a variety of sub-groups of the former Soviet citizens as 'compatriots' and can pursue policies that fall in a broad range from ethnic to civic to neo-imperial, without committing to any one of the associated discourses and without resolving the ambiguities and contradictions associated with each of the existing nation-building projects. (Shevel 2011: 199)

Vladimir Putin has always emphasised the importance of the compatriots in his annual addresses to Russian diplomats. During the first one in 2002, the theme of the compatriots and their rights was presented as a challenge to the Russian diplomatic service (Prezident Rossii 2002). Two years later, Putin placed the theme of compatriots in the context of maintaining Russian influence within the CIS (Prezident Rossii 2004). During the Medvedev interlude, the theme of compatriots disappeared from the speeches of the head of state during meetings with Russian diplomats. It reappeared, however, in 2012, with the return of Putin to the presidency. On that occasion, he repeated phrases about the necessity of protecting the rights and interests of compatriots (Prezident Rossii 2012).

SOVIET AND POST-SOVIET BILINGUALISM IN UKRAINE

The Soviet Union aspired to the amalgamation of a 'new type' of historical community, the Soviet nation. According to the official state propaganda, this community began to form during the 1970s. The mastering of the Russian language was considered to be one of the pivotal factors consolidating the Soviet nation. The then secretary general of the Ukrainian Communist Party, Volodymyr Shcherbytskyi, claimed in 1974 that

> today, as never before, the role and significance of the Russian language during the process of cultural development is growing. It is by law the second mother tongue in our republic and has become the generally recognised means of communication between all the nations and peoples of the USSR. (Masenko 2010: 139)[3]

This doctrine of a Russian–Ukrainian bilingualism remained in force in Ukraine until 1990. The main consequence of this official bilingualism, however, was the next stage of Russification in Ukraine. Education eventually spread the use of the Russian language at the expense of Ukrainian. Official reports showed that, by 1987, 48.7% of the pupils attended schools with Russian as a language of instruction (Kamins'kyi 1990: 75). At the same time, there were towns in the east and south of Ukraine, such as Donetsk and Mykolaiiv, with no school offering Ukrainian as the language of tuition. In many other cases, a few Ukrainian-speaking schools were outnumbered by Russian-language ones (Kamins'kyi 1990: 81). Nonetheless, according to the results of the last Soviet census of 1989, 67% of the inhabitants of Soviet Ukraine declared that they could freely use Ukrainian (Grynevych et al. 2004: 455). By contrast, a survey from the beginning of the 1990s showed that only 40% of the participants indicated Ukrainian as a language in which they were able to communicate easily (Yekelchyk 2009: 251).

These data illustrate the predominance of the Russian language in the public sphere of late Soviet Ukraine, although there were significant variations between regions. According to official data, Ukrainian dominated at least in western Ukraine, while the eastern and southern parts were almost totally Russified. A total de-Ukrainisation and destruction of the Ukrainian ethnos, though, was not the aim of Moscow's politics. The Soviet policy of bilingualism in Ukraine led to a clear demarcation between the social functions assigned to the Russian and Ukrainian languages. Ukrainian was referred to as the 'language of kolkhoz' and its use became a marker of 'rural provincialism' (Lysjak-Rudnyts'kyj 1994: 475).[4] The Ukrainian language was not considered a threat to the Soviet ethno-national project as long as its users did not challenge the dogma about their affiliation to the 'community of a new type', that is, to the 'Soviet nation', and continued to accept the status of Russian as 'a second mother tongue'. The Russian language, by contrast, stood for a more developed culture and universal values. The linguistic identity of the 'Soviet nation' would, of course, be based on the latter concept.

As a result, the connotations of the term 'mother tongue' became blurred in Ukrainian social consciousness. According to Larysa Masenko, the 'propaganda of two mother tongues' resulted in a specific 'mentality of a Sovietised Ukrainian', in which Russianness was not considered to be alien to or separated from Ukrainianness. Hence, Masenko suggested that 'the identity of such people remained blurred and their bond with their native culture was significantly weakened' (Masenko 2010: 140).

Respondents who associate themselves with the Soviet legacy still appear in contemporary social research on the transformations in Ukrainian society. Therefore, despite the fact that the majority of representatives of the Soviet (post-Soviet) identity are Russian-speaking, their ties with Russian culture are rather shallow. Indeed, there have always been more people in Ukraine who identify themselves with the Soviet past than with Russian culture. Except for Crimea, this has been true for all regions of Ukraine, including the Donbas and the south. According to data from 2007, 19.4% of respondents in the whole of Ukraine associated themselves with Soviet cultural tradition, and only 10.1% with the Russian one. For the eastern regions (Luhansk, Donetsk, Zaporizhzhia, Dnipropetrovsk), these shares amounted to 22.7% and 18.1%, respectively. In the southern part of the country (Odesa, Kherson, Mykolaiiv and Crimea), Soviet culture appeared more frequently in answers (26.5%), whereas the number of respondents identifying with Russian culture was almost the same as in the east (18%) (Razumkov Tsentr 2007: 6). The specifics of the Crimean situation became evident in a survey that was conducted separately in this region in 2007–8. The number of respondents who associated their identity with Russian culture (55.5%) considerably exceeded all other types of self-identification. Soviet culture was chosen by only 14.6% of the respondents (Razumkov Tsentr 2008: 52).

This data can be compared with results from similar surveys conducted in 2015, which obviously excludes Crimea, which had already been annexed by Russia by then, as well as parts of the districts of Luhansk and Donetsk occupied by the 'separatists' (Malynovs'ka 2016: 8). One year after the so-called Revolution of Dignity, the number of respondents who associated their identity with Soviet culture had decreased to 10.3% in the whole of Ukraine. Only 3.2% of participants of the survey continued to identify themselves with Russian culture, a decrease of 6.9 percentage points. As to the differences between the macro-regions of Ukraine, the inhabitants of the east and the south continued to identify more often with Soviet and Russian cultural traditions. Of the respondents from the districts in the south, 11.5% still identified themselves with Soviet culture and some 4% with the Russian one (Razumkov Tsentr 2016a). Comparing the outcomes with the results recorded seven years before, we can draw two important conclusions. First, the annexation of Crimea undoubtedly contributed to a further decrease in the number of people who identified with Russian or with culture, both on the regional and the national level. In general, there seems to be an interesting correlation between the cultural self-identification of the individual and the language they primarily employ. Russian-speaking respondents dominate the respondent group mentally attached to the Soviet legacy, as well as the group of people who have difficulty identifying with a particular cultural tradition (Razumkov Tsentr 2016a).

LANGUAGE AND IDENTITY POLITICS

Only after the Orange Revolution did the concept of *russkii mir* become an important element of Russia's foreign policy towards Ukraine and the near abroad. Yushchenko's presidency and the political struggles after the Orange Revolution shaped the context in which language and identity politics were fought out. Ukraine's president attempted to conceive of a more specific and coordinated policy of historical memory, and the commemoration of the Holodomor as a genocide against the Ukrainian nation quickly moved to centre stage (Zhurzhenko 2011). In 2006, the Ukrainian Institute of National Remembrance was created, following the Polish model. In 2008, Yushchenko established an official national holiday on the anniversary of the Christianisation of Kievan Rus' (Zakonodavstvo Ukrainy 2008) and Kyiv organised state celebrations of the 1,020th anniversary of Kievan Christianity, to which not only the Moscow Patriarch Aleksei II but also his counterpart from Constantinople, Bartolomei, was invited. The Ukrainian state thus laid claims to the prestige and symbolic capital associated with the medieval Kievan state.

After the Orange Revolution, the issue of Ukrainisation, that is, the promotion and support of the Ukrainian language in the public space, also moved to the centre of the public discourse. While Ukrainisation was supposed to be a grassroots movement, representatives of different state organs tried to support and stimulate it. Towards the end of his term, President Yushchenko issued a new 'State Concept on Language Policy'. According to this document, the Ukrainian language was 'the decisive factor and main marker of Ukrainian national identity'. At the same time, the decree defined the 'Ukrainian nation' as comprising 'all citizens of Ukraine, of all nationalities'. Command of the Ukrainian language was represented as a kind of civic duty for all residents of Ukraine 'regardless of ethnic origin, beliefs and position held'. In particular, this decree referred to people holding positions in state organs or local government. The Concept claimed that Ukrainian as a state language was 'a factor unifying and consolidating Ukrainian society' and called it a 'measure strengthening Ukrainian state unity' (Zakonodavstvo Ukrainy 2010; Shevchuk and Trach 2009).[5] The quoted document clearly assigned secondary importance to the function of the Ukrainian language as a means of communication. Language, by contrast, was above all considered as an important source of symbolic capital. The central task in the sphere of language policy in Ukraine was ascribing prestige and an enhanced place in the social structure to the Ukrainian language in public life. Against this background, a confrontation between supporters of Ukrainisation and defenders of the rights of the Russian-speaking population seemed almost inevitable.

While President Yushchenko took initiatives to reintroduce non-Soviet and non-Russian symbolic capital into the Ukrainian social space, the promoters of the *russkii mir* concept appropriated and used some of these elements for their own purposes. A good example was the official commemoration of the anniversary of the baptism of Kievan Rus'. Promoted actively by the Kremlin since 2007, the acceptance of the Christian faith by Vladimir the Great was interpreted by promoters of *russkii mir* as the founding act of that civilisational community. Ukraine had been the first to claim this anniversary as a state holiday, called the

'Day of the Baptism of Kievan Rus''. Only two days later, on 27 July 2008, the then Moscow Patriarch Alexei II approached the president of the Russian Federation, Dmitry Medvedev, with a request for state commemoration of this date in Russia (Russkaia Pravoslavnaia Tserkov' 2008). A little over one year after the appeal, and some six months after the death of its author, President Medvedev and Prime Minister Putin finally commissioned the drafting of a legal act to this effect in August 2009. The anniversary of the baptism of the Kievan Rus' became a public holiday in Russia in 2010 (Russkii Obozrevatel' 2010).

During this period, the successor of Aleksei II, Kirill I, also participated in the celebration in Kyiv of the baptism of the Kievan Rus'. Patriarch Kirill did his best to transform the holiday established by President Yushchenko into a demonstration of the unity of all of the territories covered by the civilisation of the *russkii mir*. During the solemn mass in 2009 he called Kiev 'our common Jerusalem, that of the Orthodox faith'. The head of the Russian Orthodox Church emphasised that he came to the 'holy land of Kiev' to pray to Saint Vladimir 'for our Orthodox Church and our people' (Patriarkh RPTs Kyrylo 2009).

In 2010, the head of the Russian Orthodox Church again went to Ukraine to celebrate the baptism of the Kievan Rus'. This time the visit took place in a different political situation. A few months earlier, Viktor Yanukovych had won the presidential election. Since his defeat in the 2004 elections, Yanukovych had developed an image as the defender of the 'canonical' Orthodox Church (of the Moscow Patriarchy) in Ukraine. Contrary to the organisers' expectations, however, only about 200 believers gathered for a mass in Kyiv on St Vladimir's Hill (Il'chenko 2010). Nonetheless, during a press conference in Moscow after the visit, representatives of the Russian Orthodox Church claimed that there had been thousands of people celebrating with the patriarch (Russkaia Pravoslavnaia Tserkov' 2010). During this 2010 visit to Ukraine, Patriarch Kirill publicly portrayed Yanukovych as a 'a deeply religious man' who, as a politician, was guided by his Orthodox worldview and contributed to the 'spiritual enlightenment of his people' (Televiziyna Sluzhba Novyn 2010).

The Russkii Mir Foundation and its centres were directly involved in the accumulation of symbolic capital related to commemoration of the baptism of Kievan Rus' in Ukraine. For example, in Kharkiv, the local Russian Centre organised the celebration of the 1,025th anniversary in 2013. In so doing, however, the centre referred to the Russian Federation's decree of 2010 and not to the decree of President Yushchenko issued two years earlier. Consequently, the Kharkiv branch of the Russkii Mir Foundation claimed to commemorate 'the day which laid the foundations of the history of contemporary civilisational choice made by the countries baptised in the Kievan cradle' (Russkii Mir 2013b).

It is impossible to understand the activities conducted in the sphere of language policy during Yanukovych's presidency without taking the *russkii mir* concept into consideration (Moser 2013: 121). The most notable act during his presidency was the law 'On the Principles of the Language Policy of the State', also known as the Kivalov-Kolesnichenko law, which was passed by the Verkhovna Rada in July 2012. Outwardly, its goal was to improve the language rights of the national minorities in Ukraine. According to the OSCE High Commissioner on National Minorities, Knut Vollebaek, the new law disproportionately favoured the Russian language, while also removing most incentives for learning or using Ukrainian in large parts of the country, potentially undermining Ukraine's very cohesion. Vollebaek called the new legal regulations 'controversial' at best, and advised against adopting the law in its current form, warning that 'the law is likely to lead to a further polarization of society' (OSCE 2012).

Despite these warnings and significant public protests, the Kivalov-Kolesnichenko law passed through the Rada and the Russian language gained the status of a 'regional language' in thirteen out of twenty-seven districts in Ukraine (International Alert 2017: 9). Already prior to the law, attempts to raise the legal status of the Russian language had been undertaken at the local level, not only in Crimea but also in the districts of Donetsk, Luhansk, Odesa, Kharkiv and Zaporizhzhia. Michael Moser interprets all these cases as attempts to reduce the use of the Ukrainian language in the public and in administration, or to facilitate Russian-language media's access to Ukrainian state subsidies (Moser 2013: 109–13).

According to the survey data discussed above, the Russian speakers in Ukraine consisted of a small minority of people identifying primarily with Russian culture and a much larger majority nostalgic for the Soviet past. As both of these groups were shrinking, critics perceived the law as an infringement upon the use of Ukrainian rather than as a defence of minority rights. In order to reverse this trend, Russian speakers in Ukraine became the main target group of the activities of the Russkii Mir Foundation. In this context, the flexibility of the 'Russian World' concept, being large enough to accommodate both groups, had a clear advantage over an ethno-cultural definition of Russianness.

ACTIVITIES OF THE RUSSKII MIR FOUNDATION IN UKRAINE

Several types of activity can be distinguished by means of which the Russkii Mir Foundation strives to achieve its goals. In the Russian Federation, regular congregations (assemblies) are of particular importance. The Foundation invited representatives of various backgrounds, from state authorities and politicians to intellectuals, artists, scholars and clerics. Among the latter, representatives of the Moscow Patriarchy were particularly ardent supporters of the *russkii mir*. A specific role is accorded to foreign guests, too, as their presence is meant to confirm the global scope of the *russkii mir* concept. The main goal of the congregations is thus to confirm the vitality of the global Russian community. During speeches at the congregations, the issue of Ukraine is quite often raised; however, the main target audience seems to be within the Russian Federation. Representatives of the authorities and various state institutions demonstratively rally behind the idea of a Russian civilisation produced for domestic consumption primarily.

Outside the borders of the Russian Federation, the Foundation employs two main instruments: the creation of so-called Russian Centres and a system of grants. The Foundation's website lists some goals that may be funded, such as 'the promotion of the Russian language', 'conducting linguistic research dealing with the Russian language' and 'cultural and humanitarian projects', including the 'spread and promoting of Russian-speaking mass media and other information resources sharing the values of the Russian World' (Russkii Mir 2014b; see also Chapter 9 in this volume). Moreover, the Foundation regularly provides statistical data on the number of applications submitted and selected for funding.

As mentioned above, the Russian Centres were conceived as the flagship initiative of the Foundation. Between 2009 and 2013, eleven such centres opened in Ukraine (Russkii Mir 2012: 6). They were established through joint agreements between the Foundation and selected institutions in Ukraine, usually a university or a library. Hence, the Russian Centres did not function as separate entities, but as a new element in the existing structures of Ukrainian institutions. The Foundation financed the refurbishment of rooms and provided books and equipment necessary for the implementation of the centres' mission. The first *Tsentr Russkoi kultury* was opened in a private university in Kharkiv, the Ukrainian People's Academy (NUA), in 2009. The official website of the university, however, provides no information on the functioning of the local Russian Centre in the past. Remarkably, the rector of the university, Valentyna Astakhanova, advertised the activities of the centre only on the Foundation's website, such as on the fifth anniversary of its creation (Russkii Mir 2013c).

The state universities in Kyiv, Odesa and Rivne created three other centres in cooperation with the Foundation. At present, these institutions neither promote the Russian Centre in their own promotional materials nor mention the Foundation as their partner. In Odesa, the local centre was solemnly opened at the National Mechnikov University in December 2012. On this occasion, the rector of the university, Ihor Koval, expressed his hope that 'together with the Russian side, the Russian consulate in Odesa and the Russkii Mir Foundation, we will develop and strengthen friendly relations between Ukraine and Russia' (Odessa Taimer 2012).[6] Two years later, in a changed political situation, Rector Koval strongly denied that his university had anything to do with the Foundation. He stated that, since January 2013, Odessa University had had no contact or cooperation either with the Russkii Mir Foundation or with other similar centres run by the Russian Federation (Odessa Taimer 2014). If that had been true, the Odesa centre would have lasted merely one month. By contrast, the Foundation's website reported on the activities of the Odesa centre at least until the end of May 2014 (Russkii Mir 2014c).

Indeed, reports on the Russian Centres' activities occupy a lot of space on the Foundation's website. In the first place, this allows a reconstruction of the geography of the centres' activities. A majority of the functioning institutions were located in Eastern Ukraine (Kharkiv), in the Donbas (Donetsk, Luhansk), in Crimea (Simferopol, Sevastopol) and in southern Ukraine (Zaporizhzhia, Kryvyi Rih, Kherson, Mykolaiiv, Odesa). Only two outlets (Dnipro and Kyiv) were located in the central part of the country, and only one (Rivne) in western Ukraine. Second, events organised by the centres were overwhelmingly niche events. Their form and content resemble extracurricular school activities or meetings in a seniors' club. The frequency of entries on the Foundation's website also provides some insights. In the period between 27 November 2009, when the first post appeared, and the end of February 2014, the overthrow of Viktor Yanukovych and the beginning of armed conflicts with Russia, a total of 425 entries were published. The centres in Luhansk and Donetsk showed the greatest amount of activity, with 154 entries in total. The Foundation's centres located in Crimea did not lag far behind, with 127 entries. Messages about the activity of centres in the south of Ukraine appeared much less frequently on the Foundation's website (62 entries). In sum, 80% of the activities of the Russian Centres were reported for regions in which the Russian language dominates both public and private life. Obviously, these were also the areas of Ukraine which were soon either annexed by Russia (i.e. Crimea) or involved in the ongoing fights against the so-called separatists (i.e. Donbas).

LANGUAGE AND IDENTITY AFTER THE MAIDAN

One of the first decisions of the Ukrainian parliament after the overthrow of President Yanukovych provided grist to Russia's mill. The Rada decided to repeal the Kivalov-Kolesnichenko law. The new OSCE High Commissioner on National Minorities, Astrid Thors, immediately criticised this step. She feared that the revocation of the law 'could lead to further unrest, especially in a context where language policy is such a divisive issue'. She encouraged the authorities to refrain from taking any hasty action that could lead to further escalation (OSCE 2014a). The new 'post-revolutionary' authorities in Kyiv followed Thors's suggestions. Acting President Oleksandr Turchynov declared on 3 March 2014 that he would not sign the law cancelling the Kivalov-Kolesnichenko law. Formally, this law remained in force until the end of the February 2018. Only then did the Constitutional Court of Ukraine find the 2012 law 'contrary to the constitution' and declare it invalid (Konstitutsiinyi Sud Ukraini 2018).

Nonetheless, the intent to revise the law served the Kremlin as a pretext for developing a campaign in defence of the supposedly threatened Russian-speaking inhabitants of Ukraine. In his speech before the two chambers of the Russian parliament on the occasion of the annexation of Crimea, President Putin directly linked the language issue with the political turmoil, declaring that 'those who opposed the coup were immediately threatened with repression. Naturally, the first in line here was Crimea, the Russian-speaking Crimea. In view of this, the residents of Crimea and Sevastopol turned to Russia for help in defending their rights and lives.' Russia's president asserted that 'millions of Russians and Russian-speaking people live in Ukraine and will continue to do so. Russia will always defend their interests using political, diplomatic and legal means' (President of Russia 2014).

By contrast, the OSCE High Commissioner on National Minorities, who had in the meantime visited Kyiv and Crimea, stated in her official press release that she 'found no evidence of violations or threats to the rights of Russian speakers'. On the contrary, she was 'alarmed about the risk of violent conflict on the Crimean Peninsula and the effects this could have on all communities, particularly the Ukrainian and Crimean Tatar groups' (OSCE 2014b).

This did not prevent Patriarch Kirill in September 2014 from publicly lamenting the 'tragic' news reaching him from Ukraine. According to the patriarch, 'people from an opposite camp killed all who were brave enough to confirm that they adhered to the *russkii mir*'. As a result, those who were 'not strong enough' were intimidated and 'are either silent or say something that their persecutors would like to hear' (Russkaia Pravoslavnaia Tserkov' 2014).[7] The topic of those 'silent adherents' is of particular importance for an understanding of the Russian position. The advocates of the Russian World have constantly grappled with the low level of interest in the idea of a civilisational community with Russia as an agenda for the future of Ukraine. The narration strategy applied by Patriarch Kirill sketches a completely different image of the situation. In his view, brave individuals expressing the will of the terrorised part of Ukrainian society are by no means representatives of a marginal group, but of a much larger 'silent' *russkii mir* constituency in post-Maidan Ukraine.

The logic of this defensive hero narrative was mirrored in a Russian-language compilation of 'citizen poetry' in Ukraine, inspired by the military conflict in the Donbas. Launched by the Russkii Mir Foundation, the book appeared under the indicative title 'Time of Bravery' in 2015 (Russkii Mir 2015b). This volume contained poems in Russian recalling the emotions and memories related to the mythology of the heroism of the Soviet peoples during the Nazi period, and their ensuing victory. Most of the authors were unknown to a broader public. The former head of the Russkii Mir Foundation, Viacheslav Nikonov, advertised it as 'a book about all of us'. He emphasised that 'a split within the *russkii mir* had occurred in the Donbas and now a time of trial had begun'. According to Nikonov, the war in Ukraine bore 'a fratricidal character' and had been provoked by 'external forces' (Russkii Mir 2017b: 279).[8]

Data from sociological surveys conducted in 2015 in those parts of the Donbas which were still under the control of the Ukrainian state provide a more nuanced picture. The majority of the respondents (72.4%) declared that they received their secondary education in Russian. Only 8.8% of the participants of the survey spoke 'exclusively' or 'mainly' in Ukrainian outside of the home, while 37.1% of respondents declared that in public they spoke in both Russian and Ukrainian. A majority (53.1%) asserted that in the public sphere they communicated with others 'exclusively' or 'mainly' in Russian (Razumkov Tsentr 2016a: 34–5). Obviously, accounts of a forced Ukrainisation of the Donbas, as disseminated by the Russkii Mir Foundation, seem to have had little in common with the reality on the ground.

This clearly confrontational rhetoric restricted Russkii Mir's room to manoeuvre in Ukraine. As of the beginning of 2015, only three centres are still operating on Ukrainian territory, and all of them are located in areas controlled by the so-called separatists: Donetsk, Luhansk and Horlivka. The 2016 annual report on the activities of the Russkii Mir Foundation explained this fact by suggesting that, in the remainder of Ukraine, 'extreme right and in fact Nazi parties' had come to power as a result of an 'armed coup'. The report claimed that the new authorities in Kyiv were pursuing a ruthless 'fight against the Russian language and against Russian culture'. Ultimately, under the pressure of a 'policy of glorifying Nazi predecessors and of de-communisation', the activities of all other Russian Centres in Ukraine had been suppressed (Russkii Mir 2017a: 34).[9]

Likewise, after 2014, the practical prospect of achieving the goals of Russian policy towards Ukraine with the help of compatriots virtually evaporated. That said, the compatriots did not immediately disappear from Russian public discourse on Ukraine. However, their function changed. They are no longer treated as a tool for the build-up of a positive image of Russia abroad. Instead, they allegedly provide an example circumscribing the external threats that Russia must face. Vladimir Putin warned that 'our compatriots, Russian people and people of other nationalities' (*russkie liudi i liudi drugikh natsional'nostei*) and their 'language, history, culture and legal rights, which are guaranteed among others by European conventions' were threatened (Prezident Rossii 2014).[10] Importantly, the Russian president directly connected the compatriots with the concept of the 'Russian World':

> When I speak about Russian people and Russian-speaking citizens, I mean people who consider themselves to be part of the so-called broader Russian World (*tak nazyvaemogo shirokogo russkogo mira*), not necessarily about ethnic Russians (*etnicheskie russkie liudi*), but those who consider themselves 'Russians'. (Prezident Rossii 2014)

At first glance, it would seem that a well-developed network of compatriot organisations indeed exists in Ukraine. This at least seems to be confirmed by the Internet portal for compatriots created on behalf of the Russian Ministry of Foreign Affairs (Russkii vek 2019a). It provides detailed information on the organisations involved in the compatriot movement in Ukraine. To a large extent, the data provided on this website is reproduced on the website of the Russkii Mir Foundation. Both pages, for example, provide information on compatriot and similar organisations related to Russkii Mir in Vinnytsia (Russkii vek 2019b). Five out of seven entities, however, are based at the same address, use the same email and are managed (or co-managed) by the same person. This seems to indicate that, at least as far as Vinnytsia is concerned, the organisations mentioned in the databases are mostly virtual. A more thorough and comprehensive analysis of the data contained in these databases will probably establish that this is true for other localities as well.

THE RUSSIAN LANGUAGE IN POST-MAIDAN UKRAINE:
COMMUNICATIVE AND SYMBOLIC DIMENSIONS

What, then, is the status of the Russian language in present-day Ukraine? Apparently, current surveys are likely to confirm the fears of the defenders of the Russian-speaking people. The number of respondents in Ukraine who declare Russian as their mother tongue has consistently decreased, from 30.7% in 2006 to 15.1% in 2015. The number of those declaring Ukrainian as their mother tongue increased during this period, less dramatically, from 52% to 59.9%. However, only 44.5% of the respondents of the 2015 survey speak Ukrainian at home, and still fewer (40.3%) communicate in Ukrainian in the public sphere. Participants were also asked which language they considered more prestigious as a means of communication. In response, 43% preferred Ukrainian, while Russian was chosen by only 21.5%. It is remarkable, however, that no less than 29% of the respondents declared themselves indifferent on that issue. We may suppose that Russian remains the language of everyday communication for the majority of those who are 'indifferent' (Prostir svobody 2016).

It seems that Ukrainian is slowly regaining its position after a long period of Russification. The largest part of the public sphere in Ukraine, however, is still Russian-speaking. Only 11% of the 1,000 most accessed websites in Ukraine are in Ukrainian, while 66.8% of them are in Russian. Slightly more than 22% of these websites are bilingual, however, with the basic version of the website being in Russian, supplemented by a less complete version in Ukrainian. Between 43% and 49% of the most active Facebook users are Ukrainian-speaking, whereas between 46.5% and 51.75% write their posts exclusively in Russian. The Russian version of Wikipedia is far more popular in Ukraine than the Ukrainian one.

The problems related to the functioning of the Russian language in the social sphere in Ukraine are perfectly illustrated by the case of the vice-mayor of Dnipro (formerly Dnipropetrovsk), Svetlana Epifantseva. She had been closely connected with the Party of Regions and belonged to the opponents of the 'Revolution of Dignity'. As a political gesture, the mayor of Dnipro, Borys Filatov, appointed her as deputy in 2016. Already by the end of February 2018 she had had to step down in connection with 'negative statements about the official language' (i.e. Ukrainian) and for 'deviating from the ethical rules for government officials'. The case in point had been a Facebook post written by Epifantseva, in which she claimed that people had stopped going to the cinemas because Russian films had been outlawed and only films in Ukrainian permitted (Glavred 2018).

It is worth recalling how this story was framed by adherents of the Russian World. Information about the events in Dnipro appeared on the website of the Russian RIA Novosti news agency, with the header 'in Ukraine an official was removed for her statements about the Ukrainian language' (RIA Novosti 2018). The website of the Russkii Mir Foundation also disseminated this piece, but under a different title: 'In Ukraine they have started to remove officials for their thoughts *on the Russian language*' (Russkii Mir 2018, emphasis added).[11] This is a quite typical example of manipulation of news promoted through the channels of Russkii Mir and designed to fit the image of a 'Russophobic Ukraine' (Kaitseväe Akadeemia 2017).

In this context, references to the 'communicative dimension' of the Russian language in Ukraine are of secondary importance. The Epifantseva case perfectly illustrates the transformation of the language issue in Ukraine into a struggle for symbolic capital, which in turn is implicated in a process of legitimisation and implementation of different political agendas in Ukraine.

After the overthrow of the Yanukovych regime, the Russian discourse on the role of the Russian language in Ukraine began to change. Its function as a means of attraction towards the 'idea of the spiritual unity of the Russian World' was replaced by the justification and legitimisation of Russia's aggressive behaviour towards its neighbour. Ryazanova-Clarke describes this significant reorientation in the use of the symbolic capital as a transition 'from commodification to weaponization'. In the context of the current situation in Ukraine, this means that the Russian language is 'employed to build solidarity with one part of the Ukrainian society and against the other' (Ryazanova-Clarke 2017: 451).

This approach is based on the erroneous presumption that the conflict in Ukraine is a clash between the Russian-speaking and Ukrainian-speaking parts of Ukrainian society, and that language differences mark the main point of reference for social, political and cultural cleavages in the country. On the contrary, according to a 2016 survey, the language issue retains very little divisive potential. The basic lines of political divisions in Ukrainian society are, by contrast, shaped by issues such as 'attitude towards authorities and their policy' (chosen by 42% of respondents), 'attitude towards the war in the Eastern Ukraine' (40.7%) or 'attitude towards Russia' (39.9%). By comparison, only 12.9% of the respondents chose 'Russian language and culture' and just 6% 'Ukrainian language and culture'. Of course, the respective shares differed regionally: 19.6% of the respondents in western Ukraine perceived the Russian language as a divisive factor, compared with 8% in the Donbas; by contrast, the proportions in both regions regarding the Ukrainian language as a matter of conflict (6.4% in western Ukraine and 7% in the Donbas) differed scarcely at all (Razumkov Tsentr 2016b: 58).

At the same time, the association of 'pride' with the Russian language in Ukraine is clearly receding in the wake of the Euromaidan, which openly challenged Moscow's self-conception as the centre of a common civilisation. Thus, the symbolic capital invested in the historically developed spatial structure of relations between the centre (Russia, Moscow) and periphery (Ukraine) lost its value. This could not but impinge upon the symbolic functions of the Russian language. Russia bases its attempts to 'weaponise' the language issue, within the framework of the *russkii mir* concept, upon the manipulation of facts. Figuratively speaking, the weapons launched by the promoters of the 'Russian World' on the language front in Ukraine are running out of ammunition.

CONCLUSION

At the end of 2014, the All-Russian Centre for Public Opinion (VTSIOM) published the results of a survey entitled 'The "Russian World" and How It Should Be Understood'. According to this survey, a large majority of Russian citizens had never heard of the *russkii mir*. Those who were to some degree familiar with this concept had very interesting opinions regarding the spatial reach of the Russian community. According to 75% of the respondents, the Donbas belonged to the 'Russian World'. The proportions of those willing to include Transnistria (63%), Abkhazia (55%) and South Ossetia (52%) were somewhat lower, but still close to twice as large as that of those opting to include central and western Ukraine (29%). Interestingly, many more respondents (48%) had no qualms about identifying Serbia as part of the *russkii mir*, a country far beyond the territories defined as the core area of the Orthodox civilisation in the official narrative put about between 2007 and 2013, which had mythologised Kyiv as its cradle (All-Russian Centre for Public Opinion 2014).

Whatever the credibility of the data quoted above, the mere fact that this survey was published by the All-Russian Centre for Public Opinion, a state agency subordinated to the Kremlin authorities, reveals the transformations that the *russkii mir* concept has undergone since its launch in the 2000s. The 'Russian World' and the 'compatriots' emerged as key concepts on which the Kremlin based its efforts to create its own language and culture-based version of soft power in Ukraine, aiming at the creation of a positive image and of developing mutual relations in a climate of 'brotherhood'. At the same time, the Kremlin geared its soft power initiative in Ukraine towards the promotion of a specific 'Russian' model of social identity, whose main virtue consisted in passivity and the full acceptance of the vertical paternalistic model of relations between the state authorities and society.

As it turned out, the promoters of the *russkii mir* concept underrated the changes that had occurred in the Ukrainian social space after the Orange Revolution and the Maidan. Because of these changes, the promoted social type met with resistance in Ukraine across a broad social and spatial sphere (Hudson 2015). Obviously, the experience that Ukrainian society gained in terms of their relations with the organs of state power after 2004 differed significantly from those in other parts of the former Soviet space. This, of course, did not apply to the entire society, but to a growing part of it, large enough to reduce the chance of success for such broad and ambiguous concepts as the 'Russian World' or the 'compatriots'. Russia employed these ambiguous concepts in its attempts to manipulate selected elements within Ukrainian society, using references to the status of the Russian language or to common historical memories. As a result, the boundary between 'us' and 'not us', meaning the Russian and the Ukrainian social spaces, has become much more discernible. In this sense, it facilitated the consolidation more of Ukrainian community and identity, rather than of an overarching (Great) Russian one. As a result, a significant part of the people treated by the Kremlin as 'ours' began to publicly reject this designation.

Translated from Polish by Christian Noack

NOTES

1. Translations from this document by Michał Wawrzonek and Christian Noack.
2. Translated by Michał Wawrzonek and Christian Noack.
3. Translated by Michał Warzonek and Christian Noack.
4. Translations from Lysjak-Rudnyts'kyj and Masenko (below) by Michał Wawrzonek and Christian Noack.
5. Translated by Michał Warzonek and Christian Noack.
6. Translated by Michał Warzonek and Christian Noack.
7. Translated by Michał Warzonek and Christian Noack.

8. Translated by Michał Warzonek and Christian Noack.
9. Translated by Michał Warzonek and Christian Noack.
10. Translated by Michał Warzonek and Christian Noack.
11. Translated by Michał Warzonek and Christian Noack.

REFERENCES

All-Russian Centre for Public Opinion (2014), '"Russkii Mir" i kak ego poniat?', <http://wciom.ru/index.php?id=236&uid=115074> (last accessed 1 May 2019).

Ballinger, P. (2017), 'Whatever happened to Eastern Europe? Revisiting Europe's eastern peripheries', *East European Politics and Societies and Cultures* 31 (1), pp. 44–67.

Bourdieu, P. (2000), *Pascalian Meditations*, Stanford, CA: Stanford University Press.

Curanović, A. (2012), *The Religious Factor in Russia's Foreign Policy*, London/New York: Routledge.

Glavred (2018), 'Kto takaia Svetlana Epifantseva i pochemu vokrug nee razgorelsia iazykovoi skandal', <http://glavred.info/ukraine/kto-takaya-svetlana-epifanceva-i-pochemu-vokrug-nee-razgorelsya-yazykovoy-skandal-492056.html> (last accessed 21 May 2019).

Gromyko, A. (2010), 'Russkii mir: poniatie, printsipy, tsennosti, struktura', in V. Nikonov (ed.), *Smysli i tsennosti Russkogo Mira. Sbornik statei i materialov kruglykh stolov organizovannykh fondom 'Russkii Mir'*, Moscow: Fond Russkii Mir, <https://russkiymir.ru/events/docs/%D0%A1%D0%BC%D1%8B%D1%81%D0%BB%D1%8B%20%D0%B8%20%D1%86%D0%B5%D0%BD%D0%BD%D0%BE%D1%81%D1%82%D0%B8%20%D0%A0%D1%83%D1%81%D1%81%D0%BA%D0%BE%D0%B3%D0%BE%20%D0%BC%D0%B8%D1%80%D0%B0%202010.pdf> (last accessed 1 May 2019), pp. 20–3.

Grynevych, V., V. Danylenko, S. Kul'chyc'kyj and O. Lysenko (eds) (2004), *Ukrai'na i Rosiia v istorychnij perspektyvi, vol. 2: Radians'kyj proekt dlia Ukrai'ny*, Kyiv: Naukova Dumka.

Hale, H. E., O. Shevel and O. Onuch (2018), 'Believing facts in the fog of war: Identity, media and hot cognition in Ukraine's 2014 Odesa tragedy', *Geopolitics* 23 (4), pp. 851–81.

Hudson, V. (2015), ' "Forced to friendship"? Russian (mis-)understandings of soft power and the implications for audience attraction in Ukraine', *Politics* 35 (3–4), pp. 330–46.

Iakubova, L., V. Golovko and I. Prymachenko (2018), *Russkyj myr na Donbasi ta v Krymu: istorychni vytoky, polityschna tehnologiia, instrument agresii': Analitychna dopovid'*. Kyiv: Natsional'na akademiia nauk Ukrai'ny, Instytut istorii' Ukrai'ny.

Il'chenko, S. (2010), 'Orden patriarkha – soratniku Vakhi Arsanova', *Svobodnaia Pressa*, 28 July, <http://svpressa.ru/society/article/28346/> (last accessed 31 May 2019).

International Alert (2017), *Pytannia identychnosti dlia rosiis'komovnykh v Ukrai'ni v konteksti zbroinogo konfliktu na shodi krai'ny*, <https://www.international-alert.org/sites/default/files/Ukraine_RussophoneIdentity_Spreads_UK_2017.pdf> (last accessed 31 May 2019).

Kaitsevä Akadeemia (2017), *Russian Information Warfare against the Ukrainian State and Defence Forces: April–December 2014*, ENDC Occasional Papers 7/2017, <http://www.ksk.edu.ee/teadus-ja-arendustegevus/publikatsioonid/endc-occasional-papers/endc-occasional-papers-7/> (last accessed 31 May 2019).

Kamins'kyi, A. (1990), *Na perehidnomu etapi. 'Glasnist'', 'perebudova' i 'demokratyzacija' na Ukrai'ni*, Munich: Ukrai'ns'kyj Vil'nyj Universytet.

Kazantsev, A. A. (2008), '"Suverennaia demokratiia" v sovremennoi Rossii: struktura kontsepta i ideologemy', in *Publichnoe prostranstvo, grazhdanskoe obshchestvo i vlast': opyt razvitiia i vzaimodeistviia*, Moscow: Izd-vo ROSSPJeN, <https://www.civis book.ru/files/File/Kazanzev_suv.pdf> (last accessed 10 May 2019).

Konstytutsiinyi Sud Ukraini (2018), '28 liutogo 2018 r. Zasidannia Konstytutsiinoho Sudu Ukrai'ny', <http://www.ccu.gov.ua/novyna/28-lyutogo-2018-r-zasidannya-konstytuciynogo-sudu-ukrayiny> (last accessed 31 May 2019).

Laruelle, M. (2015), *The 'Russian World': Russia's Soft Power and Geopolitical Imagination*, Washington DC: Center on Global Interests.

Laruelle, M. (2016), 'The three colors of Novorossiya, or the Russian nationalist myth-making of the Ukrainian crisis', *Post-Soviet Affairs* 32 (1), pp. 55–74.

Lysjak-Rudnyts'kyj, I. (1994), *Istorychni ese*, vol. 2, Kyiv: Osnovy.

Malynovs'ka, O. (ed.) (2016), *Migratsiia v Ukrai'ni: fakty i tsyfry*, Kyiv: MOM.

Markov, S. (2004), 'The future of managed democracy', *Moscow Times*, 30 January, <http://old.themoscowtimes.com/news/article/tmt/233370.html> (last accessed 10 May 2019).

Masenko, L. (2010), *Narysy z sotsiolinhvistyky*, Kyiv: Vydavnychyj Dim Kyjevo-Mogyljans'ka Akademija.

Moser, M. (2013), *Language Policy and the Discourse on Languages in Ukraine under President Viktor Yanukovych (25 February 2010–28 October 2012)*, Stuttgart: ibidem-Verlag.

Nikonov, V. (ed.) (2010), *Smysli i tsennosti Russkogo Mira. Sbornik statei i materialov kruglykh stolov organizovannykh fondom 'Russkii Mir'*, Moscow: Fond Russkii Mir, <https://russkiymir.ru/events/docs/%D0%A1%D0%BC%D1%8B%D1%81%D0%BB%D1%8B%20%D0%B8%20%D1%86%D0%B5%D0%BD%D0%BD%D0%BE%D1%81%D1%82%D0%B8%20%D0%A0%D1%83%D1%81%D1%81%D0%BA%D0%BE%D0%B3%D0%BE%20%D0%BC%D0%B8%D1%80%D0%B0%202010.pdf> (last accessed 1 May 2019).

Odessa Taimer (2012), 'V ONU im. Mechnikova poiavilsia Russkii tsentr', 6 December, <http://timer-odessa.net/news/v_odesse_poyavilsya_russkiy_tsentr_foto_337.html> (last accessed 31 May 2019).

Odessa Taimer (2014), 'Rektor ONU prokommentiroval zaiavlenie natsionalistov o Russkom kul'turnom tsentre', 10 December, <http://timer-odessa.net/news/rektor_onu_o_russkom_kulturnom_tsentre_995.html> (last accessed 31 May 2019).

OSCE (2012), 'OSCE High Commissioner on National Minorities urges dialogue and compromise on "divisive" language law in Ukraine', 26 July, <https://www.osce.org/hcnm/92418> (last accessed 31 May 2019).

OSCE (2014a), 'Restraint, responsibility and dialogue needed in Ukraine, including Crimea, says OSCE High Commissioner on National Minorities', 24 February, <https://www.osce.org/hcnm/115643> (last accessed 31 May 2019).

OSCE (2014b), 'Developing situation in Crimea alarming, says OSCE High Commissioner on National Minorities', 6 March, <https://www.osce.org/hcnm/116180> (last accessed 31 May 2019).

Patriarkh RPTs Kyrylo (2009), 'Kyi'v – nash spil'nyi Jerusalym', <https://www.radi osvoboda.org/a/1786585.html> (last accessed 22 May 2019).

Pikulicka-Wilczewska, A. and R. Sakwa (eds) (2015), *Ukraine and Russia: People, Politics, Propaganda and Perspectives*, Bristol: E-International Relations.

President of Russia (2014), 'Address by President of the Russian Federation. Vladimir Putin addressed State Duma deputies, Federation Council members, heads of Russian regions and civil society representatives in the Kremlin', 18 March, <http://en.kremlin.ru/events/president/news/20603> (last accessed 31 May 2019).

Prezident Rossii (2002), 'Vystuplenie na rasshirennom soveshchanii v Ministerstve inostrannykh del s uchastiem glav diplomaticheskikh missii za rubezhom', <http://kremlin.ru/events/president/transcripts/21674> (last accessed 22 May 2019).

Prezident Rossii (2004), 'Vystuplenie na plenarnom zasedanii soveshchaniia poslov i postoiannykh predstavitelei Rossii', <http://kremlin.ru/events/president/transcripts/22545> (last accessed 22 May 2019).

Prezident Rossii (2012), 'Vystuplenie na plenarnom zasedanii soveshchaniia poslov i postoiannykh predstavitelei Rossii', <http://kremlin.ru/events/president/news/15902> (last accessed 22 May 2019).

Prezident Rossii (2014), 'Soveshchanie poslov i postoiannykh predstavitelei Rossii', <http://kremlin.ru/events/president/news/46131> (last accessed 1 May 2019).

Prostir Svobody (2016), 'Stanovyshche ukrains'koi movy v Ukrai'ni u 2016 rotsi', <https://docs.google.com/document/d/1ScYcGPhLeu5Y7P8Cg1wOX1sk7lTqf3D9VhQBZgNRpac/edit> (last accessed 1 May 2019)

Razumkov Tsentr (2007), 'Identychnist' hromadian Ukrai'ny: stan i zminy', *Natsional'na bezpeka i oborona* 9 (93), pp. 3–31.

Razumkov Tsentr (2008), 'AR Krym: liudy, problemy, perspektyvy (Suspil'no-politychni, mizhnatsional'ni ta mizhkonfesiini vidnosyny v Avtonomnii Respublitsi Krym)', *Natsional'na bezpeka i oborona* 10 (104), pp. 51–72.

Razumkov Tsentr (2016a), 'Identychnist' hromadian Ukrai'ny v novykh umovakh: Stan, tendentsii, reghionalni osoblyvosti', *Natsional'na bezpeka i oborona*, 3–4 (161–2), pp. 3–57.

Rasumkov Tsentr (2016b), 'Konsolidatsija ukrai'ns'kogo suspil'stva: shliakhy, vyklyky, perspektyvy. Informatsiino-analitychni materialy do fakhovoi dyskusii', 16 December, <http://razumkov.org.ua/upload/Identi-2016.pdf> (last accessed 31 May 2019).

Religiia v Ukraine (2010), 'Patriarkh Kirill postavil Ukraine zadachu "peregruzit'" suverenitet i napravit' ego na ukreplenie Russkogo mira', <https://www.religion.in.ua/news/vazhlivo/6649-patriarx-Cyril-postavil-ukraine-zadachu-perezagruzit-suverenitet-i-napravit-ego-na-ukreplenie-russkogo-mira.html> (last accessed 1 May 2019).

RIA Novosti (2018), 'V Ukraine chinovnitsu uvolili iz-za vyskazyvaniia ob ukrainskom iazyke', <https://ria.ru/world/20180228/1515486948.html> (last accessed 1 May 2019).

Russkaia Pravoslavnaia Tserkov' (2008), 'Poslanie Sviateishego Patriarkha Aleksiia ot imeni Arkhiereiskogo Sobora Russkoi Pravoslavnoi Tserkvi Prezidentu Rossiiskoi Federatsii D. A. Medvedevu', <http://www.patriarchia.ru/db/text/428844.html> (last accessed 22 May 2019).

Russkaia Pravoslavnaia Tserkov' (2009), 'Vystuplenie Sviateishego Patriarkha Kirilla na torzhestvennom otkrytii III Assamblei Russkogo mira', <http://www.patriarchia.ru/db/text/928446.html> (last accessed 1 May 2019).

Russkaia Pravoslvnaia Tserkov' (2010), 'Okolo 5 tys. chelovek ozhidaiut patriarkha Kirilla riadom so Spaso-Preobrazhenskim soborom v Odesse', <http://www.interfax.com.ua/rus/main/44226/> (last accessed 31 May 2019).

Russkaia Pravoslavnaia Tserkov' (2014), 'Slovo pastiria', <http://www.patriarchia.ru/ua/db/text/3728244.html> (last accessed 10 May 2019).

Russkii Mir (2009), *Otchet ob osnovnykh napravleniiakh deiatel'nosti za 2008 god*, Moscow: Fond Russkii Mir, <https://russkiymir.ru/export/sites/default/russkiymir/ru/fund/docs/Report_2008.pdf> (last accessed 1 May 2019).

Russkii Mir (2012), *Otchet ob osnovnykh napravleniiakh deiatel'nosti za 2011 god*, Moscow: Fond Russkii Mir, <https://russkiymir.ru/export/sites/default/russkiymir/ru/fund/docs/Report_2011.pdf> (last accessed 31 May 2019).

Russkii Mir (2013a), *Otchet ob osnovnykh napravleniiakh deiatel'nosti za 2012 god*, Moscow: Fond Russkii Mir, <https://russkiymir.ru/export/sites/default/russkiymir/ru/fund/docs/Report_5.pdf> (last accessed 1 May 2019).

Russkii Mir (2013b), 'Khar'kovskii Russkii tsentr otmechaet iubilei Kreshcheniia Rusi', 29 July, <https://www.russkiymir.ru/news/97806/> (last accessed 31 May 2019).

Russkii Mir (2013c), 'Piatiletie druzhby i sotrudnichestva otmechaiut v Khar'kove', 21 June, <https://www.russkiymir.ru/news/97643/> (last accessed 31 May 2019).

Russkii Mir (2014a), *Otchet ob osnovnykh napravleniiakh deiatel'nosti za 2013 god*, Moscow: Fond Russkii Mir, <https://russkiymir.ru/export/sites/default/russkiymir/ru/fund/docs/Report_2013.pdf> (last accessed 1 May 2019).

Russkii Mir (2014b), 'Russkiy Mir Foundation grant provision statutes', <https://russkiymir.ru/en/grants/grant-provision-statute.php> (last accessed 20 January 2020).

Russkii Mir (2014c), 'Lektsiiu o problemakh gumanitarnykh nauk proslushali v odesskom Russkom tsentre', 20 May, <https://www.russkiymir.ru/news/119148/?sphrase_id=881745> (last accessed 31 May 2019).

Russkii Mir (2015a), *Otchet ob osnovnykh napravleniiakh deiatel'nosti za 2014 god*, Moscow: Fond Russkii Mir, <https://russkiymir.ru/events/docs/report_2014.pdf> (last accessed 1 May 2019).

Russkii Mir (2015b), 'Russkii Mir: Chas muzhestva poetov Donbasa', <https://russkiymir.ru/media/radio2/programs/all/189491/> (last accessed 30 April 2019). [Print version: *Chas muzhestva. Grazhdanskaja poeziia Donbasa 2014–2015 godov. Sbornik stikhov*, Moscow: Izdatel'stvo 'Pero', 2015.]

Russkii Mir (2017a), *Otchet ob osnovnykh napravleniiakh deiatel'nosti za 2016 god*, Moscow: Fond Russkii Mir, <https://russkiymir.ru/events/docs/report_2016.pdf> (last accessed 1 May 2019).

Russkii Mir (2017b), *Iubileinyi sbornik fonda Russkii Mir*, Moscow: Fond Russkii Mir, <https://russkiymir.ru/events/docs/Report_10_2017.pdf> (last accessed 31 May 2019).

Russkii Mir (2018), 'Na Ukraine nachali uvol'niat' gossluzhashchikh za rassuszhdeniia o russkom iazyke', <https://russkiymir.ru/news/238393/> (last accessed 31 May 2019).

Russkii Mir (2020), 'About Russkii Mir Foundation', <https://russkiymir.ru/en/fund/> (last accessed 2 April 2020).

Russkii Obozrevatel' (2010), 'Den' Kreshcheniia Rusi budet otmechat'sia v Rossii 28 iiulia', <http://www.rus-obr.ru/print/days/6646> (last accessed 22 May 2019).

Russkii vek (2019a), 'Portal dlia Rossiiskikh sootechestvennikov. O proekte', <http://www.ruvek.info/?module=pages&action=view&id=13> (last accessed 31 May 2019).

Russkii vek (2019b), 'Portal dlia Rossiiskikh sootechestvennikov. Ukraina', <http://www.ruvek.ru/?%C3%8B%E2%80%A0%C3%8B%E2%80%A0%C3%8B%E2%80%A0&cid=1&cid=1&cid=1&cid=1&cid=1&cid=1&id=631&module=country&&cid=1&&cid=1&page=5#db2%20(accessed%201%20May%202019)> (last accessed 20 May 2019).

Ryazanova-Clarke, L. (2017), 'From commodification to weaponization: The Russian language as "pride" and "profit" in Russia's transnational discourses', *International Journal of Bilingual Education and Bilingualism* 20 (4), pp. 443–56.

Shevchuk, G. and N. Trach (2009), 'Movna polityka pislia Pomaranchevoi' revoliutsii', *MAG'ISTERIUM 37: Movoznavchi studii'*, <http://ekmair.ukma.edu.ua/handle/123456789/10743> (last accessed 22 May 2019).

Shevel, O. (2011), 'Russian nation-building from Yel'tsin to Medvedev: Ethnic, civic or purposefully ambiguous?', *Europe-Asia Studies* 63 (2), pp. 179–202.

Suslov, M. (2017), *'Russian World': Russia's Policy Towards its Diaspora*, Russie.Nei. Visions 103, Paris: Ifri, <https://www.ifri.org/sites/default/files/atoms/files/suslov_russian_world_2017.pdf> (last accessed 1 May 2019).

Szostek, J. (2014), 'Russia and the news media in Ukraine: A case of "soft power"?', *East European Politics, Societies and Cultures* 28 (3), pp. 463–86.

Televiziyna Sluzhba Novyn (2010), 'Patriarkh Kyrylo: Ianukovych sluzhyt' dukhovnij prosviti svoho narodu', 18 July, <http://tsn.ua/ukrayina/patriarh-kirilo-yanukovich-sluzhit-duhovniy-prosviti-svogo-narodu.html> (last accessed 31 May 2019).

Tishkov, V. (2007), 'Staryi i novyi Russkii Mir', *Rossiia v kraskakh*, <http://ricolor.org/rus/rus_mir/proekt_rusmir/1/> (last accessed 1 May 2019).

Yekelchyk, S. (2009), *Ukraina. Narodziny nowoczesnego narodu*, Krakow: Wydawnictwo Uniwersytetu Jagiellońskiego.

Zakonodavstvo Ukrainy (2008), *Ukaz Prezydenta Ukrai'ny pro Den' Khreshhennia Kyi'vs'koi' Rusi – Ukrai'ny*, <https://zakon.rada.gov.ua/laws/show/668/2008> (last accessed 22 May 2019).

Zakonodavstvo Ukrainy (2010), *Ukaz Prezydenta Ukrai'ny Pro Kontseptsiiu derzhavnoi movnoi polityki*, <https://zakon.rada.gov.ua/laws/show/161/2010> (last accessed 22 May 2019).

Zavelev, I. (2016), 'The Russian world in Moscow's strategy', Center for Strategic and International Studies, <https://www.csis.org/analysis/russian-world-moscows-strategy> (last accessed 10 May 2019).

Zhurzhenko, T. (2011), ' "Capital of despair": Holodomor memory and political conflicts in Kharkiv after the Orange Revolution', *East European Politics and Societies* 25 (3), pp. 597–639.

CHAPTER 2

Russian in Belarus: A Feature of Belarusian Identity or Moscow's 'Trojan Horse'?

Mark Brüggemann

INTRODUCTION

With the collapse of the Soviet Union, many Russians suddenly lived in the non-Russian Soviet republics outside the borders of the Russian Federation, the self-declared successor state of the USSR. Data from the last Soviet census of 1989 provides a rough indication of the extent to which this was the case: roughly 17.4% of all Russians in the former Soviet Union lived in the non-Russian Soviet republics (Brüggemann 2017: 203–5; Comrie 1999: 837–8).

This chapter focuses on Belarus as an example of a former republic that was perceived to have been dismissed into state independence rather involuntarily in the wake of the collapse of the Soviet Union and described as a country with a weakly developed national identity (e.g. Marples 1999).[1] Since the ascent to power of President Aliaksandr Lukashenka, Belarus has not only been considered Europe's last dictatorship (Bennet 2011), but has seemingly also been characterised by a dualistic conflict between the pro-Russian power apparatus and a politically marginalised and persecuted national-minded opposition (Lastouski 2011). As far as the linguistic situation in Belarus is concerned, press coverage and academic research focus primarily on the status of the Belarusian language. Either it is seen as a marginalised language under the authoritarian rule of Lukashenka, or speaking Belarusian is treated as a linguistic marker signalling support for a political opposition that is often understood as monolithic. The aim of this chapter is twofold. On the one hand, it attempts to sketch a more differentiated picture of the relationship between languages, identities and political attitudes in Belarus. On the other hand, it explores the role of the Russian language in more detail, in terms of both actual language policy and claims raised in public and academic debates.

LANGUAGE POLICY IN BELARUS AND THE ROLE OF RUSSIAN ACTORS

Except for the early phase – that is, until the beginning of the 1930s – Russian was always the dominant language in the public life of the Belarusian Soviet Socialist Republic (BSSR). The Belarusian language, by contrast, was a subject in schools; however, only for a minority, especially in the countryside, was it also the language of instruction. Otherwise, Belarusian played only minor roles in the culture or in the academic research on 'Belarusian issues' conducted in the republic. During perestroika, the urban youth and parts of the intelligentsia started to voice concern about the general decay of the command of Belarusian in the republic and called for an improvement in the situation of the Belarusian language and culture. The defenders of the Belarusian language rallied in the Belarusian Popular Front (Belaruski Narodny Front, BNF) movement, which would later become a political party, and the Belarusian Language Society (Tavarystva Belaruskai Movy, TBM), both of which were founded in 1989 (Bieder 2001: 466–7).

Under pressure from these groups, Belarusian was finally declared the only state language shortly before the fall of the Soviet Union. The Law on Languages, adopted in 1990, stipulated that Russian retained the status of a 'language of interethnic communication between the nationalities of the USSR' (Zaprudski 2007: 107). The Law on Languages remained in force after state independence, and its preferential treatment of Belarusian was echoed by the language-related provisions of other legal acts, such as the Law on Culture of June 1991 or the Law on Education of October 1991 (Bekus 2014: 31).

In the first years after independence, the linguistic Belarusification policy and legislation found its most tangible expression in the school system, in which the proportion of first graders taught in Belarusian increased from about 15% in the 1986/7 school year to around 80% in the 1994/5 school year (Shadurskii 2016: 94). Moreover, the use of Belarusian also spread in the higher education system, which, with the partial exception of the humanities, had been the almost exclusive domain of the Russian language (Mechkovskaia 2013: 42).

The pro-Belarusian policy quickly proved rather unpopular. As Russian had, for decades, been the clearly dominant language of public life, the population had adjusted its language use accordingly (Frear

2019: 79). President Lukashenka, first elected in 1994, had already bowed to this sentiment in his election campaign and heavily promoted legal equality between the Russian and Belarusian languages. In 1995, he held a constitutionally dubious referendum parallel to the parliamentary elections, in which the population was, among other things, asked for its opinion in the language question. A clear majority, 83.3% of respondents, supported the legal equality of Russian (Vasilevich 2012). As a result of the referendum, Belarus became in legal terms bilingual; however, official documents had to be drafted in only one of the two official languages, which in practice maintained the predominance of the Russian language (Frear 2019: 80).

This revision occurred at a time in which the first effects of the pro-Belarusian linguistic policy pursued during the first half of the 1990s became apparent in the educational system. After the referendum, however, the language policy in schools was no longer geared towards increasing the use of the Belarusian language. From then on the language preferences of parents were decisive, and they opted overwhelmingly for Russian in order to provide their children with better career prospects (Zaprudski 2007: 107).

As far as the relationship between the Russian and Belarusian languages was concerned, the attitude of Lukashenka and of the relevant ministries and authorities remained virtually unchanged into the 2000s. All demands for an improvement in the status of Belarusian were rejected by pointing to the legal equality of Russian and Belarusian following the referendum, and any language 'issues' were represented as 'contrived' by the opposition, as the referendum had 'democratically' resolved the question (Brüggemann 2014). When, during the mid-2000s, sharp economic and energy conflicts emerged between Belarus and Russia, the intimidated partisans of Belarusian cherished new hopes for a change in the president's language policy. Lukashenka, however, limited himself to some symbolic gestures. One was the appointment of Paval Latushka, known for his consistent use of Belarusian in public, as Minister of Culture, and another was a new law decreeing that the primary versions of settlement or street names in official use should be the Belarusian ones, and that these should be transliterated from Belarusian for use in the Russian language (Vasilevich 2012; Brüggemann 2014: 91).

When the Russian institutions Rossotrudnichestvo and the Russkii Mir Foundation spread their activities into Belarus, they entered an environment that already displayed a highly favourable orientation towards the Russian language. This has meant, at the same time, that until now their engagement in Belarus has largely gone unnoticed and has had virtually no perceptible political impact, since their activities, in sharp contrast with the situation in Ukraine, have hardly ever become the subject of controversial debate (for Ukraine, see Chapter 1 in this volume).

Rossotrudnichestvo was initially based in the Russian embassy in Belarus, before the organisation opened a separate Russian Centre for Science and Culture in Minsk in 2010 (Rossiiskii tsentr 2018a). The centre describes its aims as 'the popularisation of the Russian language, the spread of knowledge about the richness of the Russian historical and cultural heritage and the provision of objective information about Russia' (Rossiiskii tsentr 2018b).[2] Beyond Minsk, Rossotrudnichestvo maintains Russian science and cultural centres in Brest and Homel (as of October 2018) and is considering the opening of another such centre in Mahilou (Radyio Svaboda 2018a). Rossotrudnichestvo's activities comprise institutional support for annual linguistic, cultural and historical events in various cities of Belarus, such as the 'Day of the People's Unity' or the 'Day of the Russian Language' (Rossiiskii tsentr 2018c). As of November 2018, the website of Rossotrudnichestvo in Belarus also refers to about twenty organisations of 'Russian compatriots' in the country, whose chairpersons are members of a 'Coordinating Council of Russian Compatriots' housed in the Russian embassy in Belarus (Rossiiskii tsentr 2018d). So far, these organisations have not developed any noticeable activities in the field of language policy in the country.

As the case of the Russkii Mir Foundation shows, Moscow does not seem to be particularly worried about the status of the Russian language in Belarus. Until 2013, Belarus was the only former CIS country in which the Foundation did not maintain a centre for the promotion of Russian language and culture (Wierzbowska-Miazga 2013: 28). As of now, such a centre exists only at Brest State University. The website of the centre in Brest conveys the image of a purely cultural and apolitical institution. There are reports about events such as the Olympics of Russian literature or a Pushkin festival, whereas essays, polemics or even didactic materials relating to the situation of Russian language in Belarus are completely absent (Russkii Mir 2019; Russkii Tsentr BGUIP 2019). Apart from a lack of necessity in the face of a national language policy favouring Russian anyway, the apolitical stance of the centre may also be explained by its attachment to a state university.

The annexation of Crimea and the Russian-backed separatism in the Donbas was a clear turning point in the state leadership's handling of national Belarusian identity. Lukashenka began cautiously to accentuate the importance of distinct Belarusian identity traits that had hitherto exclusively been employed by the nationalist camp within the opposition, among them the Belarusian language. In 2014, for example, the president gave parts of his speech on Belarus's Independence Day in Belarusian for the first time, and at the beginning of 2015 he even promised a 'soft Belarusification' (Petz 2015). For the first time, at least a temporary tactical alliance between Lukashenka and his Belarusian-speaking opponents appeared to be possible, with the latter calling on their friends and followers via Facebook to use the Belarusian language, 'in order not to be liberated by tanks' (Schmidt 2016).[3]

Lukashenka ran a noteworthy political risk by denying Russia the unconditional support requested in the Ukrainian conflict. By contrast, he conspicuously sought to establish good relations with the new Ukrainian leadership after the fall of Viktor Yanukovych. Against this backdrop, the Belarusian president himself, as well as Belarus and the Belarusians more generally, found themselves increasingly attacked by Russian pro-government journalists. For example in 2015, the 'alternative' election observation organisation CIS-EMO edited a report, with financial support from Russia, under the title 'Belarusian Nationalism against the Russian World', which raised concerns about a supposedly developing 'local nationalism with traditionally anti-Russian orientation':

> To prevent the Russophobic bacchanal that has swept through Ukraine from reaching Belarus, and to create an ideological basis for the progressive development of Belarusian–Russian integration, the state structures of the Russian Federation (primarily Rossotrudnichestvo) and the Russian media broadcasting on the territory of Belarus should carry out targeted work to firmly anchor the concept of the 'tripartite Russian people' in the Belarusian public consciousness, as it had prevailed in Belarus before the October Revolution. (Aver'ianov-Minskii and Mal'tsev 2015)[4]

The 'tripartite Russian people' echoes the state ideology of the Tsarist empire, according to which the Russian people consisted of Greater Russians, Little Russians (Ukrainians) and Belarusians. In the light of the above-described restraint or lack of public visibility of the Rossotrudnichestvo and Russkii Mir representations in Belarus, the quote clearly calls for more political engagement by the two institutions.

The outcome of the parliamentary elections in autumn 2016 was interpreted as another, albeit vague, signal in favour of the 'pro-Belarusian' political orientation. For the first time since the 1990s, two representatives of the political opposition became members of the Belarusian parliament. In terms of language policy, it was noteworthy that one of the two politicians was Alena Anisim, then deputy and now chairperson of the Belarusian Language Society (Piatnitskaia 2016).

The arrest of three Belarusian journalists from the Russian Internet portal regnum.ru at the end of 2016 can also be seen in the context of increasing tensions between the Belarusian and Russian governments. In the past, and on the basis of its commitment to the aforementioned identity concept uniting Russians, Ukrainians and Belarusians, the portal had been extremely critical of the Belarusian leadership. Hence, the arrest was interpreted as a warning signal towards those media outlets which questioned the independence of both the Belarusian state and of Belarusian culture in relation to Russia (Belarusinfocus 2016).

On the other hand, the state authorities continue to monitor the activities of Belarusian speakers. This is especially true when these activities take place outside governmental structures and suggest, from the authorities' perspective, a politicisation of the language issue. Examples are private-sector publishing in Belarusian or the organisation of Belarusian language courses outside the public education system (Ackermann 2017). Nevertheless, the latter, often conducted in an informal, leisurely setting, have enjoyed growing popularity in recent years, especially among young Belarusians (Lizengevic 2016).

There are no signs, however, of 'soft Belarusification' in the state school system, which is one of the decisive factors in the development of the linguistic situation. During the most recent school year for which language-related data is available, 2016/17, around 87% of all students enrolled were taught in Russian and only about 13% in Belarusian (Nienhuysen 2017). Remarkably, an initiative to create a Belarusian-speaking private university in the higher education sector emerged in September 2017, pointing to the fact that there is currently no purely or even predominantly Belarusian-speaking university in the country (Universitet imia Nila Gilevicha n.d.). This initiative was largely that of the Belarusian Language Society created in 1989 and some scholars who sympathised with it. According to its managing director, Aleh Trusau, it met resistance from supporters of Russkii Mir, writing among other places in the newspaper *Belarus Segodnia*, which is published by the presidential administration (Radyio Svaboda 2018b). Lukashenka distanced himself from the initiative and described it as 'superfluous' (Radyio Svaboda 2019).

Beyond the educational sector, the Russian language also dominates in electronic media, including radio and television in Belarus. The use of Belarusian is limited to some individual broadcasts, most likely as a strategy intermittently used by the stations to enhance their cultural standing (Aliaksandrava 2018). While it is quite common on the Belarusian Internet that news and entertainment portals offer both a Russian- and a Belarusian-language version, the Russian-language versions are frequently more comprehensive and user-friendly. In terms of content, bilingual websites in Russian display a broader range of topics, while the limited content presented in Belarusian often discusses 'opposition-sensitive' topics such as human rights or linguistic issues (Sliyashynskaya 2019).

LANGUAGES AND IDENTITIES IN INDEPENDENT BELARUS

Censuses carried out in 1999 and 2009 provide basic data on language use and national identity in Belarus. In the 1999 census, 85.6% of ethnic Belarusians declared Belarusian to be their mother tongue, but no less than 58.6% described Russian as the language they usually speak at home, compared with only 41.3% who usually spoke Belarusian at home. Of the ethnic Russians living in the country, 90.7% declared Russian to be their native language and 95.7% usually spoke Russian at home (Natsional'nyi statisticheskii komitet RB 2009). If the declaration of a 'mother tongue' is interpreted as an indicator of ethno-national affiliation, then in the 1999 census a clear majority of Belarusians emphasised their commitment to Belarusian independence from Russia.

The existence of a slight majority declaring their use of Russian as the language spoken in everyday life can be seen as an expression of linguistic 'realism'. The 41.3% allegedly using Belarusian as their 'everyday language', however, is clearly unrealistic, and can be interpreted at least in part as the desire of the respondents to distance themselves from the Russian language and its dominance in public life; like the declared affiliation with a 'native language', it may be seen as to some extent declamatory. For the ethnic Russian part of the citizenry of Belarus, by contrast, such considerations are unlikely to have played a role, as a commitment to the Belarusian language would not have been a 'meaningful' option anyway.

In the 2009 census, only 60.8% of the ethnic Belarusians named Belarusian as their mother tongue, while 37.0% named Russian (Natsional'nyi statisticheskii komitet RB 2010). Meanwhile, 96.3% of the Russians living in the country declared Russian to be their mother tongue and only 2.1% Belarusian. As for the languages commonly spoken at home, 69.8% of ethnic Belarusians specified Russian and only 26.1% Belarusian. For ethnic Russians, the corresponding shares for the language spoken at home were 96.5% for Russian and 2.1% for Belarusian. The 2009 census introduced another language-related category, that of 'another language [in addition to the language commonly used at home] that [the interviewee] freely speaks'. In this category, 12.7% of the ethnic Belarusians listed Belarusian and 15.2% Russian. Among the ethnic Russians, 23.6% named Belarusian and 0.5% Russian.

It is tempting to read the significant increase in the share of ethnic Belarusians declaring Russian as their mother tongue (almost one-quarter) or as the language commonly spoken at home (by 11.2%) as pragmatic acceptance of the de facto dominance of the Russian language, to which ethnic Belarusians have adjusted their own language use. At the same time, it could also express general acceptance of Belarus's independence after almost two decades, despite the renunciation of national language promotion since 1995. In other words, it may be that many Belarusians failed to accept that the language question and a commitment to Belarusian were as highly important in preserving the state's independence as the national-conservative opposition persistently claimed.

A joint research project conducted by German and Belarusian linguists and social scientists further nuanced the linguistic situation in the country (Trasjanka in Weißrussland n.d.). For the first time, this study included the widely used Belarusian–Russian mixed speech (BRMS) or *trasianka* as an independent category of research. Moreover, this study allowed multiple entries in the categories 'first language' and 'native language', with the aim of more appropriately mapping the realities of a multilingual country such as Belarus.

Data collected in Minsk and six smaller cities (of 8,000–53,000 inhabitants) showed, among other things, that Russian ranked second in first-language mentions (first language acquired), behind BRMS and ahead of Belarusian (Russian 42.19%, BRMS 49.55%, Belarusian 17.99%; total > 100% as multiple answers were allowed) (Hentschel and Kittel 2011: 114). This documents that, on the one hand, a majority of respondents were aware that at least one of the languages they primarily acquired was clearly distinct from the Russian language as used elsewhere. On the other hand, although Russian was mentioned as a 'first language' less frequently than BRMS, its lead over the 'titular language', that is, Belarusian, was still very large.

Interestingly, the lowest share of respondents chose Russian when asked about their 'native language'. Only 29.64% of the respondents opted for Russian, compared with 37.62% who opted for mixed speech and 48.69% for Belarusian (total > 100% as multiple answers were allowed). The introduction of the additional category of BRMS thus reduced the shares of Russian as well as Belarusian in terms of native language in comparison with the census data of 2009, with the share of Belarusian decreasing more significantly (12.11 percentage points lower, compared with 7.36 percentage points lower for Russian). Maintaining the assumption that affiliation with a 'native language' serves to a significant degree as an expression of ethno-national identity, it is notable that Russian is least likely to be chosen by ethnic Belarusians if both the Belarusian language and mixed speech are offered as alternatives. The same study confirms this interpretation by finding that, among those who called Belarusian their only native language, no less than 68.5% always or frequently used Russian in everyday life (Kittel et al. 2010: 57–8). Unsurprisingly, a clear majority (84.7%) of the respondents with Belarusian citizenship who stated that they identified with Russian culture overwhelmingly used the Russian language. At the same time, the majorities of those who stated that they were oriented towards Belarusian culture and those who claimed to be indifferent to national cultures also stated that they mostly spoke Russian (50.2% of the Belarusian-oriented, 54.4% of the indifferent) (Kittel and Lindner 2011: 638).

The results of a survey carried out in 2013 among young Belarusian nationals between the ages of 18 and 30, within the framework of the same research project, are also quite revealing in terms of language competence. According to the respondents' self-assessment, almost 100% claimed excellent language skills (writing, conversation, reading, listening) in Russian. By contrast, the respondents were less confident concerning their skills in Belarusian. High levels were still claimed in terms of listening skills (91.0%) and reading comprehension (81.6%), but significantly fewer respondents claimed the ability to write (55.8%) or hold a conversation (42.5%) without difficulty. Interestingly, 4.4% even stated that they had no competence in the language at all (Hentschel et al. 2015: 140). On the one hand, it is revealing to note the high self-esteem of the younger generation in terms of language proficiency in Russian, especially given the widespread phenomenon of language mixing in Belarus. On the other hand, the low self-esteem in terms of the active mastery of Belarusian may be interpreted either as a lack of language immersion, or as an indicator of the poor state of Belarusian language instruction in the schools.

A survey conducted in 2013 by the Independent Institute for Socio-Economic and Political Studies (IISEPS) also provided interesting results on perceptions among Belarusians of the linguistic situation. Only 21.2% of respondents considered the use of Russian by a 'significant part' of the Belarusians to be a 'huge' or a 'significant' threat to the existence of the Belarusian nation. Conversely, 37.9% saw it as a 'small' or 'very small' threat (2.9% very strongly agreed with this statement, 18.3% strongly, 37.5% partly, 26.2% weakly, 11.7% very weakly and 3.4% did not answer the question) (IISEPS 2013). These findings underpin the interpretation that, with increasing historical distance from the collapse of the Soviet

Union, the Belarusians have come to regard themselves as a consolidated nation state and attach less importance to the language question.

When asked whether knowledge of a particular language is a necessary precondition for belonging to a particular nation in the above-mentioned study, the proportion of respondents who denied this with varying emphasis (37.9% in total) was slightly above the proportion of respondents undecided (37.5%), while only 21.2% agreed with the statement. Responses to this question by supporters of Lukashenka were somewhat counterintuitive. One would have expected that supporters of the president would be indifferent to any relationship between nation and language. To the contrary, however, 29.9% of Lukashenka's supporters saw a close relationship between language skills and national affiliation, while the share among Lukashenka critics amounted to only 14.2%. This suggests that Lukashenka's supporters back a state-centred and authoritarian political positioning, and at the same time value certain national traditions.

In 2014, the cultural campaign 'Budz'ma belarusami' conducted another survey on language policy attitudes in Belarus. In total, a narrow majority demanded more state funding measures to support the Belarusian language (16.5% in favour, 36.5% rather in favour, 10.1% against, 27.3% rather against, 9.6% undecided). When asked whether a greater presence of the Belarusian language on television and radio was desirable, affirmative answers (14.3% agreeing, 30.1% rather agreeing) outweighed negative answers (4.9% against, 16.1% rather against). At the same time, however, the high proportion of respondents who stated that it was difficult to answer this question is striking (34.7%). Overall, the survey results reflect a certain level of awareness of the factually weak status of the Belarusian language, but at the same time a widespread indecisiveness as to whether concrete measures should be taken to strengthen the position of the Belarusian language and weaken the position of the Russian language (Budz'ma belarusami 2014).

In a 2015 survey by the above-mentioned IISEPS, respondents were asked what they thought distinguished Belarusians from Russians (IISEPS 2015). Beyond culture and traditions (36.3%) and history (also 36.3%), the factor 'language' was mentioned by only 24.6% of the respondents, while 32.5% of those surveyed felt that Belarusians and Russians were basically indistinguishable. The fact that language ranks here lower than culture, traditions and history obviously reflects the dominance of Russian-language use in public life and – language mixing notwithstanding – also in private life. Finally, the Belarusian education system conveys a certain awareness of the specifics of Belarusian history, culture and traditions despite some ideological bias in public school and university teaching.

The same survey explored preferences for state language regulation, and a clear majority (48.3%) argued for the currently used Russian–Belarusian bilingualism, while 20.9% of the respondents declared that any decision on this issue 'would not concern them at all', 14.5% favoured 'Belarusian only' and 13.1% opted for 'Russian only'. As a result, a renewal of the linguistic policy of Belarus as conducted during the first years of independence could currently count on little support. The same is true, however, for declaring Russian as the only state language, with the proportion of supporters of this option surprisingly being only a little lower than the share of the proponents of Belarusian as the only state language. The option 'Russian as the only state language' does not necessarily indicate the respondents' dedicated support for a 'pro-Russian' political orientation, but may have been, at least partly, chosen also by respondents who consider the supposed and actual costs of the parallel use of two state languages as unnecessary expenditure.

PUBLIC AND SCHOLARLY DEBATES ABOUT THE ROLE AND STATUS OF THE RUSSIAN LANGUAGE

During the first years of Belarus's independence as a state, nationalist intellectuals attempted to link Belarusian linguistic aspirations with a re-evaluation of the role and status of the Russian language in the country. The limited success of such initiatives is revealed by the persistence of Soviet concepts in the authoritative reference works. The lemma 'Russian language' in a linguistic encyclopaedia on the Belarusian language published in 1994 is a good example of this. It offers a historic narrative fervently opposed by the Belarusian nationalist camp, according to which an overarching 'Old Russian ethnicity' (*starazhytnaruskaia narodnasc'*) developed in the Eastern Slav settlement area after the disintegration of the proto-Slavs. This alleged 'Old Russian ethnicity', consisting of the later Russians, Ukrainians and Belarusians, is said to have communicated in an 'Old Russian language' (*stararuskaia mova*), from which only significantly later, in the course of the fourteenth century, a distinct 'Old Belarusian language' (*starabelaruskaia mova*) evolved by separation from the common linguistic 'roots' (Nikalaeva 1994). Belarusian and Ukrainian nationalists challenge this view as an expression of a Russian imperialist (linguistic) historiography, and counter it with an ethnocentric alternative model identifying the emergence of distinct Eastern Slavic languages already in the time of the Kievan Rus'. Ultimately, as Andreas Kappeler has correctly noted with reference to corresponding Ukrainian debates, this is an academically unproductive dispute, as both sides project modern national (and national-linguistic) concepts onto a historical period for which they are anachronisms (Kappeler 2017: 32).

The policy of linguistic Belarusification practised in the early years of state independence elicited strong counter-reactions, particularly but not exclusively in the ideological camp of the supporters of Russocentrism. Numerous publications and appeals called for giving the Russian language the status of an official or state language, arguing that it was the 'mother tongue' of many Belarusians (Lastouski 2011: 228–9). By contrast, the state language policy pursued by Lukashenka since the 1995 referendum was broadly supported by the 'Russocentrist' camp. This started to change in the mid-2000s, when energy disputes and economically motivated tensions between the governments of Belarus and the Russian Federation intensified. Voices cautioning against the danger of a rift between Belarus and the Russian 'brother' nation came to be more frequently uttered in the press and public debates. The roundtable 'Questions of Russian Culture in Belarus', organised in Minsk in February 2010, is a telling example. The publicist Igor Zelenkovskii discussed the role of the Russian language in the country and, pointing to the Belarusian descent of important Russian academics and writers, suggested that the Russian language had absorbed the 'best of the whole of Russia (*Rusi*)'. He warned against a renewed 'forced' linguistic Belarusification, which he believed would further provincialise Belarus in terms of science and culture (Zelenkovskii 2010). Using an argument frequently invoked by supporters of Russocentrism, he claimed that the most important works in fundamental research and the masterpieces of world literature had been written in four languages only, namely English, French, German and Russian. In this argument, the claim that certain languages occupy a dominant position in the 'world system of languages' (de Swaan 2001) is treated as a consistent historical fact.

Unlike the proponents of Russocentrism, the defenders of the Belarusian language fiercely criticised the renunciation of the Belarusification policy after the 1995 referendum. Especially in the second half of the 1990s and the early 2000s, many nationalist intellectuals discussed the supposedly 'colonial' role of the Russian language in Belarus and decried its 'pernicious' influence on the national character of Belarusians. *Nasha Slova*, the newspaper of the Belarusian Language Society, featured many contributions directed against the dominance of the Russian language in Belarus. In one of them, appearing in 2001, the then chair of the Belarusian Language Society, Aleh Trusau, addressed 'the role of the Russian language in the democratisation of our society'. In his article, Trusau identified two strains of influence by which the use of Russian in Belarus supposedly compromised democracy. He singled out a 'messianic' and 'pan-Slavic' strain on the one hand, and complained about the penetration of vulgarisms (*mat'*) into Belarusian society on the other. Suggesting monolingualism as the norm, Trusau's article argued that Belarus should strive for a system of language acquisition in schools in which one 'Western' foreign language should be studied as the first foreign language. Russian should become an option only as the second foreign language, with the possibility of replacing it with another Slavic language instead. This model, similar to ideas brought forward by other defenders of the Belarusian language, regards the actual spread and use of Russian in Belarus as an 'anomaly' that needs to be overcome in the interest of a future, 'democratic' language policy in Belarus (Trusau 2001; Brüggemann 2014: 180–8).

Trusau's reference to the penetration of *mat'*, that is, his portrayal of the Russian language as a medium infusing undesirable, morally contemptible developments into a 'pure' or 'innocent' Belarusian society, was taken further by some representatives of the national conservative right. Juryj Belen'ki, for example, the deputy chairman of the Christian Conservative Party-Belarusian Popular Front, a splinter group of the Belarusian Popular Front (BNF), claimed at a rally in November 2014 on the occasion of the 'Day of Belarusian Ancestry' (in Belarusian, *Dziady*) that, 'through the Russian language, alcoholism and other social pathologies have inflicted Belarusian families' (TUT.BY 2014).

It is no coincidence that Belen'ki made the quoted statement after the Russian annexation of Crimea. Even among the more moderate Belarusian-speaking intelligentsia, the Ukrainian crisis stimulated a resurgence of the debates about the political role of the Russian language. This sharply contrasts with the resignation which had made itself felt in the language debates of the preceding decade in Belarusian language periodicals such as *Arche*, *Nasha Niva* and *Nasha Slova*, or the Belarusian service of Radio Free Europe. The annexation of Crimea and Russia's support for separatism in the Donbas raised the question of whether the (largely) Russian-speaking nature of a country like Belarus and its situation within the sphere of influence of Russian-language media from the Russian Federation would not inevitably entail the risk of territorial claims by its eastern neighbour (Rakicki 2014).

The military conflict in Ukraine and Russia's role in it prompted critical remarks about the Belarusian–Russian relationship not only within Belarusian nationalist circles, but also by President Lukashenka. Lukashenka repeatedly criticised the ideological underpinnings of the *russkii mir* concept and denied its 'applicability' to Belarusians. In 2015, he stated in Russian in the Belarusian parliament that '*russkii mir* is not about us. We are Russian people (*russkie liudi*), but this does not mean that we are people from Russia (*Rossiiane*). We are Belarusians. Allow us to have our own worldview' (Aver'ianov 2016).⁵

Remarkably, Lukashenka accepted certain commonalities between Belarusians and Russians by using the attribute *russkie liudi* for Belarusians. At the same time, he refused their denomination as *Rossiiane*, that is, citizens of Russia, thus emphasising the separate statehood of Belarus with its distinctive Belarusian citizenship. This suggests that he was critically addressing Russkii Mir's self-declared responsibility for the Russian compatriots (*sootechestvenniki*) abroad.

Even if Lukashenka rejects the applicability of the *russkii mir* concept in Belarus, his recent comments on the linguistic situation in Belarus do not indicate that he plans to diminish the role of Russian in the country. In an interview that he gave to the Russian television station Rossiia 24 in August 2017, Lukashenka on the one hand emphasised the importance of the Russian language as a means of communication with foreign conversation partners, and on the other stressed the emotional attachment of Belarusians to the Russian language: 'How can you give up something which belongs to your soul? My soul is in there, in the Russian language, like with many Belarusians, well practically all Belarusians' (Russia 24 2017).

With this quote, Lukashenka indirectly criticised any possible turn towards linguistic Belarusification as forfeiting one's soul and thus as a morally reprehensible step. Reading this statement in context with Lukashenka's statement about the *russkii mir*, quoted above, suggests that the Russian language is the 'home' of the 'Russian people's soul', that is, a common treasure of the Russians, Belarusians and Ukrainians. At the same time, those Belarusians who display no such emotional attachment to Russian are presented as a negligible minority.

In the same interview, Lukashenka also referred to allegedly existing terminological gaps in the Belarusian language, which he related to the relatively late development of that language. He also suggested that, against this backdrop, the desire to raise the status of Belarusian was the basis of public criticism of the Russian language. Here Lukashenka confuses the linguistic areas of corpus planning and status planning (Haugen 1972). The development of terminology in Belarusian, like the development of terminology in any other language, is the subject of corpus planning and refers to the corresponding efforts of normative linguistics aimed at the development of an individual language as such, which in the case of official state languages proceeds with appropriate institutional and financial support from the state. The 'criticism of Russian' mentioned by Lukashenka, however, does not refer to the characteristics of the Russian language in the domestic Belarusian debate, but to the status of Russian and its de facto predominant role in Belarus. This blending of two different subject areas in language policies attaches a linguistic 'inferiority complex' to the critics of Russian dominance while avoiding any explicit denunciation of the 'weaker' of the two official languages.

That said, Lukashenka has gradually replaced his, at times, blunt references to Belarusian as a 'poor language' from the mid-1990s with a more benevolent view since the mid-2000s, especially in public statements made after the annexation of Crimea by Russia and the outbreak of the Donbas conflict. In a speech to the national educational council in August 2017, Lukashenka described both Russian and Belarusian as the *rodnoi iazyk* ('mother tongue'; literally 'native language') of the Belarusians. This is not only consistent with earlier public statements by the Belarusian president, but also with the language ideology of the 'two mother tongues' of Belarusians (and other non-Russian Soviet nationalities) already prevalent in the BSSR (and the Ukrainian Soviet Republic) during the 1970s and 1980s (Brüggemann 2014: 98–150). Contrary to previous statements, however, Lukashenka now explicitly considered Russian to be 'a little less' the native language of Belarusians. 'It [Russian] is our native language. Well, maybe, if I may say so, as I perceive it, well, maybe a little less than the Belarusian one. That is, less native than Belarusian.' Again, unlike in previous interviews, he did not rule out that this might change in the future, yet he suggested that this would happen only a long time after his own term of office had expired. 'Time will pass, new people will come, new generations, maybe life will change, and they will decide what language to speak' (Lukashenka 2017).

Statements like those quoted above suggest that Lukashenka rules out any specific language-policy changes that would deviate substantially from the current situation, and does not specify any conditions for their occurrence. Many representatives in the private economy, not necessarily politically close to Lukashenka, share the president's opinion that there is no point in curbing the use of Russian in Belarusian public life (Belarus Analysen 2018). Indeed, in all domains of entrepreneurial language use, Russian clearly serves as the 'unmarked', 'neutral' code. Belarusian, by contrast, is often used when the business activity is related to national issues, or when individual entrepreneurs are personally connected to the community of active Belarusian speakers. A special case is commercial advertising, in which the use of the Belarusian language can perform different functions, including emphasising the Belarusian origin of a product (Kalita 2016).

Of course linguists, too, take part in the public debate about linguistic polycentrism and the conclusions that should be drawn for language policies in Belarus. One of the most visible participants in this discussion is the Minsk-based linguist Nina Miachkouskaia. In an article published in 2005, she examined the sociolinguistic status of the Russian language outside Russia and included the situation in Belarus in her discussion (Mechkovskaia 2005). She suggested that the Russian language has become 'more cosmopolitan' and 'less marked in national respects' since the collapse of the Soviet Union, because there is no longer one single 'master'. As to the situation in Belarus and Ukraine, she mentioned some efforts among the national elites to claim a Belarusian or Ukrainian share in the cultural heritage of the Tsarist Empire and the Soviet Union, referring to the contribution of people from both countries in the development of the Russian language. On the other hand, she noted that the Russian language was increasingly supplanting Belarusian and Ukrainian in everyday use and in popular mass media. By contrast, due to the relative isolation from the lexicon of colloquial and dialectal speech, Belarusian and Ukrainian thrived mainly in the written high culture (e.g. in contributions to national history, philology and fiction).

Another prominent contributor to that debate is the Minsk-based Russianist Barys Norman. In an article published in 2010, Norman found the regional variant of Russian used by the population of Belarus developing into a distinct national variant, a *natiolect* of Russian (Norman 2010: 14). In this context, he regretted that there was no separate department for the Russian language at the Belarusian Academy of Sciences, which could assume a normative role for the specific variant of Russian spoken in Belarus, and rhetorically asked:

> what about the numerous teachers, what about the authors of school and university textbooks on the Russian language in the republic [Belarus]? Should they automatically accept the norm proposed by the neighbouring country, or in this case take responsibility for themselves – in accordance with their own sense of proportion and taste? (Norman 2010: 15)[6]

In this statement, the development of independent Belarusian norms for the Russian language appears as an act of assuming individual responsibility for the well-being of the Belarusian nation. However, Norman would prefer institutional support for the development of 'Belarusian Russian' in the form of an independent department at the Academy of Sciences, which of course also reflects the professional self-interest of Belarusian Russianists in the recognition of their work.

Besides 'native' linguists such as Miachkouskaia and Norman, 'foreign' linguists such as the American Belarusianist Curt Woolhiser also took part in the academic debate about the Russian language in Belarus. In a contribution to a collective volume published in 2012, Woolhiser noted that the norms of Russian spoken in Belarus were increasingly drifting away from the norms and standards used in Russia (Woolhiser 2012). At the same time, he was sceptical whether an independent Belarusian version of the standard Russian language would find general acceptance. In his view, the prevailing ideology of a monocentric Russian standard language, the lack of Belarusian institutions for the codification of a 'Belarusian Russian', the continued influence of the Russian media in Belarus and, finally, the fact that Belarusian already occupies the function of a marker of national identity spoke against such a scenario (Woolhiser 2012: 227).

Whether accepted in principle by Miachkouskaia and Norman or sceptically viewed by Woolhiser, the possibility of the development of an independent Belarusian variant of the Russian language has until now not resulted in any serious attempt to create a corresponding scientific institution for the standardisation of 'Belarusian Russian'. Remarkably, however, the prospect of such independence has moved into the realm of what is thinkable and perhaps even desirable in Belarusian academia since the beginning of the 2010s. An indication of the latter is the fact that the discussion has been picked up in *Belaruskaia Dumka*, a popular science journal published by the presidential administration in Belarus. In 2010, *Belaruskaia Dumka* published a contribution by the Minsk-based historian Vadim Gigin on 'Belarusian Russian'. Gigin argued that historical figures from what is now Belarus, such as the printer Francysk Skaryna (1486–1541) or the priest and scholar Simiaon Polacki (1629–80), had played a significant role in the development of the Russian language, but at the same time retained their Belarusian identities. In Gigin's opinion, it was therefore legitimate for the Belarusians to demand 'the right to have a say in the matter' as far as the norms of the Russian language were concerned, but at the same time to maintain their independent national identity and use of two official state languages (Gigin 2010).

CONCLUSION

When Belarus became an independent state after the collapse of the Soviet Union, the use of the Russian language was clearly predominant as a result of the preceding Soviet language policies. Only for a very short period in the first years of independence, that is until President Lukashenka took office in 1994 and conducted the referendum on state languages and state symbols in 1995, did it seem as if this predominance would be challenged. Irrespective of the many justifiable objections to the legality of the referendum and its implementation, large sections of the population indeed declined to reduce the use of Russian in favour of Belarusian in the mid-1990s. The pro-Russian turn in state language policy was particularly noticeable in the school system, in which parents opted overwhelmingly for Russian when choosing the language of instruction for their children. The basic features of this language policy, which in practice favours Russian while avoiding 'positive discrimination' against Belarusian, have remained unchanged to this day.

This helps to explain why new Russian institutions like Rossotrudnichestvo and the Russkii Mir Foundation have displayed little activity in Belarus until now, and have limited their endeavours to their 'core agenda' of language promotion and cultural mediation. In contrast to other countries such as Ukraine, they have avoided taking up 'general' political issues or raising controversy by acting as an active lobby of the 'compatriots' in Belarus (see also Chapter 9 in this volume).

Since the mid-2000s, the relationship between the leaders of Belarus and the Russian Federation has gradually deteriorated, initially due to conflicts about economic issues and energy policy and more recently due to Russia's annexation of Crimea and its intervention in the Donbas. In fact, President Lukashenka did not fully support Russia's position and tried to establish good diplomatic contacts with the Ukrainian government immediately after the Euromaidan. This was accompanied by some cautious signals of appreciation for speakers of Belarusian. Yet there are no signs that concrete steps in language policy will be taken in the direction of an actual return to the policies of Belarusification. Against this backdrop, fears aired by journalists in the Russian Federation about a possible victimisation of the Russian speakers in Belarus are unfounded.

In turn, ethnic Russians in Belarus, who according to the 2009 census make up 8.3% of the population (compared with around 11% in the 1999 census), do not feel much necessity to become politically active. Unlike in many former Soviet republics, they are practically non-existent as a politically organised national minority.

An important, if not the most important, explanatory factor for this seems to be the broad acceptance of the state independence of Belarus. That said, language-related surveys consistently show that the use of Russian remains clearly predominant over Belarusian, even if the Belarusian–Russian mixed speech (BRMS) is included as an alternative category. Contrary to what partisans of the Belarusian language suggested in the second half of the 1990s and the first half of the 2000s, the majority of the population apparently does not see the extensive use of Russian in public life as a threat to Belarusian national identity. Their language preferences do not prevent them from sympathising with the

Belarusian language or with people who advocate its use. At the same time, the surveys do not indicate either that Russian, as a linguistic attribute of national identity, has replaced Belarusian, or will do so in the near future. More likely, BRMS may fulfil this role: even though it is used predominantly in oral communication and has not yet undergone codification, it nevertheless displays certain conventions, that is, it has shaped linguistic norms of use, and could be developed into a variant of Belarusian that is structurally 'closer' to Russian than the current Belarusian standard language (Hentschel 2017: 37–9).

The linguistic discussion about the role of the Russian language in Belarus fits the bigger picture of the recent debates about the polycentrism or pluricentrism of other 'major' languages (Clyne 1992). There is widespread acceptance of the fact that, in the course of Belarusian independence and under the influence of the Belarusian language, the Russian used in Belarus, be it in dialectal or standard forms of language, has developed specific traits at various linguistic structural levels distinguishing it from the Russian used in Moscow or St Petersburg. There is no agreement, however, on whether this could result in the emergence of a 'Belarusian Russian' functioning as an attribute of a Belarusian national identity. Presently, the Russian language in Belarus does not, at least not to a significant extent, fulfil this role. On the other hand, its predominant use seems to be determined more by practical considerations than by 'ideological ties' with the centre of the former Soviet empire. Taking this into account, it would currently be strongly exaggerated to consider Russian as Moscow's linguistic Trojan Horse in Belarus.

Translated from German by Christian Noack

NOTES

1. The protests following the 2020 presidential election suggest that additional factors need to be taken into account in future investigations into Belarusian 'identity'. These include, for example, the rejection of violence and state repression, social self-organisation (especially in the context of the Covid-19 crisis trivialised by Lukashenka), and the question of the extent to which the Belarusian self-perception changes from the status of an object to the status of a subject of politics through the protest experience (see Petz 2020).
2. Translated by Mark Brüggemann and Christian Noack.
3. Translated by Christian Noack.
4. Translated by Mark Brüggemann and Christian Noack.
5. This and the following statements by Lukashenka (below) translated from Russian by Mark Brüggemann and Christian Noack.
6. Translated by Mark Brüggemann and Christian Noack.

REFERENCES

Ackermann, F. (2017), 'Der Verleger, der seine eigenen Bücher verbrannte', *Frankfurter Allgemeine Zeitung*, 20 March, <https://www.faz.net/aktuell/feuilleton/weiss russland-der-verleger-der-seine-eigenen-buecher-verbrannte-14945381.html> (last accessed 9 January 2020).

Aliaksandrava, H. (2018), 'Toe, shto nas iadnae', *Belarus Segodnia*, 21 June, <https://www.sb.by/articles/toe-shto-nas-yadnae.html> (last accessed 9 January 2020).

Aver'ianov, V. (2016), 'Doktrina Russkogo mira', *Izborskii klub*, 26 September, <https://izborsk-club.ru/10269#a7> (last accessed 8 May 2019).

Aver'ianov-Minskii, K. and V. Mal'tsev (2015), *Belorusskii natsionalizm protiv russkogo mira*, Moscow: CIS-EMO, <http://www.cis-emo.net/sites/default/files/images imce/extremizm_doklad_2.pdf> (last accessed 11 November 2018).

Bekus, N. (2014), '"Hybrid" linguistic identity of post-Soviet Belarus', *Journal on Ethnopolitics and Minority Issues in Europe* 13 (4), pp. 26–51.

Belarus Analysen (2018), 'Belarussische Sprache in der Wirtschaft', *Belarus-Analysen* 37, pp. 32–5, <http://www.laender-analysen.de/belarus/pdf/BelarusAnalysen37.pdf> (last accessed 31 May 2018).

Belarusinfocus (2016), 'Belarusian authorities bring in strict restrictions for supporters of union with Russia', *Belarus in Focus*, 12 December, <https://belarusinfocus.info/society-and-politics/belarusian-authorities-bring-strict-restrictions-supporters-union-russia> (last accessed 10 November 2018).

Bennet, B. (2011), *The Last Dictatorship in Europe: Belarus Under Lukashenko*, London: Hurst.

Bieder, H. (2001), 'Der Kampf um die Sprachen im 20. Jahrhundert', in D. Beyrau and R. Lindner (eds), *Handbuch der Geschichte Weißrußlands*, Göttingen: Vandenhoeck & Ruprecht, pp. 451–71.

Brüggemann, M. (2014), *Die weißrussische und die russische Sprache in ihrem Verhältnis zur weißrussischen Gesellschaft und Nation. Ideologisch-programmatische Standpunkte politischer Akteure und Intellektueller 1994–2010*, Oldenburg: BIS.

Brüggemann, M. (2017), 'Sootečestvenniki, Diaspora und Russkij mir: Die externe Sprachpolitik Russlands nach 1991', in K. Witzlack-Makarevich and N. Wulff (eds), *Handbuch des Russischen in Deutschland: Migration – Mehrsprachigkeit – Spracherwerb*, Berlin: Frank & Timme, pp. 199–219.

Budz'ma belarusami (2014), 'Iak belarusy staviacca da belaruskamounykh', *Budz'ma belarusami*, 23 December, <http://budzma.by/news/yak-byelarusy-stavyacca-da-byelaruskamownykh.html> (last accessed 1 January 2019).

Clyne, M. (ed.) (1992), *Pluricentric Languages: Differing Norms in Different Nations*, Berlin/New York: Mouton de Gruyter.

Comrie, B. (1999), 'Sowjetische und russische Sprachenpolitik', in H. Jachnow (ed.), *Handbuch der Sprachwissenschaftlichen Russistik und ihrer Grenzdisziplinen*, Wiesbaden: Harrassowitz, pp. 817–42.

de Swaan, A. (2001), *Words of the World: The Global Language System*, Cambridge: Cambridge University Press.

Frear, M. (2019), *Belarus Under Lukashenka: Adaptive Authoritarianism*, Abingdon/New York: Routledge.

Gigin, V. (2010), 'Belorusskii russkii iazyk', *Belaruskaia Dumka* 2, pp. 64–71.

Haugen, E. (1972), 'Linguistics and language planning', in E. S. Firchow (ed.), *Studies* by Einar Haugen: Presented on the Occasion of His 65th Birthday, April 19, 1971, The Hague: Mouton, pp. 510–30.

Hentschel, G. (2017), 'Eleven questions and answers about Belarusian–Russian mixed speech ("Trasjanka")', *Russian Linguistics* 41 (1), pp. 17–42.

Hentschel, G., M. Brüggemann, H. Geiger and J. P. Zeller (2015), 'The linguistic and political orientation of young Belarusian adults between East and West or Russian and Belarusian', *International Journal of the Sociology of Language* 236, pp. 133–54.

Hentschel, G. and B. Kittel (2011), 'Weißrussische Dreisprachigkeit? Zur sprachlichen Situation in Weißrussland auf der Basis von Urteilen von Weißrussen über die Verbreitung "ihrer Sprachen" im Lande', *Wiener Slawistischer Almanach* 67, pp. 107–35.

IISEPS (2013), 'Mezhdu khaosom i diktaturoi', Independent Institute for Socio-Economic and Political Studies, 4 July, <https://web.archive.org/web/20140528113959/http://www.iiseps.org/analitica/547> (last accessed 11 January 2020).

IISEPS (2015), 'Sotsiologi: vse bol'she belorusov otlichajut sebia ot russkikh', *TUT.BY*, 6 April, <https://news.tut.by/politics/442882.html> (last accessed 11 January 2020).

Kalita, I. (2016), 'Belaruskaia reklama: na shliakhu da natsyianal'naha farmata', *Jazyk a kultura* 25–6, pp. 17–29.

Kappeler, A. (2017), *Ungleiche Brüder: Russen und Ukrainer vom Mittelalter bis zur Gegenwart*, Munich: Beck.

Kittel, B. and D. Lindner (2011), 'Der soziale Hintergrund von Sprachwahlen in Belarus. Eine sprachsoziologische Analyse der "gemischten Rede"', *Kölner Zeitschrift für Soziologie und Sozialpsychologie* 63, pp. 623–47.

Kittel, B., D. Lindner, S. Tesch and G. Hentschel (2010), 'Mixed language usage in Belarus: The sociostructural background of language choice', *International Journal of the Sociology of Language* (206), pp. 47–71.

Lastouski, A. (2011), 'Crisis of Belarusian studies', *Belarusian Political Science Review* 1, pp. 227–35, <http://palityka.org/wp-content/uploads/2012/02/11_article.pdf> (last accessed 17 January 2021).

Lizengevic, I. (2016), 'Belarussisch im Aufwind', *Deutschlandfunk Kultur*, 29 June, <https://www.deutschlandfunkkultur.de/muttersprache-als-zeichen-des-widerstandes-belarussisch-im.979.de.html?dram%3Aarticle_id=358159> (last accessed 16 January 2019).

Lukashenka, A. (2017), 'Russkij iazyk, mozhet, menee rodnoi, chem belorusskii', *Naviny.by*, 24 August, <https://naviny.by/new/20170824/1503571511-lukashenko-russkiy-yazyk-mozhet-menee-rodnoy-chem-belorusskiy> (last accessed 23 December 2018).

Marples, D. (1999), *Belarus: A Denationalized Nation*, Amsterdam: Amsterdam University Press.

Mechkovskaia, N. (2005), 'Postsovetskii russkii iazyk: novye cherty v sotsiolingvisticheskom statuse', *Russian Linguistics* 29 (1), pp. 49–70.

Mechkovskaia, N. (2013), 'Iazykovoe zakonodatel'stvo v Belarusi i Ukraine kak dokumenty vremeni: sotsial'nye determinanty, pravovye reshenija i lakuny, ideologicheskii kamufliazh', in H. Gladkova and K. Vačkova (eds), *Jazykové právo a slovanské jazyky*, Prague: Filozofická fakulta UK, pp. 31–57.

Natsional'nyi statisticheskii komitet RB (2009), 'Population of the Republic of Belarus by nationality and spoken languages in 1999', <https://web.archive.org/web/20090505121015/http://belstat.gov.by:80/homep/en/census/p6.php> (last accessed 11 January 2020).

Natsional'nyi statisticheskii komitet RB (2010), 'Rasprostranenie v Respublike Belarus' i oblastiakh belorusskogo i russkogo iazykov', <https://web.archive.org/web/20131018221300/http://belstat.gov.by/homep/ru/perepic/2009/vihod_tables/5.11-0.pdf> (last accessed 11 January 2020).

Nienhuysen, F. (2017), 'Sprache als Politikum', *Süddeutsche Zeitung*, 2 June, <https://www.sueddeutsche.de/politik/weissrussland-sprache-als-politikum-1.3532349> (last accessed 16 January 2019).

Nikalaeva, V. (1994), 'Ruskaja mova', in A. Ia. Michnevich, *Belaruskaia mova. Encyklapedyia*, Minsk: Belaruskaia Encyklapedyia Imia Petrusia Brouki, pp. 459–60.

Norman, B. (2010), 'Russkii iazyk v sovremennoi Belarusi: praktika i norma', *Russkii iazyk* 6, pp. 8–15.

Petz, I. (2015), 'Eigene Sprache plötzlich bevorzugt', *Frankfurter Allgemeine Zeitung*, 17 June, p. 11.

Petz, I. (2020), 'Im Nebel', <https://www.eurozine.com/im-nebel/?fbclid=IwAR3Dxm506yJ17DKHKKi24jlZ45YSO20vjRYZaPe88wrsZOAz3crFB2XNBVc#> (last accessed 3 October 2020)

Piatnitskaia, S. (2016), 'Vybory v Belorussii: Eshche odin predstavitel' oppozitsii proshel v parlament', *Komsomol'skaia Pravda*, 12 September, <https://www.kp.ru/online/news/2507142/> (last accessed 17 January 2019).

Radyio Svaboda (2018a), 'Rossotrudničestvo: Kali my nia budzem zaimatstsa raseiskaj movai u Belarusi, iana khutka z'nikne', *Radyio Svaboda*, 4 October, <https://www.svaboda.org/a/29525657.html> (last accessed 7 October 2018).

Radyio Svaboda (2018b), 'Aleh Trusau: suprats' universytetu imja Nila Hilevicha zmahajucca i prychil'niki 'russkogo mira', i hrupouka EHU', *Radyio Svaboda*, 27 September, <https://www.svaboda.org/a/29511173.html> (last accessed 16 December 2018).

Radyio Svaboda (2019), 'S'viatkavan'nia BNR-101 na stadyëne 'Dynama' nja budze – Lukashenka', *Radyio Svaboda*, 1 March, <https://www.svaboda.org/a/29797694.html> (last accessed 2 March 2019).

Rakicki, V. (2014), 'Raseiskamoue – nepazbezhny shliakh da aneksii?', *Radyio Svaboda*, 19 March, <https://www.svaboda.org/a/25302767.html> (last accessed 25 November 2018).

Rossiiskii tsentr (2018a), 'O predstavitel'stve', Rossiiskii tsenter nauki i kul'tury v Minske, <http://blr.rs.gov.ru/ru/about> (last accessed 18 November 2018).

Rossiiskii tsentr (2018b), 'Rossiia i Belarus', Rossiiskii tsenter nauki i kul'tury v Minske, <http://blr.rs.gov.ru/ru/pages/380> (last accessed 18 November 2018).

Rossiiskii tsentr (2018c), 'Programmy podderzhki sootechestvennikov', Rossiiskii tsenter nauki i kul'tury v Minske, <http://blr.rs.gov.ru/ru/activities/91/projects/208> (last accessed 18 November 2018).

Rossiiskii tsentr (2018d), 'Organizatsii rossiiskikh sootechestvennikov', Rossiiskii tsenter nauki i kul'tury v Minske, <http://blr.rs.gov.ru/ru/activities/91/projects/199> (last accessed 18 November 2018).

Russia 24 (2017) ' "Formula vlasti" the President of the Republic of Belarus Aleksandr Lukashenko', <https://www.youtube.com/watch?v=PEGM9Z_PNKU> (last accessed 25 December 2018)

Russkii Mir (2019), 'Katalog Russkikh tsentrov', Russkii Mir – Informatsionnyi portal fonda "Russkkii Mir"', <https://russkiymir.ru/rucenter/catalogue.php> (last accessed 24 February 2019).

Russkii Tsentr BGUIP (2019), 'Novosti Russkogo Tsentra', Russkii Tsentr Brestskogo

gosudarstvennogo Universiteta imeni A. S. Pushkina, <http://www.brsu.by/rkc/news> (last accessed 24 February 2019)
Schmidt, F. (2016), 'Glückliche Menschen sprechen Weißrussisch', *Frankfurter Allgemeine Zeitung*, 7 September, p. 6.
Shadurskii, V. (2016), 'Sosushchestvovanie dvukh gosudarstvennykh iazykov v Respublike Belarus: poisk optimal'noi modeli', in P. Haslinger, M. Wingender, K. Galiullin and I. Gilyazov (eds), *Mehrsprachigkeit und Multikulturalität in politischen Umbruchphasen im östlichen Europa*, Wiesbaden: Harrasowitz, pp. 93–105.
Sliyashynskaya, H. (2019), '"One nation, two languages": Representations of official languages on multilingual news websites in Belarus', *Journal of Multilingual and Multicultural Development* 40, pp. 274–88.
Trasjanka in Weißrussland (n.d.), 'Die Trasjanka in Weißrussland – eine "Mischvarietät" als Produkt des weißrussisch-russischen Sprachkontakts', Carl von Ossietzky Universität Oldenburg Fakultät III – Sprach- und Kulturwissenschaften – Institut für Slavistik, <https://uol.de/trasjanka> (last accessed 11 January 2020).
Trusau, A. (2001), 'Rolia ruskai movy u demakratyzatsyi nashaha hramadstva', *Nasha Slova* 2, 10 January, p. 2.
TUT.BY (2014), 'V Minske shestviem i mitingom otmetili Den' pamiati predkov "Dzjady"', *TUT.BY*, 2 November, <https://news.tut.by/society/422080.html> (last accessed 11 November 2018).
Universitet imia Nila Gilevicha (n.d.), 'Misiia universiteta imia Nila Gilevicha', Universitet imia Nila Gilevicha, <http://nhu.by/> (last accessed 9 January 2020).
Vasilevich, H. (2012), 'Belarusian language: Current state and perspectives', *The Annual of Language & Politics and Politics of Identity* 6, pp. 1–21.
Wierzbowska-Miazga, A. (2013), 'Wsparcie drogą do podporządkowania. Rosja wobec Białorusi', *Punkt widzenia* 34, pp. 5–32.
Woolhiser, C. (2012), '"Belarusian Russian": Sociolinguistic status and discursive representations', in R. Muhr (ed.), *Non-Dominant Varieties of Pluricentric Languages: Getting the Picture. In Memory of Michael Clyne*, Frankfurt am Main: Peter Lang, pp. 227–62.
Zaprudski, S. (2007), 'In the grip of replacive bilingualism: The Belarusian language in contact with Russian', *International Journal of the Sociology of Language* 183, pp. 97–118.
Zelenkovskii, I. (2010), 'Bol'shoi vopros russkogo iazyka v Belarusi', *Imperiia. Informatsionno-politicheskii portal*, 2 March, <https://web.archive.org/web/20150317011654/http://imperiya.by/table19-7250.html> (last accessed 12 January 2020).

CHAPTER 3

Between Emotions and Pragmatism: The Russian Language in Kazakhstan and the 'Russian Factor'

Natalya Kosmarskaya and Igor Savin

INTRODUCTION

In terms of the size of its Russian-speaking population, the Republic of Kazakhstan is the third (Alisharieva et al. 2017: 234) or fourth country in the world (Blackburn 2019: 217).[1] The absolute number and the share of Russians in the country remains high despite strong emigrations during the first post-Soviet decade. Both the number and share of Russians are the highest among the countries of Central Asia. There were more than 3,588,000 Russians in Kazakhstan in 2018, and when combined with other Russian-speaking 'Europeans', such as Ukrainians, Belarusians, Germans, Tatars and others, the number reaches 4.3 million, or 27% of the country's population (Blackburn 2019: 231, 232). We should recall that Kazakhstan also maintains close ties with the Russian Federation as its leading strategic partner, that it became a member of the Eurasian Economic Union in 2015, and that it has joined a number of regional military and political associations under Russia's auspices. All of this explains why a whole range of socially sensitive issues related to the ethno-linguistic situation, to language policy and to the status of the Russian language have attracted much scholarly attention since the first years of independence.

From among the various publications of the 1990s and the first half of the 2000s, books by Bavna Dave (2007) and by Marlene Laruelle and Sebastien Peyrouse (2007) deserve special mention. Although they are not exclusively devoted to the ethnolinguistic problems of the country, this subject occupies an important place in both books. The authors analyse the outcomes of the policy of Kazakhisation in the linguistic sphere and trace the subsequent shifts in the status and role of the Russian language. After a certain hiatus in the coverage of this topic, there has been renewed interest in the Russian language in Kazakhstan and in related subjects in recent years.

These studies can be tentatively divided into two groups. Works of the first group, written by sociolinguists, are devoted to the peculiarities of the Russian language in Kazakhstan, seen through the lens of the theory of pluricentrism (Sabitova and Alisharieva 2015; Alisharieva et al. 2017; Shaibakova 2019). The empirical material accumulated over almost thirty years since the demise of the Soviet Union allows us to study the stages of development and the specific features of the particular Kazakh version of the Russian language.

Sociologists and anthropologists authored the second group of works, which explored the current issues of identity and the worldviews of certain ethno-cultural and demographic groups, including the Russian speakers. This relates to the entry of a new generation of Kazakhstanis into the socio-political scene. Their socialisation already took place in the period of independence, and they are accordingly called the 'Nazarbaev generation'. At the same time, a new generation of Russians and other 'Europeans' has grown up, who, unlike their parents, have not experienced the difficulties of moving from the status of 'majority' to the position of 'minority' (Jašina-Schäfer 2019a: 107). Although the authors of these works did not focus on the Russian language per se, they could not avoid addressing many relevant related topics. Among these were comparative assessments of the role and status of the Russian and titular language in Kazakhstan, the linguistic and cultural competences of various ethno-cultural groups, and their social status under the conditions of a steady proliferation of the Kazakh language in the educational sphere and public life (Alisharieva and Protassova 2016; Abdramanova 2017; Blackburn 2019; Jašina-Schäfer 2019a, 2019b; Laruelle 2019).

The problems of Russian and other 'European' minorities are frequently analysed with reference to the political discourse about the 'Russian World' and Russia's alleged specific responsibility for preserving the Russian language and culture in countries hosting people classified as 'compatriots' in Russian legislation (Jašina-Schäfer 2019b: 44; 2019a: 105–6; see also Chapter 1 in this volume). The most important feature of the Russian-speaking cultural space in Kazakhstan, however, is its supra-ethnic character. Besides ethnic Russians and other 'Europeans', it comprises Kazakhs and representatives of other ethnic groups: 'The users of the Russian language in the country today are mostly non-Russians' (Alisharieva et al. 2017: 236). Against the backdrop of the cultural and linguistic competences and attitudes of the titular ethnic group, this chapter discusses the actual role of the Russian language in Kazakhstan and the possible influence of the 'Russian factor'.

First, we briefly outline the role of Russia in the formation of the Russian linguistic space in Kazakhstan during the imperial and Soviet past. Next, we turn to recent developments in the interrelation between the Kazakh and Russian languages and sketch how the situation of the Russian language is assessed and influenced 'from above', that is, by the authorities of the republic, and how it is seen 'from below', that is, by ordinary residents. We focus our attention on the views of Kazakh students, members of the 'Nazarbaev generation', from whose ranks future elites will be recruited.

In the concluding part, we discuss two crucial questions. We ask to what extent the continued use of the Russian language and the acceptance of the Russian culture based on it currently depend on politics conducted by the Russian Federation. We also consider possible avenues for Russian politics if it were no longer to target the 'compatriots' exclusively, but also include representatives of the titular ethnic group as the main carriers of the Russian language and Russian culture in Kazakhstan.

The findings presented in this chapter are based on fifty semi-structured interviews with ordinary residents in Kazakhstan. Moreover, we conducted fifteen interviews with experts in Almaty and Petropavlovsk (Northern Kazakhstan) and ten focus-group discussions with university students in Almaty. These data were collected during the summer and autumn of 2016 and in the spring of 2017, within the framework of the international research project 'Perception of Russia in Eurasia: Memory, Identity, Conflicts' (PREMIC), 2016–17. We conducted two additional focus-group discussions in Almaty in October 2019.

THE RUSSIAN LANGUAGE IN CENTRAL ASIA: HISTORICAL AND CULTURAL ASPECTS

With the imperial conquest of vast territories, Russian language and culture essentially lost their exclusively ethnic connotations and emotional ties with the Russians as an ethnic group and began to live a 'life of their own'. In the pre-Soviet period, Russians maintained their identity, which was not an ethnic one, however. Seeing themselves and Russian culture as the engine of colonisation, attempts at linguistic Russification were only to a limited degree aimed at the assimilation of other ethnic groups, and were rather seen as an instrument for increasing the loyalty of these groups to the Russian Empire. After the 1917 revolution, similar ideas continued to inform the policy of the Bolshevik authorities. A hybrid Russian–Soviet culture formed the ideological backbone for the maintenance of the regime rather than for buttressing Russian ethnic consciousness.

Against this backdrop, the Russian language and Russian culture neither served as the main ethnic marker of Russianness, nor exclusively expressed Russian values. A Russian-cultural environment shaped the Soviet urban way of life and its inherent values and habits not only for Russians themselves, but for representatives of other ethnic groups serving as agents of empire in the peripheries, as well as for Russified autochthonous people. By no means did this 'Russianness' reflect a set of folkloric stereotypes, as can still be felt today. Many of the ethnic Russians who still reside in Kazakhstan and Kyrgyzstan, especially the residents of big cities, are suspicious of activities by the Russian agencies responsible for cultural relations and 'work with compatriots'. They are far from enthusiastic about cultural programmes offered to them in the shape of 'drinking tea from a samovar' or concerts of balalaika ensembles and Cossack choirs.

Beyond the historical background described above, the specifics of the integration of the territories now occupied by the newly independent countries of Central Asia should also be taken into account (Kosmarskaya and Kosmarski 2019: 71–9). External impulses generated incentives for the development of the peoples of the region. When they were offered participation in the Soviet mainstream of scientific and technological progress, Russians and other 'Europeans' acted as cultural mediators and formed the backbone of the scientific and industrial workforce. Any transfer of skills and knowledge required at the very least a basic understanding of one of the leading world languages and of the high culture created on its basis. The price for being absorbed by the Russian–Soviet civilisation, however, turned out to be considerable. The inherent identities, languages and traditions of the people residing in the region were severely affected, which is particularly true for those ethnic groups who developed into the contemporary Kyrgyz and Kazakhs. As former nomads without written languages before Russia's colonisation, they experienced a higher degree of Russification than their sedentary neighbours.

In the urban agglomerations and above all in the capitals (in the Kazakh SSR, Alma-Ata and the industrial cities of the north-east), close interaction between the 'Europeans' and representatives of indigenous groups unfolded. Large cities witnessed the formation of a particular layer of Kazakh and Kyrgyz urbanites during the Soviet era, very different from the rural tribesmen in their way of life and in their linguistic preferences.[2] In Kazakhstan, such Kazakhs are called 'asphalt Kazakhs' or, in a pejorative way, 'shala-Kazakhs'. Among the titular ethnic groups of Central Asian countries and their elites, Russian-titular language bilingualism or even exclusive use of Russian is still very common (see

Fierman 2012; Kosmarskaya 2014: 13–15; Kosmarskaya and Kosmarski 2019: 71–9).

THE RUSSIAN LANGUAGE IN KAZAKHSTAN SINCE INDEPENDENCE: THE VIEW 'FROM ABOVE'

With the collapse of the USSR and the independence of the Central Asian republics the status of the Russian language and the titular languages radically changed, both de jure and de facto. The latter rose to the rank of 'state languages' on the constitutional level and began to develop rapidly in terms of the scope and spheres of their use. This was especially true for the Kazakh and Kyrgyz languages. In cities above all, both languages actively penetrated social milieus in which they had hardly been noticeable in Soviet times. Such fields include primary and secondary education, media, book publishing, political life, administrative work and the urban landscape, such as street signs and place names. In the capitals and the large cities, the use of the titular languages also intensified in everyday life, thanks to an increase in the number of graduates from schools with Kazakh as the language of instruction. Changes in the labour market influenced the linguistic situation as well, caused by the increased demand for staff literate in the titular languages and, most importantly, due to the mass influx of rural labour migrants to the cities.

The Kazakh state language's progressive diffusion and its enhanced prestige and attractiveness characterises the current ethno-linguistic situation in the country (Smagulova 2016; Shaibakova 2019). At the same time, despite the gradual decrease in the share of Russians and other 'Europeans' in the population overall, the Russian language retains its function as the most important tool for accessing global culture, science and technology. Russian also continues to play an important role as the lingua franca in the wider communicative space connecting Kazakhstan with Russia and other post-Soviet countries. Moreover, according to the constitution, the use of Russian is permitted on an equal footing with Kazakh within official settings (Jašina-Schäfer 2019a: 103; Friess 2019: 151). The idea to switch to a trilingual (Kazakh, Russian, English) secondary education model, as reflected in a number of state programmes of the Republic of Kazakhstan, is the most recent innovation. It bears, however, a largely declarative character up to this point (Alisharieva et al. 2017: 238; Blackburn 2019: 232; Friess 2019: 160–1).

Post-Soviet censuses in Kazakhstan record a high Russian-language proficiency among the titular group. Due to demographic developments, the latter's share is constantly increasing among the country's population. Kazakhstan is among the few countries in the post-Soviet space in which almost all inhabitants use the Russian language in at least some contexts (Shaibakova 2019: 123). According to the 2009 census, 92% of the Kazakhs understood spoken Russian, 83.5% 'wrote freely' and 79% 'read freely' (Agentstvo Respubliki Kazahstan po statistike 2011: 24; Morrison 2017). With respect to the situations in 1989, 1999 and 2009, Marlene Laruelle notes that from census to census, the number of Kazakhs literate in Russian is increasing (Laruelle 2019: 8). The next census will show how stable this trend is.

Although linguistic 'Kazakhisation', that is, the promotion of the Kazakh language in all spheres of social life, remains an important feature of the nation-building process in post-Soviet Kazakhstan, language policy is implemented carefully and in a balanced way, taking a number of social and geopolitical factors into account. The close economic, political and military relations with Russia, as well as the fact that Kazakhstan still has a significant number of citizens who are either ethnic Russians or representatives of other groups whose historic homeland is Russia, are of utmost importance. Despite the officially proclaimed 'multi-vectoral' foreign policy, relations with Russia are the highest priority. Ex-President Nazarbaev never neglected to mention Russia first when enumerating the main foreign partners of Kazakhstan in his annual state-of-the-nation speeches (Laruelle and Royce 2019: 198).

In our opinion, recent developments including the Ukrainian crisis did not weaken, but rather strengthened the significance of the 'Russian factor' in the linguistic policies pursued by the country's leadership.[3] According to experts interviewed in Almaty in autumn 2016, the authorities issued a secret 'recommendation' to the main television channels, advising them to avoid broadcasting heated discussions about the Russian language, which were frequently demanded by representatives of the 'nationally oriented' intelligentsia and some parts of the political elite. Observers associated this move with Kazakhstan's strategic rapprochement with Russia in recent years and with the country's participation in the Eurasian Economic Union.

Alina Jašina-Schäfer has pointed to Nazarbaev's desire to strengthen the 'multinational unity' in the country in order to prevent ethnic conflicts along the lines of the Ukrainian scenario. In response to the president's proposal to punish violations of the language law, she notes that 'according to the president, in a bureaucratic or official context, a person making a query has the right to receive an answer in the same language – a clear statement that speaking Kazakh is not mandatory' (Jašina-Schäfer 2019a: 104; Shaibakova 2019: 130). Against this backdrop, it is difficult to agree with another researcher's suggestion that in recent years official initiatives in the linguistic field 'were marked by a certain hesitation and uncertainty' (Blackburn 2019: 217).[4]

Indeed, the increase in people who, to varying degrees, know Kazakh and use it in various communication situations should not be associated with politics so much as with demographic developments. The increased birth rate among Kazakhs and the ongoing outflow of Russians and other 'Europeans' from the country (albeit at much lower levels than in the 1990s) has led to an increase in the share of Kazakhs, particularly in younger age cohorts. This could not but leave its imprint on the balance of the languages of instruction in the secondary education system. In 2003, 55% of students studied in the Kazakh language, and 41% in Russian. Fifteen years later, in 2018, this ratio had changed to 66% and 31%, respectively. However, since 2015, a reversal of the trend has become noticeable, and the number of students studying in Russian has begun to increase again, from 802,000 people in 2014/15 to 910,000 in 2017/18. Due to declining numbers of ethnic Russians in secondary school, the increase was 'largely due to ethnic Kazakhs and some minorities opting for Russian language education' (Laruelle 2019: 9). According to estimates of Igor Savin, based on data received from the Agency for Statistics, Russian remains the language in which almost one-third of all schoolchildren in Kazakhstan are now receiving secondary education, including more than half a million non-ethnic Russians.

Laruelle notes that

> if Russian is enduring or maybe even expanding, it is not at the expense of Kazakh. On the contrary, it currently appears that both Kazakh *and* Russian are strengthening (or, at the very least, maintaining) their positions, meaning that the government's ambition to make virtually its entire population fluent in both languages is not unrealistic. (Laruelle 2019: 8, emphasis in the original)

THE RUSSIAN LANGUAGE IN INDEPENDENT KAZAKHSTAN: THE VIEW 'FROM BELOW'

What do ordinary citizens of the country think about the status of the Russian and Kazakh languages? How do they judge their own linguistic competencies in both languages? Here we present findings from focus-group discussions. We concentrated on the attitudes of the young generation of Kazakhstanis who grew up under the conditions of state independence and who in one or two decades' time will face the difficult task of managing the ethno-linguistic situation, requiring them to both maintain a balance of interests between the different ethno-cultural groups and take into account the requirements of globalisation.

The focus-group discussions entirely reflected the developments in the field of language policies over the years of Kazakhstan's independence. Students presented fragments of their language biographies, that is, stories about language practices in the families they grew up in; about the languages studied at school and the role parents played in their selection; where, when and how non-native languages were studied, and so on. Their accounts documented multifaceted bilingualism patterns among the urban residents of the titular ethnic group in post-Soviet Kazakhstan.[5]

Judging by the self-evaluation of linguistic skills and practices, students are at ease with the Russian language and use it extensively in their studies and for private and professional communication in the academic environment.[6] On a more general level, many participants spoke about the important role that the Russian language fulfils in the country:

R3[7] ... to this day, the place of the Russian language in our country is huge, it is of great importance. (Kazakh, male, Kazakh National University (KazNU), Dept of Sociology, 2016)[8]

R4 ... about the future Russian language in Kazakhstan? It seems to me that, as of now, it will retain its place and its status in Kazakhstan. (Kazakh, female, KazNU, Dept of Philology, 2017)

R3 ... our Russian language skills are very developed, which is necessary. (Kazakh, female, KazNU, Dept of Engineering, 2017)

We consistently recorded short approving comments on the country's bilingualism and the government's plans to add English to the curriculum:

R5 ... knowing many languages is good ... (Kazakh, male, KazNU, Dept of Ethnography, 2016)

R2 ... not only Russian and Kazakh, but also English, so that there is no bias ... (Kazakh, male, KazNU, Dept of Philology, 2017)

R5 ... as our president said, we need to speak three languages: English, Russian and Kazakh. (Kazakh, male, Kazakh-British Technological University, 2016)

The discussions revealed, however, noticeable differences in the participants' interpretations of ethno-linguistic problems in Kazakhstan. Students at 'prestigious' universities, where children from well-off families from the 'southern capital' of Almaty study and where some courses are taught in English, demonstrated a pronounced pragmatism when discussing the current role and future of the Russian and the titular languages in Kazakhstan. They most frequently spoke of the value of Russian as a tool for acquiring knowledge and for career advancement. In a similar instrumental way, many participants related to Russia, where, according to the students, science and education were better developed. In their opinion, Russia offered a larger choice of good textbooks and of academic literature in different disciplines. The students' judgements were usually detailed, offering clear justifications of the opinions expressed:

R8 The Russian language is one of the languages of the UN, so I think it will definitely keep [its role]. The integration and exchange with Russia are quite important, we constantly communicate, therefore the citizens of Kazakhstan need to know the language. (Kazakh, male, Kazakh-British Technological University, 2016)

R2 In my opinion, Russian has a future, because our government speaks Kazakh and Russian, and I earn my living with Russian as I teach it. Thirdly, I love science, and unfortunately, there is too little of the information that I would like to obtain available in Kazakh. The Russian language provides me with what I need. (Kazakh, female, KIMEP University, 2019)

R5 The Russian language is very important, you are not getting anywhere without knowing it, therefore we study it and with Russia, we have very close ties, too. You need to know it. (Kazakh, male, Kazakh-British Technological University, 2016)

R4 I joined the Russian department because it is easier for me to receive information, this database on the Internet and in the libraries, most of the stuff is in Russian. If you want to read any book of a foreign author for which there is no Kazakh translation, you read in Russian. Equally, there are very few translations of Russian writers. They say that Kazakh should have a higher status, I do not agree, but we should develop it, indeed. (Kazakh, male, Eurasian Technological University, 2016)

R2 It is the language of intercultural communication, of interethnic communication. Even despite the fact that the number of Kazakh speakers will increase, the Russian language will retain its position. As an international language. Which language do they use in Uzbekistan and Kyrgyzstan? (Kazakh, female, Kazakh-German University, 2019)

The status of the Kazakh language was discussed with the same pragmatism. The importance of this language was generally recognised, and the policy of mass bilingualism in the country likewise met with approval. Referring to personal plans to improve their command of the Kazakh language, respondents emphasised pragmatic reasons, such as the ambition to occupy a position in the public administration or to get a job with a Chinese company, and so on. Judging by our respondents, insufficient knowledge of Kazakh did not cause much distress, though:

R4 I do not know Kazakh well . . . I do not think that I should be ashamed about not speaking the Kazakh language. But I will still try to study Kazakh as in the future it might be useful for me. (Kazakh, male, Kazakh-British Technological University, 2016)

As far as their orientation towards Russian and their poor knowledge of the native language is concerned, students of this group disregard the pressure exerted on them by their social environment, and in particular by their kin:

R1 I feel hurt by such statements, like, 'well, you're Kazakh but you don't know your language'. I don't think it's such a huge problem. (Kazakh, female, KIMEP University, 2016)

Students considered knowing the traditions of one's nation to be much more important than linguistic preferences and skills:

R9 When our relatives come from the village, they jab all the time: now, you don't know the Kazakh language, you should know it. I think everyone should keep their traditions, not their language. You can speak different languages, but you need to remember your traditions. I don't see the word 'must' in front of the language. People do not have to know Kazakh perfectly. I know all our traditions, but I don't speak the Kazakh language well. (Kazakh, female, Eurasian Technological University, 2016)

In that sense, students focused on the need for the personal freedom of each individual to choose a language of communication and a professional activity. They considered social pressure unacceptable and associated it with 'nationalism':

> R6   They say that you need to know your native language. I think this is the first step to nationalism, that is, you must know your native language, and otherwise you are a nobody in this country. This should not happen. Everyone should be free to decide for themselves which language they want to use. (Kazakh, male, Eurasian Technological University, 2016)
>
> R1   We are Russian-speaking in our family and we often hear comments that we do not know our Kazakh language. Such comments are the first manifestations of nationalism, according to my observations and as another participant said already. I hear such phrases only from individuals who position themselves as nationalists and who do not like either Russian culture or the Russian language. This is very unpleasant because they themselves may have failed to attain something or lack knowledge in some field. I think they are wrong because the Russian language is a very important language in our country, for some kind of cultural improvement. (Kazakh, male, Eurasian Technological University, 2016)

A student of one of prestigious universities formulated the quintessential expediency in the approach to the languages question:

> R2   I am even against studying the Kazakh language. I myself am Kazakh, they reproach me since my childhood that I do not know Kazakh; honestly, I am tired of it. I consider language a means of communication, nothing else. It is just a tool, and when engaging with science or politics, Russian is a more convenient tool. (Kazakh, male, Kazakh-British Technological University, 2016)

We also organised focus-group discussion at several faculties of the Al-Farabi Kazakh National University with students from the regions, many of whom studied with state grants, some with Russian, and some with Kazakh as a language of instruction. These students revealed much less pragmatism and more emotion in relation to language issues. Acknowledging the benefit of knowing the Russian language like other participants, usually in a quite succinct way, they spoke more extensively and more emotionally about the Kazakh language:

R2   Now it is very prestigious and, I would say, very cool to know the Kazakh language, to be fluent in it. At least for me, for others it may be different . . . Although I am glad that I speak both languages, I prefer the Kazakh language. The Kazakh language has a very rich literature. In fact, it has many beautiful words. (Kazakh, female, KazNU, Dept of Sociology, 2016)

In addition to the pleasure associated with the beauty of the language, the second group of respondents associated its status with shame, pity and compassion:

R3   It is dismaying that the Kazakhs have largely forgotten their native language and communicate in Russian. Even in China they ask: 'please indicate which people does not speak their native language'. The right answer is 'the Kazakhs'. This is very sad. But I still think that the Russian language is necessary and unavoidable for us. (Kazakh, female, KazNU, Dept of Engineering, 2017)
R2   We studied Russian at school. It makes me sad to remember that we devoted more time to Russian than to Kazakh. We dealt with Kazakh rarely. It is a shame that we learn Russian so well in Kazakhstan. I think it is very good to speak Russian, but I would like us to switch to English in a little while, because almost all the readings are in English. (Kazakh, male, KazNU, Dept of Engineering, 2017)
R1   Sometimes I am ashamed of the fact that I as a citizen of Kazakhstan do not speak the Kazakh language sufficiently well. (Kazakh, female, KazNU, Dept of Philology, 2017)
R3   Ignorance of the Kazakh language, it seems to me, is an embarrassment, a shame. Especially when you are abroad and cannot speak your own language; that it seems to me that this is a humiliation in some way. (Kazakh, male, KazNU, Dept of Ethnography, 2016)

In students' assessments of the ethno-linguistic situation in Kazakhstan, we only twice encountered references to the national-patriotic discourse or allusions to Russia's historical responsibility for the current state of the Kazakh language. Even these cases reflected the contradictions of the situation, as the imperial past has brought benefits in some respects and has had a negative impact in others:

> R3 Relations with Russia brought enlightenment to Kazakhstan. Now that I myself studied in a Kazakh institution in the Kazakh language, I see that people who speak or study Russian think differently than people who speak the Kazakh language. No matter how terrible it sounds, those who have a Russian education think much more broadly, perhaps they even think more deeply. I think this is primarily because we parted ways with Russia, and the Kazakh language has very poorly developed until the present day. (Kazakh, female, KazNU, Dept of History, 2016)

Based on discussions with the students, we can safely conclude that the national-patriotic rhetoric has not significantly affected their views.

In general, the obvious differences in the attitudes of students of different universities concerning the ethno-linguistic situation reflect the importance of social and status boundaries in contemporary Kazakhstani society. Attitudes in the student environment towards the Russian language and Russian culture mirror similar cleavages among the older age groups of Kazakhs, among whom differences are primarily linked to social status, for example rural residents versus educated urban dwellers (Kosmarskaya and Kosmarski 2019: 86–7). Fluency in the Russian language, often paired with poor command of the Kazakh language and with a higher social and educational status, distinguish urban Kazakhs from the rural co-ethnics. Regional differences matter, too. Very good command of Russian is much more common among Kazakhs in the north-eastern parts of the country, where over a long time they have been in close contact with Russian speakers not only in cities but also in rural areas (Kosmarskaya and Savin 2018: 190–1).

As in the neighbouring countries of Central Asia, Kyrgyzstan and Uzbekistan, the growth of tensions between the Russian-speaking members of the titular groups, usually long-standing urban dwellers, and their rural co-ethnics intensified due to massive rural–urban migration in the post-Soviet period. The influx of 'villagers' only intensified the city dwellers' identification with the values of the urban lifestyle inherited from the Soviet period, including the widespread use of the Russian language (the case of Almaty is analysed in Bissenova 2017). In sum, the domains of the preferential use of the Russian language in contemporary Kazakhstani society largely coincide with residential patterns and social stratification (Blackburn 2019: 232).

IS THE RUSSIAN LINGUISTIC AND CULTURAL SPACE IN KAZAKHSTAN DEPENDENT ON RUSSIA?

Shifting the emphasis from ethnic to ideological values and priorities, the imperial-Soviet centre created in Kazakhstan (and in Central Asia as a whole) a specific model of cultural and linguistic dominance, which ultimately transformed the Russian language and the culture based on it into a supra-ethnic phenomenon. This model still determines the lifestyle, values and means of communication not just of the ethnic Russians and other 'Europeans' in these countries, but of the titular elite and of significant parts of titular populations as well. This historically based rootedness of the Russian language and culture among the titular population led to their transformation into self-reproducing local phenomena. Kazakhstani experts have repeatedly confirmed this fact.[9]

I (interviewer)	Does the Russian-speaking space exist here separately from Russia in the form of memories, in the form of a habitual cultural product?
R (respondent)	Not even memories or a habitual product. It is already a specific content. Self-reproducing.
I	Apparently, this does not depend on Russian efforts?
R	That's right. (Kazakh, male, historian, Almaty 2016)
R	The Kazakh elite and the entire Kazakh educated class is in general Russian-speaking, and the command of Russian among the Kazakhs no worse than that among the Russians.
I	Through the family?
R	In various ways, and it is self-reproducing as well. If hypothetically all Russians suddenly disappeared from Kazakhstan, the use of Russian would remain and reproduce itself in the Kazakh version . . . The Kazakh ethnocratic state itself thrives on the Russian language and on Russian culture. (Russian, male, deputy, Almaty, 2016)

The rootedness of the Russian language and culture in the local soil is also reflected in professional cultures such as literature and cinematography. Writers like Chingiz Aitmatov or Olzhas Suleimenov, the representatives of the Ferghana poetry school, as well as many young poets and writers from different countries of the region, belong to the intelligentsia from the titular nations of Central Asia writing their works in Russian (Morrison 2017; Friess 2019).

Referring to his teaching experience at the university in Astana, the British historian Alexander Morrison drew an analogy with the role of the English language in India and suggested that 'Russian is in every sense a Kazakhstani language – Kazakhstanis share in the wider Russian literary heritage, and have developed a distinctive Russophone culture of their own'. This is a 'Russophone world . . . that extends beyond the boundaries of the Russian Federation, and does not necessarily identify with it, or with ethnic Russianness' (Morrison 2017).

The opposite idea, however, also occupies a significant place in the public debate. It stipulates that the maintenance of the Russian language in the countries of Central Asia with the sizeable numbers of Russians and other 'Europeans' is a sort of 'extension of Russia', and is largely dependent on the latter country's efforts. Critics, however, perceive this idea as being a legacy of colonialism itself, and disapprove of its denial of the rootedness of the Russian language in the local environment.

On this matter, discussions in Kyrgyzstan are revealing, as the role and the status of the Russian language, recognised as an 'official' language by the constitution, are in many ways similar to the situation in Kazakhstan. Referring to materials published in Bishkek in 2011 in the journal *The Russian Word in Kyrgyzstan* with the assistance of the Russkii Mir Foundation, Georgii Mamedov has fleshed out the basic assumptions disseminated by the journal, forming the core of a debate in defence of the status of the Russian language in that country. According to the journal's authors and editors, 'the most important, if not the exclusive function of the Russian language in Kyrgyzstan is to ensure communication with Russia and with "Russian culture"'; 'the existence of the Russian language in Kyrgyzstan directly depends on the Russian government', and 'the connection with Russia through the Russian language exists not only as a rhetorical device but is actively triggered through the active work of . . . Russian and local pro-Russian institutions' (Mamedov 2012).

Mamedov himself believes that such a discourse in fact undermines the good intentions of its supporters and rather strengthens 'society's alienation from the Russian language'. Mamedov continues:

> The insistent linking of the Russian language in Kyrgyzstan with Russia, together with the almost complete absence of narratives portraying the Russian language as one of Kyrgyzstan's autochthonous languages, as a localised and organic element of the

Kyrgyzstani cultural landscape and as the most important medium of communication and expression for a significant part of the population of Kyrgyzstan, reinforces ... the following opinion. Only Russia's financial support and interests keep the Russian language alive in Kyrgyzstan, and were it not for this financial support, and if Russia lost interest in Kyrgyzstan, then there would no longer be a need for the use of the Russian language in the Kyrgyz Republic. (Mamedov 2012)[10]

Such discourses, which tightly link the fate of the Russian language in Central Asia with Russia's patronage, replicate the ideology of the 'Russian World', informing the work of most of the Russian organisations responsible for cooperation with the CIS countries. This conception suggests a focus on ethnic Russians and other 'compatriots' as the main target group in their practical work. The implicit logic seems to be that, if there are fewer and fewer Russians in the region due to migration and low birth rates, no country except for Russia will be left to preserve Russian language and culture in the region (see also Chapters 1 and 2 in this volume).

As explained above, we interpret the Russian linguistic and cultural space in Central Asia in general and in Kazakhstan in particular in a different way: as a phenomenon absorbing local cultural traditions, actively employed and developed by different ethnic groups. Does this in turn mean that Russia has no role to play and that its help is not needed? We cannot agree with this suggestion for a number of reasons.

First, the high degree of proficiency in Russian among the Kazakhs is neither a reason for nor a guarantee of positive attitudes towards Russia. Both the representatives of the ruling elites, with very diverse worldviews, and the small number of national-patriots who are very noticeable in online discussions are Russian-speaking, too.

Second, Kazakh-speaking Kazakhs, that is, the graduates of Kazakh-language schools living outside of the largely Russophone urban territories, are bilingual, too, with Russian as their second language. They might appreciate Russian cultural and educational support, which may help them to solve some of their problems in everyday life. Above all this is true for the rural youth, but unfortunately, neither they themselves nor the Russian organisations are aware of this.

Third, Russia is competing with other major players who are actively interested in winning the loyalty of the local elites and other segments of the population and have raised the stakes through their operation in Central Asia. This is primarily true of the United States and China. More recently, India has also more actively engaged in cultural, educational and humanitarian activities in the region (Letniakov and Emel'ianova 2017: 126–35).

Finally, beyond the efforts of various geopolitical actors promoting their cultures and values in Central Asia, processes of cultural globalisation affect the region. 'Global' cultural outputs reach young people first, as they use the Internet more actively than the older generations. Nazgul Mingisheva's quantitative pilot study, based on surveys among students at one of the universities of Karaganda in 2011 and 2017, clearly confirmed this. Mingisheva finds that

> be it social networks, television or music, youth in Kazakhstan appears to have been interacting with increased flows of global culture, with a particular rise in the share of culture from Asia. TV and music content produced in Kazakhstan are also increasingly preferred by young people, even if Russian and Soviet cultural elements remain important. (Mingisheva 2019: 172)[11]

All of these factors should have served as a wake-up call for Russian institutions, but so far they have produced little mobilising effect. Kazakhstani experts, by contrast, point to the efforts of China in the field of cultural promotion:

> R   Russia did not work to create a loyal space here. Americans worked, Chinese worked, Turks, Iranians, Saudis. I don't see a Russian space at all. (Kazakh, male, historian, Almaty, 2016)[12]
>
> R   Russia does not carry out any work on the problems of loyalty. (Kazakh, male, economist, Almaty, 2017)
>
> R   If Russia wants . . . if it really wants to be in this market, it needs to engage with the Kazakh environment . . . And in this respect, one can only applaud China as to how they move. Slowly, completely, calmly, without hysteria. They have opened the sixth Confucius centre, Chinese language courses, some information desks open in the libraries. (Kazakh, male, journalist, Almaty, 2016)

The Russian researchers Denis Letniakov and Natalya Emel'ianova analysed Russian soft power policy in Central Asia in a comparative perspective. They concluded that it was 'inefficient in terms of creating a positive image of Russia in the post-Soviet states'. They considered the narrowness of the target audience, that is, the focus on the Russian World, to be an important reason for this failure. Likewise, they deemed Russian soft power to be 'completely void of creativity, its actors execute in a stereotypical fashion following long-established models, not caring about their efficiency' (Letniakov and Emel'ianova 2017: 123, 124–5).[13]

An illustration of this was what we heard from one activist of a Russian organisation during an interview in Almaty in 2016:[14]

> R I know that in Kazakhstan there are several centres of the Russkii Mir Foundation, but they are practically all inactive: they opened, then they closed. There is a centre in Astana, a centre in Ust-Kamenogorsk, another somewhere else in Kazakhstan.
> I Do people know about this? Or do you know this only because you are a professional?
> R I think that only I know. There was a certain activity when they opened, then they forgot about it. The functional purpose of these centres is incomprehensible, it is unclear what they should do. There are libraries, there are electronic libraries, through them the global network of Russian resources [is accessible], which is not available through the regular Internet, but, unfortunately, they still do not use it.

Nonetheless, one should take into account some specific circumstances in Central Asia and in Kazakhstan in particular, which facilitated the 'slackening' and lack of vigilance displayed by the Russian agencies. The region simply does not receive due attention on the psychological, institutional and financial levels. According to Laruelle, Central Asia is certainly not the main target area in Russia's support of the 'Russian World' within the post-Soviet space. Central Asian elites are rather loyal both to Russia and to the ethnic Russians and other 'Europeans' living on their territory. By contrast, in the Baltic countries, in Moldova or Georgia, Russian-speaking minorities exist in a more inimical environment, and the elites of the countries reject Russian reintegration projects for the post-Soviet space (Laruelle 2015: 18; Friess 2019: 169).

A second factor deflecting Russia is both a consequence and a cause of the first, namely the persistence of dense social and cultural ties that developed between the RSFSR and the countries of the region during the Soviet era (Integratsionnii barometr EABR 2017: 15). Such networks contribute to the preservation of a sense of cultural-linguistic community. At the same time, they endure due to the similarity of cultural codes and of the mentality fostered in Soviet times. This is very relevant for Kazakhstan as well.

How does this 'interconnectedness' with Russia manifest itself in Kazakhstan? There are multiple personal contacts between Kazakhstanis and Kazakhs or Russians who had previously lived in the country and left for the Russian Federation.[15] Russian media, primarily television, still plays a very important role in the media landscape of contemporary Kazakhstan. Representatives of different nationalities and different social status groups consistently emphasise that it attracts viewers by its quality (Kosmarskaya and Savin 2018; Kosmarskaya 2020). Finally, 81% of Kazakh citizens surveyed by the Eurasian Development Bank in 2017 considered Russia to be the friendliest foreign country. Of all CIS countries, Kazakhstan displayed the strongest interest in inviting artists, writers and musicians from Russia, in purchasing and translating Russian-language books, movies, television shows, and so on (Integratsionnii barometr EABR 2017: 30, 74).

Operating in the recognisable and comfortable environment of Kazakhstani cities, in terms of mentality, cultural habits, soundscape, and so on, as most Russian organisations are, contributes to the perception that all is going well. Why bother with innovation, why demonstrate creativity, why attract additional resources to promote the Russian language and culture, if you are surrounded by peers (*svoi liudi*), if Russian is spoken everywhere, if the leaders of the two countries, according to one expert's metaphoric note, meet each other more often than their wives? Perhaps this sentiment helps to explain, for example, the tenacious unwillingness of the employees of Russian organisations working in Kazakhstan, including those of the embassy, to come to meetings with students of local universities. Several experts from higher educational institutions complained about this, pointing to the fact that representatives of embassies of other countries always readily responded to such invitations (Kazakh, female, KIMEP University, Almaty, 2016; Russian, female, Kazakh-German University, Almaty, 2019).

In our opinion, Russian efforts geared to the preservation and the development of the Russian-speaking cultural environment in Kazakhstan[16] need to be restructured in order to overcome the 'sedative' effect of the too-familiar environment inherited from the Soviet past, and to acknowledge the potential of the 'mobilising' factors described above. In fact, Russia faces a situation in which it needs to implement soft power under the conditions of tense international competition. In so doing, Russia has to recognise that its economic and ideological potential is not comparable to that which the Soviet Union could mobilise. Vladimir Mayakovsky's famous saying that he 'would have learned Russian only because Lenin spoke it' is a thing of the past.[17]

What would more adequate directions and principles of Russian policy in Central Asia look like? Instead of opening ever-new centres of Russian culture, it would be necessary to turn directly to the people as recipients of services and assistance from the Russian side. In so doing, it would be extremely important to take into account the specifics of the region as a whole, and of the individual countries.

For Kyrgyzstan, the relevant context would of course be labour migration to Russia. In this case, increasing the linguistic and cultural competences of actual and potential migrants, including those from rural areas, who have a poor knowledge of the Russian language or none at all, could become a key target of the Russian agencies' efforts.

The case of Kazakhstan is different again. It is a relatively developed country that also receives many labour migrants from Kyrgyzstan. People looking for work in Russia are, as a rule, qualified specialists (Feakins and Zemnukhova 2018). Kazakhstanis show a high interest in Russian education. Its citizens form the largest group of foreign students in the Russian Federation, with 39,700 enrolled in full-time programmes offered by Russian universities in 2017 (Shkurenko and Egupets 2019; see also Chapter 7 in this volume). In our opinion, further efforts should aim at significantly raising the number of students from Kazakhstan studying without having to pay fees, but should also ensure that among them is a large share of ethnic Kazakhs, in particular from different, traditional and modernised regions of the country. Other than in the case of the 'compatriots', there is a high probability that they will return to their homeland after graduation. This turn of events will effectively reinforce the cultural and linguistic polyphony in Kazakhstan and increase the level of 'loyalty' towards Russia that Kazakhstani experts speak about and which is a matter of concern for Kazakhstan's geopolitical competitors in the region.

Therefore it is important for Russia to continue with already tried and tested meaningful programmes instead of declamatory ones. Such programmes include, for example, support for secondary and higher education institutions operating with Russian as a language of instruction, as well as for scientific institutes, which experience a constant lack of resources in Central Asia. It is obvious that this type of assistance would contribute to the 'formation of an intellectual elite loyal to Russia' (Letniakov and Emel'ianova 2017: 124).[18] In fact, what is already being done in this area is surprisingly modest and incommensurate with the need. In 2015, for example, 160 teachers from all post-Soviet countries were invited to Russian for further training (Letniakov and Emel'ianova 2017: 124). In the Karaganda region or, say, in the Almaty region of Kazakhstan alone one might find as many teachers who would hardly refuse the opportunity to visit Russia for free and to expand their cultural and professional horizons.

More generally, Russia should target people with diverse political outlooks from different ethnic, social and professional backgrounds and age groups. These would include the urban intelligentsia interested in the classics of Russian and Soviet literature, villagers surrounded by traditional Kazakh culture, and older people who grew up with Soviet films, but also young people dreaming of going to North America to study.

Beyond the well-known, non-trivial steps should be thought of to support the Russian-speaking cultural space in the region and, in particular, in Kazakhstan. It would be worth taking the British television series *Downton Abbey* and its triumphant march around the globe as a model. Its success, and its relaunch in a widescreen version, are an indication of the high effectiveness of British soft power.[19] In a similar vein, carefully selected, and possibly, specially produced Russian films, music, television shows, theatre, and so on could cater for local audiences and meet the growing demand (especially of the young generation) for values and compassion. Beyond the linguistic background (a broad command of the Russian language) there is also a mentality ready for the acceptance of this kind of cultural production in Kazakhstani society.[20]

To conclude, the success of Russia's language and culture promotion in Kazakhstan largely depends on whether its performance can satisfy both the noticeable demand for an emotional element (often related not only to the Kazakh, but also to the Russian language), and the pragmatic language needs and expectations among different ethno-social groups and individuals in the country.

Translated from Russian by Christian Noack

NOTES

1. The differences in the assessments are probably due to the inclusion of the representatives of the titular group who are fluent in Russian in the category of Russian-speaking population.
2. According to the ethnographer Olga Naumova, in 1989 about three-quarters of urban Kazakhs did not use the Kazakh language in everyday communication (quoted in Dave 2007: 52).
3. The president's resignation in March 2019 did not significantly change the country's leadership system. As Alima Bissenova has recently put it, 'Nazarbaev is still the elephant in the room, framing and influencing the country's path' (Bissenova 2019: 271).
4. Blackburn refers to the 'stop-start process of promoting Kazakh as the state language' and 'delays in the long-anticipated shift from Cyrillic to Latin script which has now been postponed till 2025' (Blackburn 2019: 232).
5. Extreme cases would include, on the one hand, being born into a family of Russian-speaking Kazakhs (often urban for more than one generation) in Almaty or another large city, followed by education in a 'Russian' school and then at a university in

Russian, producing an individual whose command of Russian is at the native level combined with poor knowledge of Kazakh (Russian-titular bilingualism); or, on the other hand, being born in a Kazakh-speaking region, followed by education at school in the Kazakh language and then study at a university in the capital, where, under the influence of the environment and the requirements of the curriculum, a gradual development of Russian as a second language takes place (titular-Russian bilingualism).

6. Other micro-studies reflect similar findings on the language practices and preferences of students in Kazakhstan (Asylbekova et al. 2013: 92–6; Alisharieva and Protassova 2016: 86).
7. Numbers indicate the identification of a student within one separate group discussion.
8. All respondents' quotes have been translated by Natalya Kosmarskaya and Christian Noack.
9. The interviews have been translated from Russian by Natalya Kosmarskaya and Christian Noack.
10. Translated from Russian by Natalya Kosmarskaya and Christian Noack.
11. Translated from Russian by Natalya Kosmarskaya and Christian Noack.
12. Respondents' quotes translated from Russian by Natalya Kosmarskaya and Christian Noack.
13. Translated from Russian by Natalya Kosmarskaya and Christian Noack.
14. Interview translated from Russian by Natalya Kosmarskaya and Christian Noack.
15. In 2017, 3.5 million journeys were counted from Kazakhstan to Russia, and 3 million in the opposite direction (Turisticheskie potoki 2018). These large numbers reflect the density of human contact across the border of Russia and Kazakhstan, which is the longest land border in the world (c. 7,500 km).
16. To a certain degree these conclusions also apply to other countries of Central Asia with a sufficiently developed Russian linguistic and cultural space (Kyrgyzstan, Uzbekistan).
17. This is a line from Vladimir Mayakovsky's poem 'Nashemu Iunoshestvu', first published in the second number of the journal *Lef* in 1927. It was frequently quoted in Soviet propaganda.
18. Quote translated from Russian by Natalya Kosmarskaya and Christian Noack.
19. According to a 2015 rating of the attraction of soft power exerted by different states in the world, Britain constantly takes the lead position, which experts attribute to the quality of British films and television series. Russia first appeared on this list in 2016, and has not yet risen above twenty-sixth place (Nochevka 2019).
20. Nazgul Mingisheva's research on young people in Kazakhstan, especially girls, found that they are interested in popular Korean animated films and K-pop series, because the latter transmit morality and emotionality. Mingisheva draws an analogy with Soviet films and animated films, often known to young people through communication in the families, which also 'taught to be kind' (Mingisheva 2019: 173, 175).

REFERENCES

Abdramanova, S. (2017), 'Ethnic identity of Kazakhstani young people in relation to language', *Eurasian Journal of Philology: Science and Education* 2, pp. 140–7.

Agentstvo Respubliki Kazakhstan po statistike (2011), *Itogi Natsional'noi perepisi naseleniia Respubliki Kazahstan 2009 goda. Analiticheskii otchet (proekt)*, <http://www.myshared.ru/slide/372836/> (last accessed 19 January 2021).
Alisharieva, A. and E. Protassova (2016), 'Lingvisticheskoe samosoznanie mnogoiazychnykh studentov Kazakhstana', *Kazanskii Pedagogicheskii Zhurnal* 3, pp. 83–7.
Alisharieva, A., Zh. Ibraeva and E. Protassova (2017), 'Kazakhstanskii russkii: vzgliad so storony', *Ab Imperio* 4, pp. 231–63.
Asylbekova, A., S. Akhmettaeva and Zh. Erezhepova (2013), 'Problema bilingval'noi iazykovoi podgotovki studentov gumanitarnykh spetsial'nostei v Respublike Kazakhstan', *Sotsiologicheskie issledovaniia* 9, pp. 92–6.
Bissenova, A. (2017), 'The fortress and the frontier: Mobility, culture, and class in Almaty and Astana', *Europe-Asia Studies* 69 (4), pp. 642–67.
Bissenova, A. (2019), 'Social change unsettles Kazakhstan', *Current History* 118 (810), pp. 271–5.
Blackburn, M. (2019), 'Discourses of Russian-speaking youth in Nazarbaev's Kazakhstan. Soviet legacies and responses to nation-building', *Central Asian Survey* 38 (2), pp. 217–36.
Dave, B. (2007), *Kazakhstan: Ethnicity, Language and Power*, London: Routledge.
Feakins, M. and L. Zemnukhova (2018), '"I'm not a Gastarbeiter anymore": Liminal mobility of young Kazakh IT professionals in Russia', *Discourse: Studies in the Cultural Politics of Education* 39 (5), pp. 752–66.
Fierman, W. (2012), 'Russian in post-Soviet Central Asia: A comparison with the states of the Baltic and South Caucasus', *Europe-Asia Studies* 64 (6), pp. 1077–100.
Friess, N. (2019), 'Young Russophone literature of Kazakhstan and the "Russian World"', in N. Friess and K. Kaminskij (eds), *Resignification of Borders: Eurasianism and the Russian World*, Berlin: Frank & Timme, pp. 149–74.
Integratsionnii barometr EABR (2017), *Report no. 46*, St Petersburg: Tsentr integratsionnykh issledovanii Evraziiskogo banka razvitiia.
Jašina-Schäfer, A. (2019a), 'Where do I belong? Narratives of rodina among Russian-speaking youth in Kazakhstan', *Europe-Asia Studies* 71 (1), pp. 97–116.
Jašina-Schäfer, A. (2019b), 'Everyday experiences of place in the Kazakhstani borderland: Russian-speakers between Kazakhstan, Russia, and the globe', *Nationalities Papers* 47 (1), pp. 38–54.
Kosmarskaya, N. (2014), 'Russians in post-Soviet Central Asia: More "cold" than the others? Exploring (ethnic) identity under different socio-political settings', *Journal of Multicultural and Multilingual Development* 35 (1), pp. 9–26.
Kosmarskaya, N. P. (2020), 'Kakoi vidit Rossiiu molodezh postsovetskikh stran? Mneniia studentov Kazakhstana', *Rossiya i sovremennyi mir* 1, pp. 186–203.
Kosmarskaya, N. and A. Kosmarski (2019), '"Russian culture" in Central Asia as a trans-ethnic phenomenon', in K. Platt (ed.), *Global Russian Cultures*, Madison, WI: University of Wisconsin Press, pp. 69–93.
Kosmarskaya, N. P. and I. S. Savin (2018), 'Chto dumaiut kazakhstantsy ob otnosheniiakh s "severnym sosedom"?', *Central Eurasian Studies* 1, 175–95.
Laruelle, M. (2015), *The 'Russian World': Russia's Soft Power and Geopolitical Imagination*, Washington DC: Center on Global Interests.
Laruelle, M. (2019), 'Introduction: The Nazarbaev generation: A sociological portrait', in M. Laruelle (ed.), *The Nazarbaev Generation: Youth in Kazakhstan*, Boulder, CO: Lexington Books, pp. 1–21.

Laruelle, M. and S. Peyrouse (2007), *'Russkiy vopros' v nezavisimom Kazakhstane. Istoriia, politika, identichnost'*, Moscow: Natalis Press.
Laruelle, M. and D. Royce (2019), 'Kazakhstani public opinion of the United States and Russia: Testing variables of (un)favourability', *Central Asian Survey* 38 (2), pp. 197–213.
Letniakov, D. and N. Emel'ianova (2017), 'Strategii "miagkoi sily" v postsovetskoi Tsentral'noi Azii: Rossiia vs SShA, Kitai, India', *Mir Rossii* 26 (4), pp. 118–42.
Mamedov G. (2012), 'Russkii iazyk v Kyrgyzstane: diskurs i narrativy (po materialam zhurnala "Russkoe slovo v Kyrgyzstane")', *Shtab*, 17 September, <http://www.art-initiatives.org/ru/content/russkiy-yazyk-v-kyrgyzstane-diskurs-i> (last accessed 1 November, 2019).
Mingisheva, N. (2019), 'Cultural globalization and youth identity construction', in M. Laruelle (ed.), *The Nazarbaev Generation: Youth in Kazakhstan*, Boulder, CO: Lexington Books, pp. 167–76.
Morrison, A. (2017), 'Russian beyond Russia', *Eurasianet.org*, 4 April, <http://www.eurasianet.org/node/83296> (last accessed 17 October 2019).
Nochevka, F. (2019), 'Velikaia televisionnaia derzhava. Britanskie serialy prevratilis' v odno iz samykh moshchnykh orudii britanskoi "miagkoi sily"', *Kommersant*, 29 September, <https://www.kommersant.ru/doc/4101318?-from=main_4> (last accessed 20 December 2019).
Sabitova, Z. and A. Alisharieva (2015), 'The Russian language in Kazakhstan: Status and functions', *Russian Journal of Communication* 7 (2), pp. 213–17.
Shaibakova, D. (2019), 'Russian language in Kazakhstan in the 21st century', in A. Mustajoki, E. Protassova and M. Yelenevskaya (eds), *The Soft Power of the Russian Language: Pluricentricity, Politics and Policies*, London: Routledge, pp. 123–33.
Shkurenko, O. and A. Egupets (2019), 'Chto Rossiia i Kazakhstan znachat drug dlia druga?', *Kommersant*, 20 March, <https://www.kommersant.ru/doc/3917333?from=main_spec> (last accessed 10 August 2019).
Smagulova, J. (2016), 'The re-acquisition of Kazakh in Kazakhstan: Achievements and challenges', in E. Ahn and J. Smagulova (eds), *Language Change in Central Asia*, Berlin: De Gruyter, pp. 89–107.
Turisticheskie potoki mezhdu Rossiei i Kazakhstanom v 2017 godu (2018), *Vesti: Ekonomika*, 13 November, <https://www.vestifinance.ru/infographics/11561> (last accessed 10 August 2019).

CHAPTER 4

Speakers of Russian in Ireland: 'What unites us is language, but in all other respects we are different'

Feargus Denman

INTRODUCTION

This chapter presents an analysis of roundtable discussions among speakers of Russian living in Ireland. The discussions were facilitated as part of 'Our Languages/Nashi iazyki', a project undertaken to investigate multilingualism and sociolinguistic dispositions among Ireland's Russian-speaking population between 2008 and 2011. The chapter introduces the Irish linguistic context as of 2009, when these discussions were recorded, before proceeding to analysis of six roundtable discussions. The chapter adopts a typographic distinction such that *Ln*anguage denotes a species of language or, what is normally termed – and often named as – a language, whereas *l*anguage denotes finite quantity of linguistic content.[1]

HOW MUCH IS RUSSIAN SPOKEN IN IRELAND?

Irish society is frequently represented as having been relatively homogeneous for most of the twentieth century, at least in the southern Republic, or as defined by dichotomies between Britishness and Irish nationalism – especially in Northern Ireland.[2] However, the proportion of non-Irish-born residents grew from 6.1% in 1991 to 10.4% in 2002 to 15% in 2006 (Mac Gréil 2011: 15–16). Over this period, attitudes to the social category 'Russians' among the general population were counted among the most significantly improved (Mac Gréil 2011: 66).

The population of Russians in Ireland is not commensurate with the population of persons speaking Russian, and it is not a simple matter to quantify the Russian-speaking population, though there are official figures. The Irish state census did not include any question about languages other than Irish and English until 2011, when 22,446 people reported speaking Russian at home; in 2016, the slightly lower figure of 21,707 was returned. Yet estimates frequently exceed the census indications by a factor of four or five.[3] One reason for this disparity is that the added census question allows just one language other than English and Irish to be specified as being spoken at home. Census figures therefore exclude persons by whom Russian is spoken, but not at home, or households where Russian is not named within a broader repertoire of languages spoken. For example, the 13% of persons speaking Russian recorded in 2011 as Russian nationals represents fewer than half the total number of resident Russian nationals – 5,936 – returned in the same census. Irish nationals accounted for 20% in 2011, which rose to 29% as of 2016; Latvians accounted for 27% (down to 23% in 2016) and Lithuanians for 14% (falling to 9%) (Central Statistics Office 2012, 2016).

The higher estimates reflect an inference on the basis that many nationals of former Soviet Union (FSU) states avail of Russian as a language of wider communication. Immigrants from the Baltic states, rather than from Russia itself, constitute the major portions of this population, and Russian speakers in these states have faced particular push factors for emigration, such that the proportion of Russian speakers emigrating from Baltic states exceeds domestic proportionality (Aptekar 2009). There are also significant populations from Belarus, Moldova, Georgia and Ukraine. Thus, for a variety of reasons, the number of people speaking Russian may not be reflected in official figures.

There have been numerous initiatives to foster community and collective support. In 2007, the Council of Russian Compatriots established a committee in Ireland, and further initiatives include the annual celebration of 9 May as Victory Day and an annual festival of Russian culture around *Maslenitsa*, the beginning of Lent in the Eastern Orthodox calendar. Cultural associations and newspapers celebrate and simultaneously create Russian speakers' community in Ireland: a Society of Russian Speakers in Ireland (SORUSSI) was formed in 2001 and the Russian-language newspaper *Nasha Gazeta* has been in print since the same year. This paper has grown from a rate of monthly to weekly publication. Russian-language content now appears in the linguistic landscape throughout the country in shops where Russian is spoken.

Numerous websites address and serve speakers of Russian in Ireland, the largest of which is virtualireland.ru with 20,000 registered users. There also exist social media groups, which typically convoke a community of Russian speakers, rather than Russians as such. Thus, membership of 'Russoglot Ireland' [*Russkoiazychnaia Irlandiia*] in Facebook far exceeds membership of the 'Russians in Ireland' [*Russkaia Irlandiia*] group.[4] All this notwithstanding, Sofya Aptekar found, as of 2009, the institutionalisation of 'ethnic communities of Russian-speaking migrants' to be relatively weak (Aptekar 2009).

CONCEPTS OF LANGUAGE-BASED COMMUNITY

In dealing with languages such as Russian and English, one operates within a specifically European tradition according to which members of a *L*nanguage-based community 'are united in adherence to the idea that there exists a functionally differentiated norm for using their "language" denotationally' (Silverstein 1996: 285). Institutionalisation of a standard form of *L*nanguage requires of members of such a community their deference to the institutionally maintained norms, so that 'the standard that informs a language community's norm thus becomes the very emblem of the existence of that community' (Silverstein 2000: 122).

Following Dell Hymes, Silverstein distinguishes between *language community* and *speech community*. The concept of 'speech community' has been subject to a degree of criticism: 'it must be admitted that "speech community" is not precise enough to be considered a technical term' (Mesthrie et al. 2000: 37). However, concepts of discourse-based and *L*nanguage-oriented community remain significant both academically and as elements of language ideology – 'beliefs about language articulated by users' (Silverstein 1979). In Silverstein's terms, the concept of

> patterned linguistic usage-in-context—'rules of use'/ in short—of who, normatively, communicates in which ways to whom on what occasions, may be termed 'speech community', while that of 'a population manifesting regularity of usage based on allegiance to norms of denotational code' may yet properly be termed 'language community'. (Silverstein 1997: 129)

As he notes, only the latter concept has bearing upon the conventional understanding of languages – for example, Russian – as 'lexically distinctive and grammatically regular ways of representing referents' (Silverstein 1997: 129).

Russian cultural-semanticists have explored a Russian 'language picture of the world' (RLPW, in Zalizniak et al. 2005, 2012).[5] This culturally framed linguistic relativity categorises identity in discrete ethno-national terms, with *L*nanguage a crucial property. Just as dictionaries and written grammars prescribe standardised *L*nanguage, so the RLPW prescribes – or describes so as to inscribe – defining features of Russian mentality. This scholarship is germane to a neo-Slavophile concept of *russkost'* (Kelli 2013), in that native command of Russian is taken to imply a worldview underpinned by the intrinsic specificity of Russianness.

The Russian Federation has sponsored a number of entities with the express purpose of affirming the unity of a global, Russian-language-based sphere of interests. These include the Russkii Mir Foundation and the World Association of Russian Press (WARP). Where such a concept of *L*nanguage is firmly established, even if it is removed from a particular register or rhetoric of nationalism, that *L*nanguage remains readily available for emblematisation as a seal of community. In the former Soviet sphere, Russian speakers have been addressed as a single audience and interest group. Thus, the director of the Mir broadcasting corporation, Batyrshin, states of his viewership and market, 'we are in the first instance united by the Russian language' (Ryazanova-Clarke 2014: 256). The concept of a 'Russian World' functions similarly to that of *Francophonie*, relying on a like ambivalence between strictly linguistic, national and statist levels of interest (Laruelle 2015: 23). The concept serves to unite speakers of the language with a coordinated concept of cultural heritage.

Addressing the annual congress of the World Association of Russian Press in 2008, President Vladimir Putin analogised the Russian (*rossiiskaia*) diaspora to its homeland, Russia: open yet unified by virtue of the Russian *L*nanguage. In such discourses of diaspora, the concept of 'homeland' assumes dispersal in relation to the ideal of a common point of origin, with *rodina* encapsulating a moral core. The language brings this diversity into communion with the country/state (*Rossiia*), rather than a strictly cultural Russianness (as *russkaia*):

> The Russian [*rossiiskaia*] diaspora is one of the largest in the world. It is unique in that it is open to people of different nationalities. It is as open as our homeland [*rodina*], as Russia [*Rossiia*]. All this diversity of religions, ethnic groups and traditions is united by the Russian [*russkii*] language. The greater your influence the greater its role in global politics, economy and the social sphere. (Putin 2008)

However, as becomes apparent by attention to facilitated discussions among speakers of Russian living in Ireland, the unitary *L*nanguage does not in itself give rise to a self-conscious community of speakers. The different ways in which one may be termed a speaker of Russian are not formally defined, nor strictly sustained.

'OUR LANGUAGES'

The 'Our Languages' research project launched in 2008, asking 'Who in Ireland speaks and understands Russian?' The target population was not conceived of as a single community, but as an aggregate comprising various ethnicities and nationalities and at the intersection of diverse groups (Singleton et al. 2009). Fifteen roundtable discussions took place at eleven locations, six of them in Dublin. The present chapter focuses on those events in Dublin.

The research question of the project was originally 'Russian-speakers in the Republic of Ireland: who are they?' (Smyth 2008). The later wording shifts the emphasis away from Russian speakers as 'other', and towards the discussion of languages and of Russian speaking within Ireland. There were three major strands to this project. The first of these was a sociolinguistic survey, gathering data to capture the social realities of language repertoire, attitudes and practice among people with a knowledge of Russian. The survey was live at www.tcd.ie/Russian/our-languages from September 2008 through the beginning of 2010. A second strand of the project comprised autobiographical narratives – life stories – in which participants offer a personal chronicle, structured and themed according to their own inclination. Upon completing the survey, all survey respondents were invited to indicate interest in contributing to the collection of life histories. The third strand of the project was conducted between February and June of 2009 in fifteen roundtable discussions. A fourth instrument within the project was family observation with regard to transmission, conducted and analysed by Svetlana Eriksson (2011, 2013).

The question 'Who in Ireland speaks and understands Russian?' does not establish formal criteria for its target audience. The profile of participants in the project was therefore shaped by self-selection and networks of acquaintance. In such instances, the difficulty of reaching hard-to-access populations, such as undocumented and marginalised immigrants, tends to skew social research towards more socially integrated, more educated, and professional elites (Atkinson and Flint 2001). The project attempted to correct against this bias by distributing paper copies of the survey to Eastern European-oriented shops and public libraries throughout the country, as well as disseminating the link to the project website online.

Roundtable discussions took place at eleven locations, determined in relation to survey responses. The project invited 'any group of Russian-speaking people in any place in Ireland wishing to organise a roundtable discussion' to make contact. Twenty roundtable discussions were scheduled, and a poster was distributed to public libraries and placed in regional newspapers. Between six and thirteen participants were present at each of the roundtable events in Dublin. There was an overlap of participants across these events, with repeated attendance by several participants. Each discussion began from a prompt respectively towards discussion of family life (I), integration (II), multilingualism (III), social life (IV), diaspora (V) and Russian as a language of wider communication (VI). Beyond the initial prompt, participants conversed freely, with minimal moderation from the facilitating researcher.

Initial transcription of the roundtable recordings was produced by an L1 speaker of Russian. My analysis of the discussions involved coding the content of the discussions and further annotation of the transcriptions while listening to the recordings in order to identify distinct speakers' voices. Participants are identified according to the order in which they first speak and according to reflexive grammatical inflection of gender. Thus, 'I.f3' denotes the third female/feminine speaker identified in the course of the first roundtable discussion; 'VI.m1' marks the first male/masculine speaker in the recording of the sixth roundtable discussion.

ANALYSIS

The following analysis proceeds in three sections. First we consider the connection between language and identity in the Russophone discourse. This connection is articulated in principle with regard to an Irish context in which discussants observe the disjuncture between the titular – *rodnoi*/'native' – L*n*anguage of Ireland and the vernacular speech of the Irish. It also involves complication at the levels of personal heritage, for speakers who are not simply monolingual nor monocultural in their genealogical or autobiographical selves, and who further experience a sense of change or rupture in their linguistic identity while living in anglophone Ireland. The second section of the analysis examines the ways in which discussants affirm their community, or rather the fact of a Russian-speaking community, in Ireland. Third, we turn our attention to the ways in which discussants negotiate moments of disjuncture that arise in the course of discussion, where perspectives are unaligned.

LANGUAGE AND IDENTITY IN IRELAND

Participants explore the link between language and identity through observations on the specific context of Ireland. They are sympathetically perturbed by the question of Irish national language:

> I.f4 And since English here, the expansion [. . .] Gaelic, not many speak it any more. The Irish also have their problems with language.⁶

There is a degree of curiosity about Irish Gaelic, though acquisition of the language is not necessitated by any imperative of social integration:

> III.f4 I tried to learn Irish, but I gave up, it's a very difficult language, it takes a lot of time. I said, no, maybe later.

Irish Gaelic does present a motivating point of contrast vis-à-vis potential outcomes for heritage language conservation. One may hope 'our' children will master their heritage languages (Russian and Moldovan in the case of this speaker's household), unlike classmates 'who learn Irish as a foreign language in their own native country'.

In the present geopolitical order, English is the lingua franca and it replaces Russian for a new generation:

> VI.f4 Now, our generation, like, young people, they of course have switched to English and their language of international communication will be English.

Ireland is for practical purposes an English-speaking country and more pressing questions pertain to the possible prospect of children experiencing confusion or conflict between heritage and culture:

> I.f6 In the [case of a] child, can we avoid this division between Russian culture and Irish-anglophone [. . .]
> I.m1 Anglo-Saxon, yes.

The question of Irish Gaelic is left for the Irish themselves to resolve,⁷ though it may retain a spectral significance:

> I.f7 Interestingly, we have distinguished the Russian and let's say the Irish culture, Russian language and Irish language.
> I.m1 Do you mean Gaelic? Gaelic or English?

I.f7 English, English
I.m1 It's interesting how you mix them up, though, all the same, unconsciously.
I.f7 Never mind. [general laughter]

On the topic of Gaelic language within Irish society, participants identify a paradox in Irish national pride not being expressed through the emblematic and first official Irish L*n*anguage. One speaker echoes a self-representation of the Irish, marking their own vernacular (English) *l*anguage to query the pride in their national identity:

III.f5 It's strange, if they are so proud of their *national identity* [in English] and their independence from England, why don't they want to talk Irish?

III.f5 emphasises the apparent contradiction between their claim to a proud 'national identity', as they might put it, and the fact of its being asserted, so to speak, in English. This *l*anguage signifies the lacuna of an unproblematically singular Irish L*n*anguage.

The dissonance between an Irish anglophone understanding of 'nationality' as citizenship and a Russian understanding of nationality (*natsional'nost'*) as ethno-national identity also occasions comment:

IV.f1 When I become a citizen of Ireland, they'll ask, well, *where are you from* [in English]; Well I know I can't say that I am *Irish*. I can say I, *I am a citizen of Ireland* [in English].

This speaker – who holds Azerbaijani citizenship – again uses specific English *l*anguage to establish a context of dialogue between the English-speaking Irish and her formally and subjectively evolving identity. Many of the instances of code-switching and hybrid speech similarly perform the departure of Irish speech community from simple L*n*anguage community as well as the division between Russian L*n*anguage community and Irish mainstream society. Ireland presents a context in which the complications in the correspondence between named language and personal identification may be assumed from the outset.

With regard to Ireland as a linguistic context of the prospects for Russian, the discussants show a certain optimism. It may already, speculatively, along with Polish and Chinese, have supplanted Irish in 'popularity' [*populiarnost'*].[8] Considering the prospects for Russian, one parent predicts that within twenty years:

III.f4   Twenty per cent of the population, of the Irish, will speak it, for sure.

This prognosis is queried by another, who notes that

III.f1   You are very bold, it seems to me, twenty per cent, [. . .] the Russian language is diminishing in russoglot families, very few russoglot parents seem concerned about maintaining the language among their children.

But the optimism of III.f4 is bolstered by the prevalence of cultural activities in Russian and the fact that Russian speakers are transmitting the language to their children, as she claims, even in mixed marriages. At a later event, she suggests that the Irish themselves appreciate the value of Russian as a language offering greater opportunities than Irish Gaelic.

Besides the Irish sociolinguistic context, participants raise complications in their personal background. The woman hoping that her children should grow up with both their heritage languages, Moldovan and Russian, in a subsequent discussion reflects on the sociolinguistic situation of her home country:

IV.f2   It's interesting, interesting every time for me to come to these discussions, because I am not [a] russoglot, I was only born in Russia, but [in Moldova] to speak in Russian was even more prestigious than in one's native tongue.

Identifying in this instance as a Moldovan – specifying her civic nationality as 'one among *moldavane*' – she claims both Russian and Romanian/Moldovan as native languages – alternately naming her non-Russian language both as Moldovan [*moldavskii*] and also by its official glossonym as Romanian [*rumynskii*] (this reflects complications discussed by Ciscel 2008). Thus, her own language accommodates and suggests flexibility between different perspectives on Moldovan language. On a previous occasion, however, she recounts:

III.f4   They ask me, and are you a Moldovan? I say, no, I am of Russian stock, but I lived in Moldova.

Yet, at a subsequent event, the same woman states

IV.f2   But this place of birth then gets complicated. I come from Russia [. . .] but I am at root a Moldovan and my parents are Moldovans, they simply went to Russia to earn money and I was born there.

Many speakers experience dissonance in relation to an implicit imperative to have a singular sense of one's place in the world:

> I.f3 I don't feel at home in my homeland, and I don't feel at home here, though I do have family, friends, I don't feel at home here. So, where is my home?

Contending with incongruences amidst a diversity of language, birthplace, ethnicity and nationality, they report seeming paradoxes of subjectivity vis-à-vis simple categories, where such categories are implicitly exhaustive:

> II.f1 I am not Russian, I also have a much mixed blood, and therefore this question is very complicated – who are you, in fact, or of what ethnicity [*natsional'nost'*], what's your nationality. Like, a grandfather of mine was a Jew, my grandson is a Latvian, and, well, I am Russian. It's unfathomable.
>
> V.f4 Look I, for example am called [a Turkic name] and I am from Ossetia. Who am I? A Russian Ossetian? A Soviet woman, as you say, yes? Because, I was born in an Ossetian family, but I do not speak Ossetian, I only speak Russian. As, quite simply, I grew up in Russian culture. And so, who am I?

On top of personal narratives in which heritage confounds the assumptively simple ethno-national correspondence of language and identity, migrants experience a disruption to their provisionally familiar sense of self in relation to language. Since arriving in Ireland and having left a Russophone milieu, many participants note an unsettling impermanence in their command of Russian. Attrition and interference – inadvertent hybridisation – occasion reconsideration of their relationship to their first language:

> I.f7 I am worried that I am beginning to lose the Russian language, because at work I speak in English, at home with my beloved, I speak English – I'm losing Russian.

One man repeatedly emphasises his dismay at the inconstancy of his native language – 'moi russkii–rodnoi' – during a return trip to Latvia:

> I.m2 I had problems speaking in Russian. I found that it's sometimes simpler for me to describe a situation in English than immediately to communicate in Russian.

For several speakers, it is observed specifically in connection with workplace habits and habitus:

> VI.f1 Sometimes it's easier to switch into English.
> VI.f2 It's much easier for me in English now.

And some participants do not hesitate to draw others' attention to departures from standard practice, for instance in orthography on name cards:

> II.m2 We have mixed Cyrillic with Roman lettering and some have even mist . . . forgotten that it's not written like 'N', [they're/you're/we're] even losing letters already.

In the preceding analysis we have seen how the speakers of Russian living in Dublin assume a relationship between language and identity that should ideally comprise a binary correspondence of national vernacular and personal affiliation. However, personal genealogy and variability in linguistic repertoire makes this simple binary correspondence difficult to sustain, certainly in practice if not as an ideal.

AFFIRMING COMMUNITY

Such complications as are discussed above notwithstanding, participants in these discussions affirm their community. Speakers of Russian in Dublin invoke collective identities on various scales, in broad terms of being immigrant foreigners in Ireland, ethnic Russians (*russkie*), expatriated Russians (*rossiane*), post-Soviet denizens, and as speakers of Russian. The different ways in which one may be termed a speaker of Russian are not strictly distinguished by *russkogovoriashchie* (literally, 'Russian-speaking') versus *russkoiazychnye* ('Russian-languaged', or 'russoglot'). These words appear to function as synonyms, though one or the other tends to predominate in each event. Although the latter term might appear the more semantically restrictive and potentially definitive classification, the former is defined as denoting persons with linguistic command primarily of Russian:

V.f4 For example, I am not [a] *russkaia*. I am an Ossetian, but I still say that I . . .
V.f3 And for this there exists such a term as Russian-speaking [*russkogovoriashchii*] – one carrying [*nositel'*] the Russian language. It is as simple as that.
V.f4 Which is to say that Russian is one's first language, yes?
V.f2 That's what I think.

These terms do not have a clearly defined purview. One participant affirms that 'we' russoglots who have come to Ireland are an exceptionally well-educated, valuable group, necessarily distinguished from immigrants from former British colonies, whom he assumes to have simpler passage to Europe and knowledge of English as a given:

II.m1 Coming here are Russian-speaking people [. . .] not even a middle stratum, and certainly not a low stratum – like, say, the Indians, the Pakistanis, who from the off learn English there at home with the prospect of coming to Europe – coming here we can say are adventurers, people above average, or with higher education, that is, people who have passed an extremely high threshold . . . And our specificity, of our diaspora, is not that we are Russians, russoglots, but because we met a higher level of selection, and for this reason we have a different standard of the average russoglot person who's made it to Ireland [compared with other immigrant cohorts].
II.f5 You are confusing Russians from Russia, and russoglots from Latvia
II.m1 I am speaking about russoglots; from Latvia, that's a more recent development.

This conclusion suggests that 'russoglot'/'Russian-languaged' should be understood in terms of native Russians, rather than a more broadly construed Russian-speaking or ethnically Russian diaspora. However, the meaning of these words can vary even in individual persons' usage. The Moldovan discussed above identifies as a member of the russoglot population in Ireland in one instance and later states the contrary. In one discussion, she states 'I am not [a] russoglot, I was only born in Russia' (IV.f2; see p. 100); on another occasion, she does identify as one among russoglots in Ireland, dissociating herself from Moldovan others (III.f4; see p. 107).

The equivalence of being Russian-speaking and being Russian – or Russified – is debatable:

> IV.m1 Well, let's not say Russians, but Russian speakers, because for me, 'Russians' is everyone from the Soviet Union.

In discussions of Russian diasporic community, it becomes apparent again that terms do not bear self-evident definition:

> V.f4 I am simply trying to understand what is [meant by] diaspora. Shall we define it? Perhaps, there is a Russian church, I think that people chat there and this is what unites them. There are Russian shops. There are places where Russians go.
> V.m2 Russians, you say? Russian speakers, let's say.
> V.f4 Let's in that case say what is [meant by] Russian speakers.
> V.m2 Well, yes, otherwise we end up in a mess.
> V.f4 Come on, let's first define diaspora and then who are the Russian speakers, yes?

The potential for confusion reflects the ambiguities of 'diaspora' – understood both as a general phenomenon and as a particular local community – but also of 'Russian', which involves recursive implications of ethnolinguistic affiliation, a *Ln*anguage-based incidental community, and a legacy of Russification processes expanding the extent of the Russian.

Collective experience of Soviet realities is one of the things assumed in common for various participants. A man from Moscow suggests that the conversation is confused because the participants are not clear on whether they mean to discuss 'Russian speakers' (*russkogovoriashchie*) or 'Russians' (*russkie*) or, indeed, Soviets:

> V.m2 It is worth underscoring what we are talking about now – Russian-speaking. It seems to me we are getting lost. [. . .] I was thinking about this just last night. Who am I – Russian or Soviet? Basically, Soviet. Setting aside the fact that I am Russian, I am probably Soviet, if one is not to count a Tatar four hundred years ago. I am Soviet.

Where this man describes the Soviet mentality of immigrants from Russia, another participant sees typical *russkaia* curiosity. However, for the man, it is rather a matter of

V.m2   the spirit of the great Soviet state in some sense; people of smaller countries, people from Russia, as in, the collapse of the USSR – a great power, a superpower [. . .] The mentalities differ greatly.

Affirming a common heritage, participants invoke 'our post-Soviet culture' (in which one writes the family name first, rather than one's given name, reflecting a different relation to the ego) and professional socialisation:

IV.f4   For us in post-Soviet countries the [Western manner of conducting a job] interview is simply unfamiliar ground.

This assumption of a common Soviet formation can be contrastively juxtaposed to a broadly conceived Western form. Indeed, assuming the point of view of the Irish repeatedly facilitates discussion of 'our' coherence as a group. It may be easier to affirm 'our' identity assuming the objectivising gaze of Irish society:

III.f4   Culturally, you find, integration and an intercultural connection, [. . .] I feel that with the russoglot population it has already taken place. The Irish accept us, you know?

The binary of 'us' and 'them' facilitates the construal of collective identities. Thus, distinguishing between the Irish and one of 'our' people is simply a matter of seeing how someone walks:

IV.f4   You know, somehow on the street our faces are distinguishable. If someone carries himself one way, well that's one of us; but if that way, then it's an Irishman.

At the end of an event, one man implies that those present have spoken in one voice, regretting that

II.m1   [. . .] we have not had [a/the] second voice, the Irish.

Complementing the vicarious external perception of Russian-speaking diasporic unity, participants also variously contrast 'our' immigrant community from that of other expatriated cultural identities:

II.m1   The Chinese diaspora, for example, in any country will strive for segregation, simply by culture. [A] Russoglot diaspora in various countries, not only in Ireland, strives more for assimilation.

Nobody voices disagreement on this point. However, twelve minutes later at the same event, another insists:

> II.m6 There is generally no diaspora as such, but nonetheless Russians do not assimilate. They remain Russians. Those who have come who have some initial Russian base, they remain Russians. They do not assimilate. [. . .] Perhaps there will not be a diaspora, as such, as a group, but Russians remain Russians. They do not assimilate.

He is supported on this point by II.f2, who observes that this is, for whatever reason, a property of *russkoiazychnye*. Without direct remark upon her having expanded the point of reference from Russians to the Russian-languaged, II.m1 returns the emphasis more nicely to ethnicity:

> II.m1 This phenomenon is well known. There are ethnicities that assimilate and ethnicities that are assimilated.

Russians and Russian speakers are distinguished from other immigrant bodies not so compatible as 'we' in comportment and temperament, such as the Chinese:

> II.m1 We are too European a nation to feel ourselves apart from Europe, unlike the Chinese.

Or those from Africa:

> III.f4 It's easy for them to accept us; it's difficult for them to accept, let's say, people from African countries.

And Russians in diaspora are said not to form a local community, unlike Jews, Armenians and Ukrainians:

> V.m3 But who supports one another? Jews, or rather those who consider themselves Jews. Armenians support each other, western Ukrainians support each other. That is to say, not all Ukraine, but specifically the west.

This conversation comes to focus on the regrettable absence of 'our' community in diaspora. At that point, V.f4 asks for a definition of the word 'diaspora', because she suspects that the discussants do not have a common understanding of the term or concept and V.f3 admits:

> V.f3   To be honest, I wanted to look in the dictionary to translate it.

As noted above, one way in which the collective identity as speakers of Russian can be affirmed is by assuming the objectivising perspective of native Irish society. Yet, while the external vantage point and a principle of contrast facilitates the affirmation of common identity among speakers of Russian, it is also necessary on occasion to draw the distinction between immigrant bodies where the Irish may fail to discern 'our' people. The Irish may fail to discern the distinction, but 'we' must draw it for them:

> II.m2   When I came here in ninety-eight, for them any person with a more or less, say, shorn head, in a leather jacket, would be called Russian. Says I, sure they're Lithuanians!
>
> III.f4   When a Moldovan woman's stolen something, they say 'a Russian'. Of course, this is a shame, well, what can be said, we are all *russkoiazychnye*, and so we end up taking the blame collectively.

With guidance, the Irish may be brought to perceive the distinctions:

> VI.f4   When they say, where are you from, I say that I am from Russia, specifically from Russia. It's just, there are many Russian speakers, but, look, Ukrainians, they are Ukrainians, Lithuanians, they are Lithuanians, the comportment of us all is varied.

This woman proudly reports that once her husband advised colleagues of the array of Eastern European identities, he was later reassured of their enlightenment:

> VI.f4   Now at his work, the Irish have started to differentiate, too. Ah, [they say], you were right. In certain moments, yes, that was Lithuanians, Latvians, Poles, you really are different. This is very important.

It also the case that within the Russian-speaking community, 'we' must be careful not to be too crudely construed as a monolith. There are undesirable elements, especially amongst a criminal class that can be identified by its use of obscene *l*anguage – Russian *mat*:

> V.f4   But when Latvia, Lithuania, Poland and so on got in [to the EU], this circle expanded and then people came here, not only intelligentsia people, not only the well-educated. [. . .] So, when you hear, in principle they speak Russian, you just hear complete obscenity flowing out of their mouth.

This woman is emphatic that she does not want the Irish to conflate that sort of person with the kind of person whom 'we' represent:

> V.f4   Now we don't want that people should think the same of us. Like, when we first came here, when people said that we're all from Russia. To you Irish it seems that we are all, how to say it, of one face, all the same.

With regard to the affirmation of collective identity, the participants in these roundtable discussions show an awareness of the ambiguities persisting in the terms by which they index a basis for common interest. In order to affirm solidarity, it can be expedient to assume a perspective from outside the group, so that 'we' can assume a vicariously objectivised solidity. However, this manoeuvre is unsatisfactory when the external perspective evidently fails to discern in 'us' the identity we might wish to claim.

DISJUNCTIONS OF HISTORY

We noted above how family histories belie an assumed simple binary of language and identity. There is also difficulty encountered in questions of general history. For example, one academic from Riga recalls the collapse of the Soviet Union as a positive moment of renewal: 'I welcomed this.' The collapse is lamented by another and of these two participants the former was born in Moscow, whereas it is the latter who comes originally from Riga and claims confident command of Latvian. Despite this competence, he felt no inclination to integrate during the course of Latvian national renewal:

> II.m6   For me this was a cataclysm, and I do not wish to integrate into that society. [. . .] I know the language, I know the cus-

tomary conduct, but this is not my language, not my way of doing things.

Nonetheless, his initially more optimistic counterpart was also later disillusioned: 'All Russoglots were obliged to keep quiet, [we/they] didn't have a right to speak up' (I.f4).

While a majority of Russian speakers in Ireland come from the Baltic region, their historic experience does not inform others' affective identity. Speakers of Russian from the Baltic states lament insult and injury, which those from the Russian Federation might not care to discuss:

> I.m1   I am going to move you away from your trauma, from the Baltics, simply to approach our theme.

And among those from the Baltic states, while memories of Latvian independence may have grown congruent, there is adamant disagreement between generations as to the possibility of hybrid identity in a national community:

> I.f5   In Latvia it's really like this, as you are either a Latvian [*latysh*] or Russian [*russkii*].
> I.f3   I completely disagree.

The younger of these two participants, I.f3, speaks Latvian and Russian. She feels that living in a particular state, one ought to have command of that state's (titular) language:

> I.f3   Living in Latvia, I have command of Russian and Latvian, too, as a second language, because I feel that, yes, they have offended us, they have wounded us and so forth, but living in this country, in this state, you ought to know this language.

Memories of the Soviet Union itself vary with personal background. On the one hand, in a positive vein, the Soviet Union made everything simple:

> II.m2   [I]t was convenient in that there was no need to think; everything had been thought of for you, everything was sorted.

One can further take pride as a former Soviet citizen, 'because, morally, emotionally, we had something that nobody else will have' (II.m2). From another point of view, though, the Soviet Union is seen in a wholly negative light:

> VI.f4   The thirtieth of December, nineteen twenty-two.
> VI.f2   A black date, I don't remember it! [laughter]
> VI.f4   Why black date?
> VI.f2   Because the most terrible thing that happened in our century was the formation of the Soviet Union, you realise?

Attempting to account for this incongruence of perspective, participants seek to place each other in time and place of origin, or by nationality:

> VI.f3   In what year approximately were you born? [laughter]. The seventies?
> VI.f2   In seventy-eight.
> VI.f3   But, I, look, we, like, we bore no hardship from Soviet power. We were very happy, we really were satisfied. And one cannot throw away a chunk of our life saying that it was bad. [. . .] It was an effort towards a better society.

One may seek to address the divergence of perspective via simpler categorisation, yet nuances multiply:

> VI.f2   I disagree, because I don't accept propaganda.
> VI.f3   But where are you from? From Latvia, from Lithuania?
> VI.f2   No, I am from Ukraine.
> VI.f3   Well, I'm from Ukraine! [laughter]
> VI.f4   And I am a Russian.
> VI.f1   But are you a Russian by passport or by place of birth? [laughter]

These attempts to specify grounds on which to account for the divergence of perspectives cannot attain a final consensus:

> VI.f4   The position of the former republics is that someone owes somebody something, and Russia is altogether guilty. But I can say as a woman from Russia, that we lived in such [. . .] destitution, that … Really, Moscow, Saint Petersburg, central Russia was not at all the same thing as in remote Siberia. They pumped everything out of there. But all the

republics, Latvia, Lithuania, Estonia, well, I can't say about Georgia or Armenia, but Ukraine, Belarus, everyone lived very well. Everyone lived very well.

VI.f2 I can't say that, no. You didn't live in Ukraine, you do not know, you cannot answer thus that Ukraine lived very well.

At this point, VI.m1 interjects 'Ukraine is also a big country', with VI.f1 adding, 'We also need to define the timeframe. What Ukraine are you speaking about?' The terms in play are in this manner unsettled even as discussants seek to coordinate their points of view.

With regard to post-Soviet Russia, VI.f4 claims that 'all Russians [*russkie*] now are grateful for what happened, that these republics finally fell away', as this allowed the Russian state to take on the responsibility for its own people. By way of contrast, a mathematician from Moscow reports that he misses a degree of solidarity present in the Russian Federation, and arising from a unifying resentment of the Russian Federation as an oppressive state:

II.m3 To a certain extent, to a great extent, in Ireland this figure of an enemy is far less starkly formed, and it's possible that in certain situations the absence of this common enemy is for some an impediment to integration.

But especially painful for VI.f4 is the fact that commemorations of the Great Patriotic War and proud defeat of Nazism are soured by contrasting perspectives on Russia's role in the Soviet empire. The myth of the Baltic states' voluntary accession to the USSR persists (see Mendeloff 2002; Sokolov 2011), confronting people with differing and objectionable historical narratives:

VI.f4 [I]n the year 1939, before the start of the Second World War, Latvia, Lithuania and Estonia were last acceding to the Soviet Union, because Hitler was at the border and they all made the request.

The place of Soviet Socialist Republics within the Soviet Union is a vexed topic:

VI.f4 [I]t's painful and a pity, when people say invaders and so on. [laughter] [. . .] At work, a woman was speaking, she was trying, we were speaking together in Russian, but a girl from India says, 'you understand'? As in, you share a language? I say, well, 'yes, you know, so, there was this big country, the Soviet Union, and so on and so forth and at a time we were able to speak one language'. [. . .] And then this girl, I think she's from Latvia or Lithuania, 'Russia, Russia was an occupying force.' I say, 'Why? Why?' I got so upset, it just overwhelmed me.

Noting that her colleague was from a Baltic state, VI.f4 associates that political space with an untoward disagreeableness. In a conversation that had begun in assumed sympathy, with comity based in a shared language for communication, the divergence of historical narratives causes a rupture.

Yet history can also be reimagined so as to depict a firm backdrop of Irish attitudes to 'us' and to the Russian. There is a striking example of mythologised national sympathy towards the end of one discussion, when III.m1 states that an enduring, benign disposition is evidenced by a statue of Lenin that stands 'to this day' in Belfast. He interprets this as acknowledgement of the inspiration drawn from Russia at the time of Ireland's struggle for independence from the United Kingdom. In fact – aside from the fact that Belfast remains within the United Kingdom – the statue has a far more recent history, marking the entrance to the Soviet-themed gay venue 'Kremlin' only since 1999.

In light of these complicating divergences, speakers regret a lack of cohesive identity for the Russian-speaking diaspora: a stable sense of 'our own' (*nashi*) is not available. The first-person plural pronoun's indexical reference can be limited to the particular group gathered or taken to represent a total body of Russian-speaking immigrants in Ireland. Other 'we' positions span a range of overlapping populations. The challenge of refining the definition of who 'we' are as a body within Ireland is repeatedly acknowledged:

II.f4   You understand, we all live in different spheres of life.
V.f6   All of our isolated circumstances, you see.
VI.f1   The language just by itself cannot unite [us].

It can seem that the specificity of so many unique cases might overwhelm the possibility of sharing experience. In this regard, the project's role in bringing the participants together is salient:

V.f5   But then why have we gathered here at all?
V.m2   We were asked. It was requested.

All the same, another participant muses,

> I.m1 An interesting topic, why are we drawn together, although we are so different, we are united by language and culture.

In a subsequent discussion, he repeats that this unitary *Ln*anguage delimits the identity of a common population:

> II.m1 Within our russoglot diaspora at this moment there are people who are European, people who are non-European, there are people who are entirely Eurasian, for example, Tajiks or from the Caucasus, and we are diverse. We cannot now find for ourselves a common language except for Russian. [. . .] We are diverse. We have only the Russian language.

At the same roundtable, the man from Riga affirms, with qualification,

> II.m2 We cannot even identify ourselves as Russian, there can be, right, a russoglot Arab, a russoglot Jew, a russoglot Ukrainian, a russoglot Latvian, but all the same it is some sort of social body.

V.m2 reverses the emphasis:

> V.m2 What unites us is the language but in all other respects we are different.

Either way, the unity of the *Ln*anguage, at least, withstands those contradictions that confound the specification of its associated community.

In order to simplify the discourse of identity, some participants report an inclination to fudge details. The bilingual woman from Moldova at one point notes her inclination not to identify by country of origin; it is simpler to claim to be from Russia (omitting in this instance to mention that she was indeed born in Russia):

> III.f4 I always have to explain where Moldova is. I decided one time to say, more briefly that I'm from Russia. And then it's simpler. [. . .] It's not necessary to explain anything further.

A young woman from Latvia notes how she plays on stereotypes. She can identify as Latvian or Russian, depending on the impression she wishes to convey when meeting Irish people:

I.f3   If I want people to relate to me at ease, normally, entering new company, new society, I say that I am a Latvian. If I know that in this company there may well be problems or something of that sort, I say that I am Russian and all the problems go away

As both these women indicate, simple narratives are appealing and convenient, but only as a provisional construct and necessarily by artful elision.

CONCLUSION

These conversations between speakers of Russian living in Ireland rest upon mutual comprehension through language in an unaccustomed environment. As a context for linguistic diversity, Irish society has changed dramatically in recent decades. The titular and first official language of the state is not the dominant vernacular and it is very rarely, if ever, dominant in speakers' language repertoire. Moreover, the beginning of the twenty-first century was a period of unprecedented economic growth and social change, with immigration greatly augmenting the variety of languages spoken in the country. 'Our Languages' captures a snapshot of a moment five years after a referendum rescinding birthright citizenship – widely perceived as a response to increased rates of immigration – and in the immediate aftermath of the 2008 economic crash. Within this context, the situation of Russian is a particular case.

First, the Russian language has a complex history of associations. It is the titular language of a polity reinvented in the relatively recent past and the heritage language of a richly variant heritage. Since the end of the twentieth century, the population of people speaking Russian in Ireland has risen from the tens and hundreds to the tens of thousands. This population has not come from a single country. It is not uniform in its economic standing, nor cultural formation; it comprises a body that is ethnically diverse with varying repertoires of spoken and heritage languages, which has come to share social space at a particular historic moment.

The question of community that is based in language involving speakers of Russian in Ireland is fraught with overlapping associations and divergent perspectives on a variety of themes. The difficulty of settling upon a sense of the reference population begins with semantic ambivalence in terms for the russophony of Russian speakers and/or speakers of Russian (*russkogovoriashchie, russkoiazychnye*). While it is possible to stipulate an ostensibly simple criterion such as that Russian be dominant or claimed as a native language, different speakers' usage and questioning of such terms complicates investigation of the collective entity. Discussants themselves note the scope for ambiguity in terms such as 'nationality' and 'diaspora', both in Russian and in translation.

In a language-based community, it may be assumed that a Russian-language picture of the world might provide all true speakers of Russian with a common outlook. Indeed, this is to some degree posited by several of the roundtable participants. And just as the French state has sought to foster and sustain francophone community on a global scale, the Russian Federation sponsors a number of entities addressed to Russian speakers *en masse*. The community envisioned by *Russkii Mir* – a Russian World, with something of a Russian (*russkii*, if not *rossiiskii*) worldview – rests on the assumption that a unitary *Ln*anguage should lend its identity to lived heterogeneity.

However, as becomes apparent in the course of discussions among speakers of Russian living in Ireland, the assumption of *Ln*anguage does not lend itself to a readily articulated concept of its speakers' community. While Helen Kopnina alerts us to the fact that a similar body of speakers asserts notions of community, culture and ethnicity (Kopnina 2005: 96, 203–7), we do not find it so easy to put this sensibility into words. Rather than rest with the parenthetically simplified assumption of an 'actual group of people (Russian migrants)', we must contend with the different ways in which actual speakers of Russian can be categorised and the fact that to the extent they constitute a group, its existence is subject to constant negotiation.

Speakers of Russian, themselves not of monocultural origin, experience a recontextualisation of (their) linguistic identity in Ireland. Most do not find a simple, shared sense of collective identity through categorisations on the basis of language, birthplace, ethnicity and/or nationality. Even the putative permanence of 'native' language competence is subject to relativising change.

Nonetheless, the discussants affirm their community, or rather the fact of Russian-speaking community in Ireland. Perhaps the most dependable basis for positing 'our' community is through the identification of others, hence the contrast drawn between 'our people' and other populations, such as the Chinese, Africans or Westerners. Furthermore, it is assumed that from an external vantage point, 'our' coherence as a group might appear plain. However, from this point of view, the Irish may fail to discern distinctions that 'we' would wish to draw between the peoples of Eastern Europe, or between Russian speakers of insalubrious character and the identity 'we' more properly wish to claim.

More specifically, discussants encounter and negotiate many moments where their perspectives are incongruent. Experiences and estimations of the Soviet Union diverge, as do attitudes to the 'Russianness' of speaking Russian. Speakers regret that they cannot simply articulate the cohesive identity of (the/a) Russian-speaking diaspora: 'We are diverse. We have only the Russian language' (II.m1).

Ten years have passed since the roundtables discussed above took place. Ireland has experienced economic recovery, and a new generation of Irish-raised speakers of Russian is now entering adulthood. Perhaps, as in Israel, this heterogeneous body of immigrants may come to be perceived as possessing a new Russian-Irish ethnicity. There is little precedent for such hybrid diasporic identities in Ireland, and civic nationalism could continue to predominate over the salience of ethnicity. Some participants are confident that Russian will be spoken in Ireland by virtue of its strength as a world language and the institutional or intrinsic resilience of Russian culture. However, as the transnational rhetoric of Soviet ideals recedes into memory and political relations between Russia and the EU have become fraught, it is to be hoped that the observed destigmatisation of 'Russian' in Ireland will not be reversed. As Laitin (2004) found, speakers are likely to emphasise elements of their identity deemed best for thriving in a local context. Further research will reveal how a sense of community among Irish speakers of Russian may develop. As is the case wherever one provides a medium of mutual understanding, at the least this capacity implies a potential for reflexive negotiation of common interests and ongoing discussion of divergent perspectives.

NOTES

1. Within this schema, *L*anguage (with upper-case italicised initial) denotes the faculty of language or more broadly conceived framework of possibility for meaningful speech, the metaphysical concept of *logos*.
2. From this point, references to an Irish political and social context are confined to the Republic of Ireland.
3. An article in *The Irish Times* in February of 2012 (Wholey 2012) suggested a figure of 200,000, but this is exceptionally far above other estimates. Another article in the same period (Mullally 2012) suggested approximately 70,000–80,000, and a community-generated publication gave a figure of between 60,000 and 100,000 (Tarutin and Posudnevsky 2012: 52). Addressing a student society at Trinity College, in February 2018, the ambassador of the Russian Federation in Ireland cited a figure of 80,000.
4. There are 12,774 members of *Russkoiazychnaia Irlandiia*, rising to 23,290 and then to 26,996, versus 553 members of *Russkie v Irlandii*, down to 480 and then up to 1,364, as measured in May 2016, February 2018 and September 2018. Another group exists as 'Russian Ireland' [*Russkaia Irlandiia*] – 'a group for Russians-in-spirit, lovers and

supporters of Russia' – with membership growing from 2,300 to 3,300 and then 3,870 over the same period (statistics collated from online groups by the author, Feargus Denman).
5. 'Picture of the world' here echoes Humboldt's concept of *Weltansicht*, but also Weisgerber's *Weltbild* (Sériot 2004). The concept is also found in Czech and Polish ethnolinguistics; Danka Široká (2013) presents an overview of these literatures.
6. Translations of all quotes from Russian in this chapter by the author, Feargus Denman.
7. This notwithstanding, in February 2019 the appointment of a Moscow linguist as one of ten Irish language planning officers in Uíbh Ráthach became national news: 'a Russian man has been tasked with devising a plan to save the Irish language in a part of the Kerry Gaeltacht' (Mac an tSíthigh 2019).
8. Census data from 2011 and 2016 indicate that Polish is spoken in the home by more people (> 130,000) than speak Irish daily outside the education system (c. 73,000); the figures for Russian exceed those for Chinese, but are lower than Lithuanian and Romanian (both < 40,000) (Central Statistics Office 2012, 2016).

REFERENCES

Aptekar, Sofya (2009), 'Contexts of exit in the migration of Russian speakers from the Baltic countries to Ireland', *Ethnicities* 9 (4), pp. 507–26.
Atkinson, Rowland and John Flint (2001), 'Accessing hard-to-reach populations: Snowball research strategies', *Social Research Update* 33 (1), pp. 1–4.
Central Statistics Office (2012), *This Is Ireland: Highlights from Census 2011, Part 1*, Dublin: Stationery Office.
Central Statistics Office (2016), 'Census 2016 -Non-Irish Nationalities Living in Ireland', <https://www.cso.ie/en/releasesandpublications/ep/p-cpnin/cpnin/introduction/> (last accessed 19 January 2021).
Ciscel, Matthew H. (2008), 'Uneasy compromise: Language and education in Moldova', *International Journal of Bilingual Education and Bilingualism* 11 (3–4), pp. 373–95.
Eriksson, Svetlana (2011), *Family and Migration: The Intergenerational Transmission of Culture, Language, and Cultural Identification in Russian-Speaking Families in the Republic of Ireland*, PhD dissertation, University of Dublin, Trinity College.
Eriksson, Svetlana (2013), 'The same but different: Negotiating cultural identities by migrant children in Irish mainstream classrooms', *Irish Journal of Applied Social Studies* 13 (1), pp. 38–52.
Kelli, Katrina (Caitriona Kelly) (2013), 'Retsenziia na knigu A. A. Zalizniak, I. B. Levontinoi, A. D. Shmelev "Kliuchevye idei russkoi iazykovoi kartiny mira"', in A. V. Pavlova (ed.), *Ot Lingvistiki K Mifu: Lingvisticheskaia Kul'turologiia V Poiskakh 'etnicheskoi Mental'nosti'*, St Petersburg: Antologiia, pp. 278–88.
Kopnina, Helen (2005), *East to West Migration: Russian Migrants in Western Europe*, Aldershot: Ashgate.
Laitin, David D. (2004), 'The de-cosmopolitanization of the Russian diaspora: A view from Brooklyn in the "far abroad"', *Diaspora: A Journal of Transnational Studies* 13 (1), pp. 5–35.
Laruelle, Marlene (2015), *The 'Russian World': Russia's Soft Power and Geopolitical Imagination*, Washington DC: Center on Global Interests.
Mac an tSíthigh, Seán (2019), 'Russian man appointed Irish language officer in

Kerry Gaeltacht', *Raidió Teilifís Éireann*, 21 February, <https://rte.ie/news/ireland/2019/0220/1031818-victor-bayda-irish-language> (last accessed 5 May 2019).

Mac Gréil, Micheál (2011), *Pluralism and Diversity in Ireland*, Dublin: Columba Press.

Mendeloff, David (2002), 'Causes and consequences of historical amnesia: The annexation of the Baltic states in post-Soviet Russian popular history and political memory', in Kenneth Christie and Robert Cribb (eds), *Historical Injustice and Democratic Transition in Eastern Asia and Northern Europe*, London: Routledge, pp. 79–117.

Mesthrie, Rajend, Joan Swann, Andrea Deumert and William L. Leap (2000), *Introducing Sociolinguistics*, Edinburgh: Edinburgh University Press.

Mullally, Una (2012), 'Dublin's Russian Revolution', *The Irish Times*, 21 February.

Putin, V. V. (2008), 'V. V. Putin vystupil na prieme, posviashchennom KH Vsemirnomu kongressu russkoĭ pressy', Government of the Russian Federation, <http://archive.government.ru/special/docs/1461/> (last accessed 29 February 2019).

Ryazanova-Clarke, Lara (2014), *The Russian Language Outside the Nation*, Edinburgh: Edinburgh University Press.

Sériot, Patrick (2004), 'Oxymore ou malentendu? Le relativisme universaliste de la métalangue sémantique naturelle universelle d'Anna Wierzbicka', *Cahiers Ferdinand de Saussure* 57, pp. 23–43.

Silverstein, Michael (1979), 'Language structure and linguistic ideology', in Paul R. Clyne, William F. Hanks and Carol L. Hofbauer (eds), *The Elements: A Parasession on Linguistic Units and Levels*, Chicago: Chicago Linguistic Society, pp. 193–247.

Silverstein, Michael (1996), 'Monoglot "standard" in America: Standardization and metaphors of linguistic hegemony', in Donald Brenneis and Ronald K. S. Macaulay (eds), *The Matrix of Language: Contemporary Linguistic Anthropology*, Boulder, CO: Westview Press, pp. 284–306.

Silverstein, Michael (1997), 'Encountering language and languages of encounter in North American ethnohistory', *Journal of Linguistic Anthropology* 6 (2), pp. 126–44.

Silverstein, Michael (2000), 'Whorfianism and the linguistic imagination of nationality', in Paul V. Kroskrity (ed.), *Regimes of Language: Ideologies, Polities, and Identities*, Santa Fe: School of American Research, pp. 85–138.

Singleton, David, Sarah Smyth and Ewelina Debaene (2009), '"Second language acquisition and native language maintenance in the Polish diaspora in Ireland and France" and "Our languages: Who in Ireland speaks and understands Russian?": The rationale, structure and aims of two Dublin-based research projects', in Maciej Duszczyk and Magdalena Lesińska (eds), *Spolczesne Migracje: Dylematy Europy i Polski; Contemporary Migrations: Dilemmas of Europe and of Poland*, Warsaw: Centre of Migration Research, University of Warsaw, pp. 196–220.

Široká, Danka (2013), 'A linguistic picture of the world and expression of emotions through the prism of expressive lexis', *Journal of Education Culture and Society* 2, pp. 297–308, <https://jecs.pl/doi/10-15503-jecs20132-297-308/> (last accessed 18 January 2021).

Smyth, Sarah (2008), 'Russian speakers in the Republic of Ireland: Who are they? A sociolinguistic study of hybrid identities', <http://people.tcd.ie/Profile?Username=ssmyth> (last accessed 28 April 2019).

Sokolov, Boris V. (2011), *Mificheskaia Voina: Mirazhi Vtoroi Mirovoi*, Moscow: Iauza.

Tarutin, Sergey and Viktor Posudnevsky (2012), *Russians in Ireland/Russkie v Irlandii*, Dublin: Irish–Russia Enterprise Centre.

Wholey, Jennifer (2012), 'Irish–Russian links celebrated', *The Irish Times*, 16 February.

Zalizniak, Anna A., Irina B. Levontina and Aleksei D. Shmelev (2005), *Kliuchevye idei russkoi iazykovoi kartiny mira*, Moscow: Iazyki slavianskikh kul'tur.
Zalizniak, Anna A., Irina B. Levontina and Aleksei D. Shmelev (2012), *Konstanty i peremennye russkoi iazykovoi kartiny mira*, Moscow: Iazyki slavianskikh kul'tur.

CHAPTER 5

Media Use of Russian Speakers in Germany

Olga Tikhomirova

INTRODUCTION

Patterns of media consumption among the Russian-speaking community in Germany and its impact on their political outlook came into sharp focus in the wake of the 'Lisa case'. In January 2016, a young Russian girl in Berlin was reportedly kidnapped and allegedly raped by Arab immigrants. Both facts were later disproved. As it turned out, Lisa had run away from home with her boyfriend. Nonetheless, Russian-language media in Germany heavily publicised the story, and the aggressive coverage of the story triggered street protests in a Berlin district with a significant share of Russian- and Soviet-born residents. These residents accused the German authorities of overly lax immigration control and security. The several weeks of commotion that followed completely surprised the German authorities, who found themselves unprepared to communicate with residents who evidently believed in a completely different narrative from the one that they based their actions on. It quickly became obvious that the German authorities considered most Russian speakers in the country to be so-called Russian-Germans (repatriates from the USSR), while in fact these repatriates constitute only one part of the Russian-speaking community. In fact, the German government was able to liaise with these Russian-Germans, yet (completely) failed to connect with other groups of Russian speakers in the country.

This 'Russian' resentment in the Marzahn neighbourhood in Berlin was quickly exploited by a new political force, the far-right Alternative for Germany (AfD). The party had received surprisingly good results in several recent regional elections, running an anti-immigration campaign. It was the first to come to this district and interact directly with the Russian-speaking community there. It was also the first to print and distribute election leaflets in the Russian language. For the federal election in September 2017, the AfD even put six Russian speakers on its party slate. As a populist party, the AfD promised what the inhabitants of this district were evidently waiting for: public and social security, higher pensions, protected borders, and support for and preservation of occidental Christian traditions. In the same vein, it advocated higher birth rates against foreign infiltration and demanded an independent foreign policy, attempting to capitalise on contemporary anti-American feelings. The subject of this chapter is whether or not the AfD's expectations were justified, and how they were linked to the media consumption of the Russian speakers as a target group.

RESEARCH DESIGN

The developments described above generated many academic studies and much public discussion in Germany (Schmalz 2017). This surge of interest in the Russian-speaking community and the visible lack of understanding of its structure and views motivated the Boris Nemtsov Foundation to study the issue in greater detail. The Foundation commissioned IPSOS Public Affairs to carry out a survey on the media use of Russian speakers in Germany, which was conducted in August and September 2016 and the results of which were first presented publicly at the Nemtsov Forum in Berlin in October 2016 (Boris Nemtsov Foundation for Freedom 2016). In the course of the survey, 606 people with a 'Russian background' were questioned. The target group hence consisted of immigrants from Russia and the countries in the Commonwealth of Independent States (CIS) who were at the time of the interview at least 18 years old and who were permanent residents of Germany. The sample was based on an onomastic analysis of names and surnames, which categorised names according to an assumed ethnic background.[1] The interviews were conducted by phone (using both stationary and mobile phone data banks). Each interview, based on a questionnaire, lasted on average a little under half an hour. Besides the usual questions about education, occupation and time of emigration, the questionnaire contained questions referring to three main topics: (1) the level of integration, according to respondents' self-perception; (2) the respondents' patterns of media consumption and their trust in the media they consumed; and (3) their attitudes and views regarding current political debates in Germany (i.e. their perception of the migration 'crisis', of terrorism and of the security situation in general). This chapter is based on the findings of the survey.

In the first place, the objective of the survey was to gain a better understanding of media influences on the Russian-speaking diaspora and to map the patterns of media consumption of the Russian-speaking community, defined by language, habits and other characteristics.

In a broader sense, the Boris Nemtsov Foundation conducted this research also to advance one of its main goals: the promotion of European values among Russians, not only among those who live in Russia but also among so-called global Russians. To some extent, the study of the Russian-speaking community in Europe was conducted to determine whether there is a set of common universal values shared by the Russian-speaking community and to test the hypothesis that Russia is part of European civilisation.

DIVERSITY IN GERMANY'S RUSSIAN-SPEAKING COMMUNITY

Russian speakers in Germany are a significant group within German society. The total number of Russian speakers of different origins in Germany is estimated to amount to 4 million people (Lokshin 2020). According to statistics presented by the German political scientist Dr Andreas Wüst, 3% of all voters who could participate in the parliamentary elections in September 2017 were Russian speakers (Wüst and Faas 2018: 7). This diaspora is very diverse, with differences depending on the time of emigration, age, education level, ethnic origin, income and other characteristics. Overall, there are two large groups of immigrants from Russia, including those who fled from the USSR and former Soviet republics after the fall of the Soviet Union.

First are the so-called *Aussiedler* (resettlers), that is, people with German origins whose ancestors migrated to Russia during the seventeenth and eighteenth centuries. Article 116 of the German Basic Law entitled these people to receive German citizenship in 1949, although this started to matter in practice only in the 1980s. In total, 2,377,791 resettlers moved to Germany from the USSR and its successor countries between 1950 and 2016, mostly coming from Russia and Kazakhstan (Bund der Vertriebenen 2018). Not all of them maintained Russian as their primary language of communication, and their children and grandchildren may not even speak Russian.

The second most important group consists of Soviet Jews. A resolution of the federal Conference of the Ministers of the Interior signed on 9 January 1991 extended the application of the HumHAG (Gesetz über Maßnahmen für im Rahmen humanitärer Hilfsaktionen aufgenommene Flüchtlinge), the law regarding measures for accepting refugees in the context of humanitarian relief, to include Jewish immigrants, who received the opportunity to leave the former USSR countries. This is described in section 23(2) of the AufenthG (Gesetz über den Aufenthalt, die Erwerbstätigkeit und die Integration von Ausländern im Bundesgebiet – German Immigration Act); however, since the beginning of 2004 this has excluded immigrants from the Baltic States, which had by that time become members of the European Union. The applicants must match a number of criteria, in addition to being of Jewish ethnicity or having at least one Jewish parent. Among others, they may not belong to any other confession and need proof both of elementary German-language skills and that they will be accepted by a Jewish community in Germany. Experts estimate the number of Jewish immigrants coming from the post-Soviet space to Germany between 1991 and the present day to amount to between 200,000 and 250,000 people (Tolts 2015: 24).

Other Russian-speaking Germans are immigrants who came for different reasons over the last twenty-five years, among which political asylum, family reunion, marriage, work or business are the most important. Their number is estimated at up to 350,000, but they cannot be as easily counted as a result of their varying legal and residence conditions (Bund der Vertriebenen 2018). In all likelihood, this group is quite evenly spread throughout Germany.

The demographic data of the survey conducted by the Boris Nemtsov Foundation shows that 95% of respondents were born outside Germany. The majority came to Germany between 1990 and 2009, with two-thirds coming during the 1990s. These respondents mostly came from Russia (40%) and Kazakhstan (39%); another 9% came from Ukraine and 4% came from Kyrgyzstan. Family reunification was the main motivation to migrate, and most respondents were ethnic German resettlers (78%); 11% came through the Jewish refugee programme. It is worth mentioning in this context that more than 20% of the 80 million people living in Germany have a migrant background. The main home countries for these people are Russia along with the former Soviet countries (27%), Poland (25%) and Turkey (11%) (German Federal Statistical Office 2016).

Our respondents were quite equally spread across age groups: 38% of the Russian speakers questioned were between 36 and 54 years old, 30% were older than 55, and 32% were between 18 and 35.

Language behaviour is one of the key parameters and key criteria of integration. It also helps to explain patterns in media consumption, as language preference determines the choice of the most influential channels of information access. Therefore, our respondents had the choice between answering the questions in Russian or in German. It is noteworthy that 87% of respondents opted for German. At the same time, more than 60% considered Russian to be their native language, 27% said that they spoke Russian fluently, 9% rated their Russian skills as intermediate and 2% as basic. For German-language skills, the picture is different: 21% called German their native language, 43% claimed to be 'fluent' in it, 28% estimated their command as 'intermediate' and only 7% as 'basic', despite the fact that 78% considered themselves German resettlers. Russian was chosen as the language of communication within their immediate family by 43% of the respondents, while 24% preferred German. The remaining third used both languages.

Despite these different language preferences, the majority of the respondents said they felt comfortable in Germany. Four out of five respondents said that they had integrated into German society. While 83% of the respondents described themselves as integrated in German society, only 3% felt completely unintegrated. German-language skills and the respondents' ages correlated with their levels of perceived integration. It is obvious that people of Russian origin who speak German feel much more integrated. Among those who affirmed fluent language proficiency, 55% affirmed themselves to be very integrated. The same is true for the younger generation: 58% of respondents aged 18–35 years old described themselves as well integrated, whereas only 43% of respondents aged 36–54 and 26% of those over 55 shared this perception.

Roughly 44% of respondents identified themselves as German, and nearly one-fifth identified as European. Those respondents who were fluent in German in most cases also identified themselves as German.

RUSSIAN-LANGUAGE NEWS OUTLETS IN GERMANY

Understanding the patterns of media use among Russian speakers in Germany is central to the work of the Boris Nemtsov Foundation. Several Russian-language media outlets in Germany have shared with us their experiences in communicating with their audience. There is a large variety of Russian-language sources of information (or disinformation) controlled, openly or covertly, by the Russian authorities.

The Institute for Strategic Dialogue and the Institute of Global Affairs at the London School of Economics and Political Science (LSE) researched the influence of media and social networks on the Russian diaspora during the 2017 election campaign for its report titled *Make Germany Great Again* (Applebaum et al. 2017). According to this report, the Russian-speaking community enjoys access to a full range of media outlets from the Russian Federation. Local cable providers, for example, offer such a service. However, there are also a number of Russian-language media outlets produced in Germany.

Print media in particular is quite diverse. Entertainment magazines and newspapers are interspersed with information and advertisements (Kurennoy 2006). At the same time, Russian speakers can buy Russian newspapers in Germany, such as *Izvestia*, *Komsomolskaya Pravda* or the *Moskovskii Komsomolets* with a special edition for the readership in Germany.

It is worth mentioning that there are a number of online communication options for Russian speakers in Germany. There are up to 100 different groups in social networks like VKontakte and Odnoklassniki (both of Russian origin), and Facebook has hundreds of thousands of users.[2] There are also online forums.[3] These networks, as well as various messaging services, became places for the dissemination of the call to rally on the streets of Berlin in the 'Lisa case'.

Boris Feldman is the publisher of the media holding Rusmedia Group, which prints three Russian-language newspapers: *Russkaia Germaniia* (*Russian Germany*), *Russkii Berlin* (*Russian Berlin*) and the *Rejnskaia gazeta* (*Rhein Gazette*). Feldman himself edits *Russian Germany*. All of these are also available in online editions. The Rusmedia Group has been working in Germany for more than twenty years (Rusmedia 2018). The weekly audience of the print version of *Russian Germany* attains 200,000 readers. Nearly half of these readers are between 30 and 49 years old. The daily audience of the Russkij Berlin radio station, which is part of the same media organisation, is 350,000 people of the same age group as the audience of the newspapers.

The most popular topics among the readership are the migration crisis, pensions and Donald Trump. While Donald Trump has preoccupied the minds of the global audience for the past years, he was also the top news issue in Russian media in late 2016 and early 2017. He was even more frequently mentioned than president Vladimir Putin, who is usually the top newsmaker in Russia. Russian retirement pensions were a highly relevant issue for a substantial part of Russian-speaking citizens, who are recipients at present or in the future. Both preferences may thus be understood as further evidence of Russian media influence.

Refugees, by contrast, are a hot political topic all over Europe, and the subject is frequently presented in a very partisan way. This includes in Russian-language media in Germany. *Russian Germany* conducted an online poll among its subscribers which showed that their Russian-speaking audience is very suspicious about refugees (Russkaia Germaniia 2018). Almost 4,000 users took part in this poll. One-fifth responded that Germany is not a country for refugees and they should return to their countries of origin. Almost one-third expressed the opinion that any other country should accept refugees, but not Germany. Only 2% said that Germany must give asylum to refugees due to humanitarian reasons, and even fewer respondents volunteered that they themselves came to the country as refugees some time ago. In another poll regarding attitudes towards the European Union, users named immigration policy as the most important issue, and more than 40% thought that it should be changed (Russkaia Germaniia 2018).

A Russian-speaking television station in Germany, OstWest (formerly RTVD), also has experience in communicating with local television audiences. This channel is viewed mostly in Germany but also in Austria and Switzerland, with approximately 100,000 households watching the channel. It has a 24-hour broadcast service and produces its own programmes that target Russian-speakers living in Europe. According to OstWest Director General, Peter Tietzki, the channel's audience is aged 45 years old or older and made up of about 45% male and 55% female viewers. The largest share, one-third, are pensioners, and 70% have higher education. Tietzki states that OstWest's viewers are mostly looking for entertainment content in the Russian language; they want to see movies and TV series that they are familiar with from when they still lived in Russia or the USSR.[4]

The third important media outlet for Russian speakers is Deutsche Welle, a German public media holding that offers a Russian-language service. Its budget has increased significantly in recent years, from 320 million euro in 2015 to 360 million euro in 2018. The Russian-language service is one of the outlet's current priorities (Deutsche Welle 2016, 2018). While for most of its history Deutsche Welle has targeted audiences abroad, it now acknowledges the need to broadcast in Russian within Germany too. The obvious reason is to challenge possible disinformation spread by Russian state channels, including the propaganda channel RT. Since 2017, Deutsche Welle has provided its content to the Russian-speaking community inside the country as well, making use of, among others, an agreement with OstWest. The launch in late spring 2017 of a special political television show, *Quadriga*, to discuss the 2017 German elections in Russian clearly shows Deutsche Welle's new awareness of its need to have a Russian-language service to communicate with the domestic Russian-speaking electorate. The Russian case is by no means unique, however, as various minorities living in Germany have become the target of foreign authoritarian regimes, with Turkish citizens being the most important group besides the Russian-speaking population. More generally, the advance of communication technologies, especially the Internet, has erased borders, in some cases rendering geographical borders and limitations obsolete in terms of communicating with foreign audiences. The adaptation process is slow, however. As mentioned above, Deutsche Welle does not have its own broadcasting channel within Germany and depends on partner broadcasting companies or on the Internet to distribute its Russian content within Germany.

In 2018, another German regional public broadcasting institution, Westdeutscher Rundfunk (WDR) in Cologne, an important member of the German public broadcasting consortium providing content for the First and Third German television channels, decided to launch a Russian service. WDR also offers a half-hour news programme in Russian on its radio channel COSMO.

MEDIA CONSUMPTION OF RUSSIAN SPEAKERS IN GERMANY

Regarding their media use, respondents to the Boris Nemtsov Foundation's survey were asked about the media outlets they preferred, the frequency of their access to media, the language of these media, and whether they trusted Russian or Western media more. Moreover, the survey included questions about their attitude towards European values and their level of tolerance towards people who are not like them.

The respondents used both Russian-language and German-language media outlets. Two-thirds of the respondents said they use the Internet and watch television every day. Of the Internet users, 37% mostly browsed Russian-language sites, with 'mostly' referring to more than two-thirds of the total consumption time. Of the television viewers surveyed, 40% said they mostly watched Russian television (Tables 5.1 and 5.2).

There are several explanations for these preferences. On the one hand, many respondents obviously felt more comfortable with the Russian language than with German or English. On the other hand, the themes, approach and style of presentation of Russian media content resonate better with the expectations of people with Russian backgrounds. Beyond that, long-standing habits also play an important role in the selection of sources of information. The people who prefer Russian media do so because they find the communication style familiar and because they are accustomed to the topics, attitudes and values. Furthermore, Russian media, especially television channels, provide their audiences with free-of-charge access to high-quality content, including popular blockbusters and up-to-date shows.

This may explain the fact that the respondents trusted Russian media more than Western media. For 32% of respondents, Russian television was the most trustworthy source of information on politics and current affairs. Only 19% trusted Western media, compared with 30% who considered Russian media as a more trustworthy source of information on politics and current affairs.

The preference for certain sources of information influences people's attitudes towards sensitive issues, including security and human rights. In general, audiences who watched Russian television channels were more critical towards the German authorities and their decisions as well as more aggressive and more suspicious towards the USA. These people are ready to believe and to disseminate conspiracy theories. In their worldview, 'real democracy' does not exist and politicians are always lying about it. By contrast, the audiences who preferred German-language channels showed more positive attitudes towards democracy. Those who watched German television believed that Germany respects human rights, and they were less anxious about becoming a victim of a terrorist attack. These differences are also noticeable in the way people perceived major threats to Russia and the efficiency of different economic models. The survey examined these differences among two respondent groups: those who watched Russian-language and German-language television channels respectively more than 60% of their media-use time (Table 5.3).

Refugees are a very sensitive issue, especially for immigrants to Germany, including Russian immigrants. In general, 72% thought that there were terrorists among them, while 49% supported the idea of closing the borders. Only 20% said that refugees were able to successfully integrate into German society. Russian television viewers are significantly more sensitive to this topic, as seen in Table 5.4.

In order to find out about their level of tolerance, responses to a question about attitudes towards different social groups were also taken into consideration. Answering the question 'How would you perceive living in the same neighbourhood as . . .: positively or negatively?', our interviewees could choose between five groups: drug addicts, heavy drinkers, LGBT people, immigrants, and Muslims. The questionnaire also contained separate questions asking about the respondents' attitudes towards immigrants and refugees.

Seventy-four per cent of respondents found it acceptable to live near Muslims, 67% near immigrants, 49% near homosexuals, 16% near heavy drinkers and 8% near drug addicts. When asked about their perception of immigrants in general, 52% of the respondents agreed with the statement that immigrants would increase crime rates, 38% considered that migrants were the ones taking on hard and unpleasant work, 34% acknowledged the immigrants' contribution to the culture of their host country and only 18% believed that immigrants were taking jobs away from native Germans. As far as refugees were concerned, 72% of Russian-speaking respondents agreed with the statement that there were terrorists among refugees and merely one-fifth believed in the refugees' ability to successfully integrate into German society.

HOW TO UNDERSTAND THE OUTCOME OF THE SURVEY?

Elena Koneva, a sociologist who participated in preparing the survey on behalf of the Boris Nemtsov Foundation, suggested two methods of classifying the Russian-speaking community based on the analysis of the collected data. The generational model is based on factors like the year of immigration, language habits, intensity of contacts within Germany and the existence of ties to the home country, self-perception of the level of integration, and media consumption habits.

Based on these characteristics, four groups were identified among the respondents of the survey, which we called the 'New Generation' (34%), the 'Middle-Aged People' (36%), 'Citizens' (14%), and 'Latecomers' (16%):

- *New Generation*: This is the youngest and one of the two best integrated groups. They migrated to Germany in the 1990s, most likely as children. They have many connections in Germany and few in Russia or other countries of origin. They readily share European values and generally show loyalty to the German government, though they can be quite critical. This group is the most tolerant; however, they too do not want more refugees coming to Germany.
- *Middle-Aged People*: This forms the biggest group of Russian-speaking Germans. They are mostly middle-aged people who immigrated primarily from Russia and Kazakhstan in the 1990s. Their families are well integrated and fluent in German. They are very close to the New Generation group in terms of values but are more mature and self-confident. This group is less tolerant than the New Generation and they are even less friendly to other immigrants and refugees.
- *Citizens*:[5] This group consists of respondents aged 55 years and older. They immigrated in the 1990s and are well integrated. They have good language skills as well as the strongest connections in Germany. They care less about freedom and human rights; however, they are

more relaxed on the issue of immigrants and refugees compared with the other groups.
- *Latecomers*: This group is the least integrated. In many cases, the Latecomers belong to the second wave of immigration, having followed their children and relatives. They are of the same age as the Citizens, but they have very poor language skills and, in their self-perception, the lowest integration level (57%). The members of this group are the most devoted viewers of Russian-language television. They often refused to answer questions, and they represent the least tolerant group.

The second method of classification, which is based on the attitudes of the respondents towards minorities, refugees and other nationalities, offers the opportunity to identify two large groups among the Russian-speaking community in Germany: the conservative, Russian-oriented 'patriots' and a more cosmopolitan, German- or Europe-oriented faction.

The key features of these two groups are:

- *Russian-oriented*: This group comprises 17% of the respondents, including the biggest share of the latecomer group (56% are aged 55 years and older). They are the least integrated segment. They retain many connections in Russia and have few in Germany. Often they migrated relatively recently, following their children; 43% of them came to Germany during the period 2000–9. They believe that Russia should pursue its national interest even if this leads to conflicts with other countries. They see Russia as a source of international political stability; nonetheless, they believe Russia should invest more in its armed forces to face current security risks. As to the recent crisis, they are convinced that Russia has the right to influence external and internal political decision-making in Ukraine.
- *German-oriented*: This comprises 18% of the respondents, including the biggest share of the Middle-Aged People and the New Generation. They came mainly from Russia and Kazakhstan and immigrated before 1999 (82%). They perceive themselves as fully integrated and they have many connections in Germany but few in Russia. Besides considering themselves integrated, they see themselves as Germans in the first place. They are relatively tolerant of minorities, accepting at least three out of the five social groups referred to in the survey. About 70% think that it is important to live in a democratic state and they believe that Germany adheres to human rights principles.

Attitudes towards the media are entirely different in both groups. At the same time, the Russian-oriented group is much more interested in politics and current affairs (78% vs 58% of the German-oriented group).

It is interesting to note that in the Russian-oriented group, 67% of respondents trusted Russian television and only 28% trusted Russian-language websites. At the same time, among the German-oriented group, only 17% trusted Russian television or believed that Russian-language websites were a reliable source of information (Table 5.5).

Furthermore, the Russian-oriented group demonstrates less tolerance and integration. They are notably more concerned with security and refugee issues (Table 5.6). In particular, when they were asked if they would consider it acceptable to live next to different minority groups, only 30% of the Russian-oriented group accepted homosexuals, in contrast to 92% of the German-oriented group. Furthermore, 74% of the Russian-oriented group also thought that the presence of immigrants made crimes more likely to take place, while only 33% of the German-oriented agreed with that statement.

POLITICAL ORIENTATION OF THE RUSSIAN-SPEAKING COMMUNITY IN GERMANY

Did the wooing of the Russian-speaking electorate by right-wing populists pay off in the 2017 federal elections in Germany? Previously, the Russian-speaking community had traditionally supported the Christian Democrats, with the party receiving up to two-thirds of Russian speakers' votes. However, the AfD's aggressive election campaign focusing on the migration crisis had already proved successful in the previous regional campaigns. They succeeded in building up an image of being a new political force different from the traditional elite. After the 2017 elections, researchers at the University of Duisburg-Essen and the University of Cologne studied the voting results among the Russian and Turkish communities in Germany (Goerres et al. 2018: 4–10). They questioned about 500 German citizens with Soviet and post-Soviet backgrounds as well as 500 Germans with Turkish backgrounds. The main results are shown in Table 5.7.

Table 5.7 shows that the share of votes among Russian speakers more or less corresponded to the average percentage totals of these parties across Germany, except for one party and that was not the AfD but the left populist party Die Linke.

At the same time, according to an announcement on the AfD's Russian-language webpage, in Lower Saxony and Thuringia, 'the electoral districts populated mainly by Russian Germans, the AfD party showed phenomenal results': more than 50% and more than 35%, respectively (Russlanddeutsche für die AfD 2017)

The authors of the research cited above also observe that one-third of those Russian voters who supported AfD in 2017 did not take part in the previous federal elections in 2013. One-third of those who did vote in 2013 had at that time supported the CDU/CSU (Goerres et al. 2018: 6). According to the study, the turnout was significantly lower among Russian speakers than overall. Only 58% of Russian-speaking German citizens took part in voting, while the overall turnout was 76.2%. Obviously, the AfD failed to mobilise those parts of the Russian-speaking electorate in Germany that would have been most likely to share the party's outlook, that is, the Latecomers or the Russian-oriented group.

Remarkably, the next elections in which the Russian-speaking community in Germany participated were the Russian presidential elections in 2018. A comparison of the results of the Russian citizens' voting in Germany at the Russian embassy in Berlin and the consulates around the country in 2012 and 2018 shows that the turnout increased almost threefold, and votes in favour of Vladimir Putin nearly doubled from 49.7% to 81.1% (Strana.ua 2018). Unfortunately, it is very difficult to establish the number of Russian speakers in Germany who hold both a Russian and a German passport and who would be entitled to cast their votes in both countries. As tempting as it would be to read participation in the Russian presidential elections as a further indicator of politicisation and cleavages among the Russian speakers in Germany, there is simply not enough factual evidence to support such an interpretation.

CONCLUSION

Over recent years, the Russian-speaking community in Germany – the biggest in Europe – has become an important factor in domestic policies. Only on 17 May 2017, however, did Angela Merkel become the first German Chancellor to receive representatives of the Russian-language community in Germany.

In response to the 'Lisa case', the Federal Ministry of the Interior and its agency for political education set up new programmes to exert influence on the country's Russian speakers, attempting to promote tolerance and to facilitate networking between different civic action groups of Russian speakers. One of the explicit goals of these programmes was to increase the involvement of the Russian-speaking residents in German public affairs. Government agencies actively sought to connect with existing Russian-language civil society organisations to stimulate discussions and, where possible, an exchange of ideas and thoughts in the Russian language. Another aim was to cross-link existing Russian-language civic organisations and associations, for example through online portals like the Dialogplattform des Bundesverbands russischsprachiger Eltern (The Dialogue Platform of the Union of Russian-speaking Parents).[6] This platform has been holding meetings for Russian-speaking community members in different regions of Germany since 2017. Recent topics of these discussions have included 'perspectives for Germany after the elections', 'the future of nuclear energy in Germany' and 'migration policy'. These discussions involve prominent Russian speakers living in Germany as well as Russian members of different political parties (including the AfD), and are a sign of obvious progress in establishing an open dialogue.

These activities of German NGOs, German parties and the German authorities, especially those of the Federal Ministry of the Interior and its civil education agency, are a clear sign of a changing perception of the Russian-speaking community. It is now understood and treated as an important part of the German electorate. Russian speakers have gained visibility. At the same time, they are still mistakenly perceived as a fairly homogeneous group. As Dmitri Stratievski reminds us, however, 'Germans of Soviet origin represent over 80 nationalities' – most of whom are members of this Russian-speaking community (Stratievski 2017). Despite the latest efforts at inclusion, Russian speakers are still poorly represented in German politics. The community is not a homogeneous group, and their outlook varies significantly, in particular concerning the latest conflicts on the territory of the former Soviet Union.

Table 5.1 Frequency of media use to get information about politics and current affairs (%)

Type of media	Daily	At least once a week	At least once a month	Less than once a month	Never	Don't know/ refuse to answer
Internet	68	14	2	3	13	0
TV	66	18	3	4	8	1
Newspaper	24	34	5	8	28	1
Radio	53	10	3	7	27	0

Table 5.2 In which language do you use the media (%)?

Type of media	In Russian	In German	In English
Internet	37	59	4
TV	40	59	1
Newspaper	16	83	1
Radio	8	91	1

Table 5.3 Perceptions and opinions according to media consumption (% of respondents)

	Watch Russian TV > 60% of time	Watch German TV > 60% of time
Perception of human rights and security		
Likely to become a victim of a terrorist attack	33	23
Security measures are sufficient	17	31
Germany respects human rights	24	42
Preferred economic model		
Free market economy	32	65
State-run economy	24	18
Don't know/refuse to answer	43	17
Threats to Russia		
Corruption	60	54
Religious extremism	27	18
EU enlargement	11	21
Conflict with the West	32	41
Separatism	9	16
Authoritarian government	7	20

Table 5.4 Attitude towards immigrants and refugees according to media consumption (% of respondents)

	Watch Russian TV > 60% of time	Watch German TV > 60% of time
Terrorists are among them	79	69
Close borders	59	46
Make crime problems worse	64	47
Take jobs away from natives	21	12
Most refugees can successfully integrate	16	19
Do the hard and unpleasant work for the country	43	40
Could enrich the culture of the country	25	49

Table 5.5 Media used to learn about current affairs (comparison of two groups: Russian-oriented and German-oriented)

Type of media	Russia-oriented		German-oriented	
	Daily	In Russian	Daily	In German
TV	79	57	74	58
Internet	70	51	64	64
Newspaper	63	–	63	–
Radio	43	–	57	–

Table 5.6 Comparison of attitudes of the two major groups

Views and attitudes	Russian-bound (%)	German-oriented (%)
– towards minorities		
Consider it acceptable to live next to . . .		
drug addicts	6	16
heavy drinkers	11	29
homosexuals	30	92
immigrants	60	99
Muslims	62	98
– towards immigrants		
Agree that immigrants . . .		
take jobs away from natives	29	6
could enrich the culture	30	46
do hard work	50	38
make crime problems worse	74	33
– towards refugees		
Agree that . . .		
refugees can successfully integrate into their new society	23	28
Germany must close borders entirely	63	31
there are terrorists among refugees	88	63

Table 5.7 Distribution of votes in the 2017 federal elections in Germany

	Russian respondents (%)	Turkish respondents (%)
CDU/CSU (Christian Democrats)	27	20
SPD (Social Democrats)	12	35
Linke (Left Party)	21	16
Grünen (Green Party)	8	13
FDP (Liberals)	12	4
AfD (Alternative for Germany)	15	0
Others	5	12

NOTES

1. This procedure works well for people from Russia and its successor states; nevertheless, it is unable to capture Russian Germans who have German names and surnames (e.g. Karl Müller).
2. For example, Mix Markt, 'Наши люди в Германии' (Our people in Germany); 'Vsë o germanii' (All about Germany), <https://ok.ru/germany.de> (last accessed 15 January 2021).
3. See <http://www.allrussian.info/>, which has more than 60,000 users (last accessed 15 January 2021).
4. Telephone interview, Bonn/Berlin, 3 May 2017.
5. The term is the English equivalent of the German 'Bürger', which carries a somewhat ironic connotation in contemporary Russian, referring to those Russian speakers who have 'arrived' in German society.
6. <https://www.bvre.de/dialog-plattform.html> (last accessed 18 January 2021).

REFERENCES

Applebaum, Anne, Peter Pomerantsev, Melanie Smith and Chloe Colliver (2017), '*Make Germany Great Again*': *Kremlin, Alt-Right and International Influences in the 2017 German Elections*, London: Institute for Strategic Dialogue/Institute of Global Affairs, <https://www.isdglobal.org/wp-content/uploads/2017/12/Make-Germany-Great-Again-ENG-061217.pdf> (last accessed 25 September 2018).

Boris Nemtsov Foundation for Freedom (2016), *Boris Nemtsov Foundation's Survey: Russian-Speaking Germans*, <http://nemtsovfund.org/en/2016/11/boris-nemtsov-foundation-s-survey-russian-speaking-germans> (last accessed 25 September 2018).

Bund der Vertriebenen (2018), *Aussiedlerstatistik seit 1950* [Statistics on Resettlers since 1950], <http://www.bund-der-vertriebenen.de/information-statistik-und-dokumentation/spaetaussiedler/aktuelle-aussiedlerstatistik.html> (last accessed 15 May 2018).

Deutsche Welle (2016), *Income Statement for the Fiscal Years 2016 and 2015*, <https://www.dw.com/downloads/50965501/income-statement2016.pdf> (last accessed 22 January 2021).

Deutsche Welle (2018), *Income Statement for the Fiscal Years 2018 and 2017*, <https://www.dw.com/downloads/50885946/income-statement2018guv.pdf> (last accessed 22 January 2021).

German Federal Statistical Office (2016), *Migration 2016: Net Immigration into Germany at 500,000*, <https://www.destatis.de/EN/FactsFigures/SocietyState/Population/Migration/Migration.html> (last accessed 15 May 2018).

Goerres, Achim, Dennis Spies and Sabrina J. Mayer (2018), *Deutsche mit Migrationshintergrund bei der Bundestagswahl 2017: Erste Auswertungen der Immigrant German Election Study zu Deutschtürken und Russlanddeutschen*, Universität Duisburg-Essen, 2 March, <https://www.researchgate.net/project/First-Migrant-Election-Study, http://udue.de/migrantenwahlstudie/> (last accessed 15 May 2018).

Kurennoy, Vitaly (2006), *Strukturnyi analiz russkoiazychnykh pechatnykh SMI v Germanii*, Kyiv: Eurasia Heritage Foundation, <https://refdb.ru/look/3411844-pall.html> (last accessed 25 September 2018).

Lokshin, Pavel (2020), 'Wieviele Wie viele Russischsprachige leben in Deutschland?', *Mediendienst Integration*, 3 December, <https://mediendienst-integration.de/artikel/wie-viele-russischsprachige-leben-in-deutschland.html> (last accessed 25 January 2021).
Rusmedia (2018), *Mediadaten*, <http://www.rusmedia.de/upl_files/733a6162d2ccc078 221e2de4f849cc3c.pdf> (last accessed 15 May 2018).
Russkaia Germaniia (2018), *'O bezhentsakh v Germanii i Evrope' Surveys*, <http://www.rg-rb.de/index.php?option=com_rg&task=pollarchive&limitstart=6> (last accessed 25 September 2018).
Russlanddeutsche für die AfD (2017), 'Rezul'taty vyborov v Bundestag 2017', <https://russlanddeutsche-afd.nrw/ru/news/2017/09/btw-fazit-ru/> (last accessed 14 November 2018).
Schmalz, Tatjana (2017), *Zur medialen Integration der Russlanddeutschen nach dem Fall Lisa im Jahr 2016*, Master's thesis, Humboldt-Universität zu Berlin, <https://nemtsovfund.org/cp/wp-content/uploads/2018/07/Schmalz-Tatjana-Masterarbeit-2017-Zur-medialen-Integration-der-Russlanddeutschen-nach-dem-Fall-Lisa-im-Jahr-2016.pdf> (last accessed 8 November 2018).
Strana.ua (2018), '"Dostala idiotskaia propaganda". V seti sporiat, pochemu v Germanii u Putina udvoilos' chislo izbiratelei', <https://strana.ua/news/130595-v-hermanii-u-putina-udvoilos-chislo-izbiratelej.html> (last accessed 22 January 2021).
Stratievski, Dmitri (2017), 'Russian-speaking Germans: Who are they?' *Intersection*, 25 November, <http://intersectionproject.eu/article/russia-europe/russian-speaking-germans-who-are-they> (last accessed 8 November 2018).
Tolts, Mark (2015), 'Demography of the contemporary Russia-speaking diaspora', in Zvi Gitelman (ed.), *The New Jewish Diaspora: Russian-Speaking Immigrants in the United States, Israel and Germany*, New Brunswick, NJ: Rutgers University Press, pp. 23–40.
Wüst, Andreas M. (2014), *Wahlbeteiligung von Menschen mit Migrationshintergrund. Impuls*, Presentation, Friedrich-Ebert-Stiftung, Bonn, 7 June, <https://www.fes.de/index.php?eID=dumpFile&t=f&f=16711&token=5bd7a48bdb1c0038e8393c5455b-f66796d8406cf> (last accessed 20 January 2021).
Wüst, Andreas M. and Thorsten Faas (2018), *Politische Einstellungen von Menschen mit Migrationshintergrund. Gutachten*, Empirische Sozialforschung, vol. 9, Berlin, Friedrich-Ebert-Stiftung, <http://library.fes.de/pdf-files/dialog/14347.pdf> (last accessed 20 January 2021).

CHAPTER 6

The Role of Russian for Digital Diplomacy in Moldova

Dmitry Yagodin

INTRODUCTION

The language issue was the cornerstone of perestroika across the national republics of the late Soviet Union. In *The Moldovans: Romania, Russia, and the Politics of Culture*, Charles King (2000) argues that language politics was especially dramatic in Soviet Moldova's transition to independence. The language reform of the late 1980s aimed to replace Russian with Moldovan as the state language. Nowhere in the national Soviet republics did this question receive more attention than in Moldova (King 2000: 133). The reform led to mass demonstrations in large industrial cities, to separatism and to the military conflict in Transnistria in the eastern part of the country: 'it was in Transnistria where loyalty to the Soviet system was strongest and where the language reforms, particularly the required language tests mandated by the new laws, promised to have the greatest impact' (King 2000: 187).

The Transnistria war involved the deployment of the Russian army. It ended with a ceasefire agreement and with a special autonomous status for the region being introduced to the Moldovan constitution in 1994. Since then the conflict has been frozen. Fast forward to the more recent past, and we find a Moldova still divided, including by conflict over language issues.

Roughly 4 million people live in Moldova, half a million of them in Transnistria. Although Transnistria is only a small, pro-Russian (and officially Russian-speaking) breakaway region, a narrow strip on the map bordering western Ukraine, the language debate preoccupies the whole territory, not least due to Moldova's relations with the EU and Russia. These major powers aim at closer ties with Moldova and have been unable to escape the language issue. For decades, speakers of the majority language in Moldova insisted that they themselves spoke Moldovan, which is strictly speaking a dialect of the Romanian language. In 2013, however, the Constitutional Court ruled that the correct name of the official language of Moldova was Romanian. The ongoing debate regarding the proper naming of the national language precludes identity-building and allows more justification for policies about the status of the Russian language, which is spoken by a quarter of the population.

For Russian ideologists, Moldova is part of the 'Russian World'. The concept broadly designates a borderless and geographically diffuse space that unites Russian speakers around the world (see also Chapters 1 and 9 in this volume). The post-Soviet space by default overlaps with the 'Russian World', and Transnistria is a good example of that. The rest of Moldova, however, is more ambivalent about its identity issues. Approximately half of the population favours a closer relationship with the European Union. The other half, if not explicitly pro-Russian to the same extent as Transnistrians, demands that politicians take into account the complexity of ethnic and language identities. In June 2014, Moldova signed an agreement with the EU that created mechanisms for closer economic and political association. It came into force on 1 July 2016 despite strong resistance among pro-Russian politicians. The integration process was problematic. At the end of 2016, Moldova elected Igor Dodon as its new president, who could not overrule the decisions of the parliamentary government but who promised to cancel the agreement and called for a closer relationship with Russia.

This brief summary of the past thirty years of Moldova's history shows how the country remains torn by political uncertainties, acute language issues and a continuous national identity crisis (Ciscel 2007). Any external influence, such as public diplomacy initiatives by foreign governments, comes to play a crucial role in such circumstances. Since the end of the 2000s, the development of social media has equipped governments with new digital tools of communication. Digital diplomacy, as it is called, has been welcomed by some and criticised by others. Scholars have also questioned the benefits and effectiveness of this form of government interaction with foreign audiences. Studies have suggested new normative models and theories of public diplomacy (Gilboa 2008). This chapter follows the strand of research that considers digital public diplomacy as a tool for socio-political change (Bjola 2015). The empirical approach chosen here operationalises digital diplomacy as three processes: agenda-setting, conversation-generation and presence-expansion (Bjola and Jiang 2015).

In this chapter I look into this new phenomenon from a language-use point of view. I compare how two foreign government organisations, the EU delegation and the Russian embassy in Moldova, use Facebook pages as their foreign policy tools. I look into specific language choices they make to communicate with Facebook audiences in Moldova. The analysis presented here explores how the two Facebook pages were tuned to interact with Moldovans. I assess the communicative effectiveness of the EU's and Russia's digital diplomacy with specific questions about languages used, key messages and their sources, and the quantity and quality of the target audience reactions.

POST-SOVIET RUSSIAN

In the post-Soviet space, the Russian language is an important source of Russia's influence and must be a critical factor in the EU's integration politics. The common language and the large number of Russian speakers define Russian foreign policy in this region and distinguish it from Russian public diplomacy strategies elsewhere (Forsberg and Smith 2016: 132). Following the disintegration of the USSR in 1991, roughly 25 million native Russian speakers existed outside Russia (Hyman 1993). By 2010, this figure was 22 million (Aref'ev 2017: 251). In addition, in the post-Soviet states beyond Russia there are many more people who know Russian and use it in everyday life as their first language or as a lingua franca. The total number of people in the national Soviet republics who could speak Russian was 120 million in 1990 (Aref'ev 2017: 253). The confusing mixture of native speakers of Russian, ethnic Russians and other Russian speakers is the legacy of Soviet language policies. In the national republics of the Soviet Union, titular languages had lower status than the Russian language. The central Soviet government privileged the spread of the Russian language, which led to Russification, characterised by Brian Silver as 'the psychological transference of persons from a non-Russian to a Russian identity' (Silver 1974: 46). Russian is used mostly by older generations of former Soviet citizens and it is especially prevalent among the political and business elites (Rotaru 2018: 38). Regional intergovernmental organisations, often led by Russia, also prefer communicating in Russian.

Following the collapse of the Soviet Union, the Russification process reversed. The position of the Russian language weakened due to policies of de-Russification across the new states (Pavlenko 2009). Titular languages gradually replaced Russian in official use, and some of them also switched from Cyrillic to Latin scripts. Russian was no longer the primary language spoken in schools. Fewer Russian-language schools were opened. Fewer students attended them. The number of students in Russian schools in Moldova fell by two-thirds between 1991 and 2011 (Aref'ev 2015: 35). The Russian language lost its attractiveness among the youth. Younger generations are choosing English as their first foreign language (Blauvelt 2013; Mkhoyan 2017). Students who want to study abroad find more international programmes taught in English outside Russia (Fominykh 2016). While the Russian government actively develops and sponsors the export of higher education, it also prioritises language promotion and encourages the Russian universities to continue teaching mostly in Russian (Mäkinen 2016). Such a policy limits its cultural influence to advanced and native speakers of Russian. A more inclusive approach could attract more non-Russian speakers from the former Soviet Union, and introduce them to the language. Meanwhile, the number of Russian speakers in the post-Soviet space has been rapidly decreasing. It dropped from 120 million to 94 million from 1990 to 2010, and is expected to fall to 65 million by 2025 (Aref'ev 2017: 253).

In Moldova, language policy is a major issue in the country's domestic and foreign politics (Prina 2015). The Russian language is widely used for interethnic communication and is strongly influenced by the position of Transnistria, where it remains the primary language. Nearly half of Moldova's remaining population also know Russian to some extent and use the language in a much wider range of contexts than officials usually report (Muth 2014). However, the proportion of active Russian speakers, who use the language in everyday life, in Moldova excluding Transnistria is 14% (Aref'ev 2015: 33). This number is low when compared with the average of 42% throughout all former Soviet republics and territories. Only in Tajikistan, Uzbekistan and Turkmenistan is this proportion lower. Include Transnistria within Moldova and the proportion reaches 24%. This is higher than in Azerbaijan and Lithuania, but lower than in Armenia and the other seven former Soviet republics.

Russian is important for Moldova's public space due to its substantial presence in popular culture and a large number of Russian-language media outlets (Saari 2014: 63). In Transnistria in particular, Russian is the language of mass media that have a powerful ideological effect on attitudes towards Russia and regional politics in general. For example, on Transnistrian television, regular weather forecasts begin with the temperature, precipitation and wind direction in Moscow, some 1,300 km away. Then the weather in Kyiv, Chisinau, Tskhinvali and Sukhumi is reported. These locations are the capitals of Russia, Ukraine, Moldova, South Ossetia and Abkhazia, the last two being disputed pro-Russian territories in Georgia. Thus, Transnistrian television places Russia first and Ukraine ahead of Moldova, and the forecast shares breakaway solidarity with otherwise meteorologically irrelevant places in Georgia.

The surprising combination of these forecast locations demonstrates the 'banal nationalism' (Billig 1995) of Transnistrian everyday routines and its representations of nationhood. In other words, the forecast implicitly links Transnistrians to the geographical and political East.

LANGUAGE AS A SOFT POWER RESOURCE FOR (DIGITAL) DIPLOMACY

This chapter draws on theoretical debates about digital diplomacy as a tool of soft power. It places an emphasis on the new conditions created by rapidly developing communication tools, the ongoing crisis of transnational and global politics, the growing connectivity of networked society, and the specific position of the Russian language in the post-Soviet space and in Moldova in particular.

Soft power, defined as 'the ability to get what you want through attraction rather than coercion or payments' (Nye 2004: x), relies on the ideological work of culture, of which language is a central component. According to Nye's definition, the recourse to war in Eastern Ukraine in 2014 was a failure of Russia's soft power. The ongoing conflict highlights the political tensions between Russia and other states of the former Soviet Union. These tensions can be seen as persistent attempts by Russia to re-establish control over its sphere of geopolitical (and cultural) interest. The Kremlin's main justification for the conflict was the protection of the Russian-speaking diaspora.

Studies of soft power traditionally focus on the cultural hegemony of the USA. But there is also a growing interest in studying soft power in other regional centres (e.g. Hill 2010; Lai and Lu 2012; Thussu 2013). Studies that address Russia's soft power (e.g. Tsygankov 2006; Popescu 2006; Sherr 2013) often refer to the country's influence in hard power categories, emphasising Russia's aggressive foreign politics. Political scientists generally consider Moldova and Transnistria as objects of foreign politics and international relations between Russia and the West (Hill 2012; Samokhvalov 2014). As a result, mixed national identities and internal cultural dynamics go unnoticed when it comes to making big political decisions. However, as Nye points out, 'soft power depends more than hard power upon the existence of willing interpreters and receivers' (Nye 2004: 16). It is, therefore, necessary to go beneath the surface of the immediate political agenda and search for interactions that are not coercive and lie within a more subtle dimension of power.

The role of digital communication tools is a nascent discussion in theorisations of soft power. The Internet makes public diplomacy more complex but, at the same time, more visible and hence accessible for research. The rise of interactive online media, social networking sites and blogging challenges traditional one-way communication models and opens space for the revision of soft power theories. Such a task was largely anticipated in the 1990s, when Manuel Castells (1996) described the crisis of the nation state as leading towards the conditions of the 'network state'. New online communication technologies enable social connectivity on an unprecedented scale, with various social media and networking websites comprising the ecosystem of connective media (van Dijck 2013). For diasporic cross-border interactions, this means new forms of cultural identification (Alonso and Oiarzabal 2010) and the emergence of digital diasporas (Brinkerhoff 2009; Laguerre 2010). This trend in media studies reconsiders the concept of diaspora not as a phenomenon of displacement but as a formation based on connectivity, in which media technologies play a crucial role (Tsagarousianou 2004: 52). This is why scholars often describe them in conjunction with the concept of soft power (Nye 2004; Melissen 2005; Seib 2009; Hayden 2012) and contrast it with economic and military hard power.

How does the idea of soft power relate to public and digital diplomacy? As Eytan Gilboa theorises it, public diplomacy is 'presented as an official policy translating soft power resources into action' (Gilboa 2008: 61). Theorists of public diplomacy distinguish between different models, depending on the actors implied, communicative tools and the character of interaction. For example, Robert Entman suggests the concept of mediated public diplomacy, which consists of 'targeted efforts using mass communication (including the Internet) to increase support of a country's specific foreign policies among audiences beyond that country's borders' (Entman 2008: 88). Whereas earlier theories focused on one-way communication and direct influence, recent public diplomacy literature advocates collaborative interactions, building dialogic relationships between countries (Cowan and Arsenault 2008; Zaharna et al. 2013). The definition of Castells (2008) emphasises the diplomacy of public and civil society organisations rather than of government agencies. This vision deprives modern nation states of their sovereignty in exchange for a global public sphere and horizontal communication networks and ultimately argues for the creation of the network state as a new form of international governance. These are two extreme positions on a large spectrum of diverse forms.

Similarly, there is no clear definition of digital diplomacy. It may be simply 'the use of social media for diplomatic purposes' (Bjola 2015: 4), or a more nuanced approach 'in which foreign ministries employ social media in their nation-branding activities' (Manor and Segev 2015: 89).

In more abstract terms, it is also a form of diplomacy 'practiced through information-rich, highly interactive environments' (Singh 2015: 181). In a broad sense, digital diplomacy is the 'use of the Internet and information communication technologies (ICTs), from video conferencing to social media platforms, to help state and non-state actors to manage international change' (Bjola and Holmes 2015: 207). The diversity of interpretations indicates multiple ways in which subjects of foreign politics may pursue their goals and evaluate their achievements.

THE RATIONALE FOR THE STUDY

Take modern digital media into account and the lingua franca status of the Russian language looks stronger than the reported decline in social statistics. Among the Internet services of the post-Soviet nations, many websites use Russian and there is a significant number of Kremlin-sponsored resources that connect the scattered diaspora (Gorham 2011) and stimulate regional ties. This is the power of language promotion coupled with the economic and cultural benefits of information and communication technologies. This conflation seems to have changed the status of the Russian language abroad. Digital connectivity at once enhanced the notion of 'global Russian' but also put forward new 'tensions that emerged from the dislocated and deterritorialised position of Russian in the contemporary world' (Ryazanova-Clarke 2014: 3). Multiple issues emerged regarding language policies, laws, minority rights and identity struggles. Moreover, in the western part of the post-Soviet space, these developments coincided with the growing economic and security interests of the European Union.

Starting in 2010, the EU has exercised a concerted foreign policy through so-called EU delegations endowed with an official diplomatic status. The delegations coordinate their actions with the embassies of all member states. In the case of Moldova, this means that the EU delegation represents the interests of, among others, thirteen member states that do not have diplomatic missions in the country, and this leads to a stronger overall external action (Baltag and Smith 2015). One of the challenges is that the working language of the delegation meetings is English, and that the EU staff do not necessarily know the local languages. As Dorina Baltag points out, for EU diplomats working in countries like Belarus, Ukraine and Moldova, 'knowing at least Russian is extremely important' (Baltag 2018: 93).

In terms of digital diplomacy, Russia and the EU have similar preferences regarding particular communication platforms and social media for the purpose of directly influencing foreign audiences. The European External Action Service (EEAS) has made Twitter and Facebook its main tools of public diplomacy in the field (Collins and Bekenova 2017). The Russian Ministry of Foreign Affairs prioritises these two services too (Ministry of Foreign Affairs of the Russian Federation 2018), although Russia has developed its own alternatives that are sometimes more popular in the neighbouring countries. The Delegation of the European Union to the Republic of Moldova uses only Facebook (European Union in the Republic of Moldova – EURM). The Russian embassy in Moldova uses both Facebook and Twitter, although the latter mostly copies links from the former. Thus, to analyse the digital diplomacy of the two organisations I focus on their Facebook pages. In Moldova, however, Facebook is not the most popular form of social media. According to Alexa.com (2021), it was ranked seventeenth among all websites in Moldova. Moldovans more often use Russian services such as Ok.ru (ranked fourth) and Vk.com (ranked fifth). Therefore, the use of Facebook as the main social media platform does not appear optimal.

In my analysis of the role of the Russian language for the EU's and Russia's digital diplomacy in Moldova, I focus on their Facebook publishing activities during 2017. This was the year when Moldova for domestic political reasons entered a new period of relations with Russia and the EU. The newly elected president, Igor Dodon, and his Socialist Party are known to be pro-Russian and opposed to the pro-EU government. Dodon openly criticises Moldova's integration plans with the EU and promises to cancel the EU agreement when the Socialist Party gets to control the parliament.

In his public appearances, President Dodon regularly emphasises the importance of the Russian language to Moldova and of maintaining strong relations with Russia. This position of the president has benefited Russia's public diplomacy by providing authoritative support for the Russian embassy to promote the value of the language. Dodon has criticised past decisions of the Moldovan government, including the education reform of 2014 which limited the use of Russian in Moldovan schools, and has argued for a policy reversal. In March 2017, the Facebook page of the Embassy of the Russian Federation in the Republic of Moldova (ERFRM) shared a news report in which a Russian television channel quoted the Moldovan president as saying that 'we should return to the compulsory study of Russian in schools [. . .] It is an advantage over our other neighbours' (ERFRM 2017b).[1] In September of that year he reiterated his position, strongly objecting to the government policy that, according to him, limited the use of Russian as the language of interethnic communication in Moldova (Dodon 2017). Part of his concern was related to the national media regulator's decision prescribing that proper names, such as toponyms, should follow Romanian phonetic transcription in the Russian-language media, contrary to established linguistic norms.

To assess the communicative effectiveness of the EU's and Russia's digital diplomacy I approached the two Facebook pages with data mining techniques (retrieving metadata through the Facebook interface Graph API) and quantitative comparisons. I selected several examples to illustrate the results. This is the network ethnography approach (Hine 2000; Kozinets 2009; Boellstorff 2010). The advantage of digitised networked content is that it is relatively easy to extract. But it also presents scholars with the challenge of linking virtual and real-life phenomena. The sheer volume of data available can become an obstacle to reaching a deeper understanding of the studied phenomenon (Kozinets 2009: 182). Therefore, network ethnography encourages supplementing data mining with observations and contextualisations.

The Facebook page of the European delegation (EURM) became active in July 2011 and had published 1,860 posts by the end of February 2018 (estimated in March 2018), that is, around 0.8 posts a day. The Facebook page of the Russian embassy (ERFRM) was launched in October 2014 and had published 758 posts in the same period (around 0.6 a day). During the time when both pages were in use, they had a relatively similar publishing frequency (four to five weekly posts on average). The primary data sample of this study includes only the posts that the two Facebook pages published during 2017, which produced two subsamples of 353 (EURM) and 225 (ERFRM) posts. In focusing on them, I wanted to find out how Facebook users reacted to the messages. I collected information about all the available reactions (numbers of likes, shares and comments for each of the posts). I paid special attention to the languages used in the posts and the content sources, distinguishing between the pages' own stories (appearing as added photos, videos and status updates) and stories borrowed from external sources (tagged as 'shared' in the retrieved metadata). I also analysed the hyperlinks of the borrowed posts, to get a sense of what sources were used, in which languages and how often.

My theoretical approach was based on the premise that practitioners and diplomacy experts have long questioned the effectiveness of digital diplomacy. Scholars have struggled to provide predictive analytical models to assess it. A simplified descriptive approach, especially with the focus on social media functionality, was suggested by Corneliu Bjola and Lu Jiang (2015), who pointed at three goal-orientated aspects of digital diplomacy: agenda-setting, conversation-generation and presence-expansion. The rest of this chapter uses this framework to structure the analysis.

THE LANGUAGE OF AGENDA-SETTING

Agenda-setting is related to information dissemination, as the process of delivering specific mediated content to the audiences. The purpose is not so much to influence what they think but to make sure their attention is drawn to something they could think about (McCombs and Shaw 1993). Borrowing from this classic communication theory, Bjola and Jiang (2015) suggest studying digital diplomacy as it directs foreign audiences to some topics and diverts them from others. The primary task of agenda-setting is to 'construct an issue as salient and worthy of attention for their audience by repeatedly providing relevant information on that issue' (Bjola and Jiang 2015: 74). The difference with traditional mass media agenda-setting theories lies in a different understanding of audience. In the twentieth century, the audience was an abstract, vaguely defined mass of people. As digital technologies developed into social media such as Facebook, YouTube and the like, the mass audience turned into fragmented smaller audiences of 'special interest and personal interest communities' (McCombs et al. 2014: 794).

In the light of the transformation in the audience, the mere reach of digital diplomacy, measured quantitatively, is less relevant than the character and nature of communities it targets. Nevertheless, it makes sense to compare agenda-setting practices by addressing the question of how much public attention digital diplomacy can potentially draw. What is the size of the special interest communities for different digital diplomacy agents in Moldova? How do the language choices targeting these communities correspond to language use in Moldova overall?

As of the end of 2017, the EU delegation to Moldova had a Facebook page (EURM) with 12,889 followers. At the same time, the Russian embassy's Facebook page (ERFRM) had 2,070 followers. This may be compared with the number of Facebook users following the pages of the US (about 40,000) and Romanian (close to 4,000) embassies to Moldova at the same moment. These numbers help contextualise the limited scope of digital diplomacy in relation to a country with about 4 million inhabitants. Of the four major foreign actors, Russia had gained the lowest following.

On Facebook, agenda-setting capacity is reflected in user reactions, the most basic of which are user likes. The maximum amount of user reactions (likes) per single Facebook post, which was 1,242 for EURM and 709 for ERFRM, reveals the absolute capacities that the two pages were able to reach during the studied period. As a very rough estimate, these numbers compared with the above-mentioned numbers of followers indicate that ERFRM was able to offer content that suited the interests of a larger proportion, close to 30%, of its smaller audience. EURM has a larger base of assumed followers, but fewer than 10% reacted favourably to its content at the peak of attention. A different perspective opens up if we look at how many users on average liked each of the posts that the two pages published on Facebook. The approximately sixfold difference (90 likes per post for EURM and 14 likes per post for ERFRM) is of the same order as that between the total number of followers of the two pages.

In a discussion about the role of language in digital diplomacy it is crucial to distinguish between different linguistic choices. What languages did the embassies use in their Facebook pages? ERFRM overwhelmingly relied on one language: 91% of its posts were in Russian. The remaining minority of the posts were in Romanian (8%), with only one post in English (less than 1%). EURM was more diverse in its language use. Half of the posts (49%) were in Russian. The use of Romanian was also common (33%). An important difference is that EURM also published posts where a message in Russian was duplicated in Romanian or vice versa (12%). In addition, a small proportion of posts were in English (6%). These observations illuminate essentially different approaches between EURM and ERFRM. The overwhelming use of Russian by the Russian embassy contrasts with the more balanced strategy of the EU delegation. But within this balance there are also traces of the prioritising of Russian. Notably, one EURM post written in Russian announced the opening of 'EU Neighbours' (www.euneighbours.eu), an online portal about the EU's relationships with neighbouring countries. The announcement informed users that the portal already had versions in English and Russian and only planned to open a version in Romanian (EURM 2017b).

While this post provoked neither discussion nor critical comments by the users, it can be paralleled by the opposite effect that a lack of information in Russian could cause. An earlier announcement post by EURM (2017a) was part of the EU promotion of higher education abroad, and turned out to be perceived in the context of language politics. For potential students, planning their studies in foreign schools or universities, the language of instruction is already an important question and a possible limitation for enrolment. The language used in education promotion messages, though less crucial in influencing the applicants, may help and encourage the public to spread the word as well as spark unexpected discussions about precisely who is targeted and how. When EURM promoted the EU's 'Erasmus+' programme's offer of 590 scholarships to Moldovans, the text of the announcement was in Russian (EURM 2017a). It also included a poster in Romanian and linked to the website of the programme's office in Chisinau (www.erasmusplus.md). The information was obviously useful and received high numbers of Facebook likes and shares (300 and 208, respectively). The feed of eight comments generally praised the initiative, though one of the longer comments surprisingly picked out a language issue:

> There is no Russian version of the website. The Russian language in Moldova by law is the language of interethnic communication. I doubt that the EU wants to invite the Moldovans of Ukrainian, Gagauz, Bulgarian, Jewish and other descent, who communicate with each other in Russian, less than the Romanian-speaking Moldovans. At least I really hope not. (EURM 2017a)[2]

Although the website promoting the EU's educational programme in Moldova was indeed in Romanian and English, in contrast to the official EU delegation website that in addition had a version for the Russian speakers, the comment points to something more important than merely a question of the language of public diplomacy. It highlights the inconsistency of communication and language policies at different levels of the EU's official interactions with foreign publics. On the one hand, the EU is well known for its concern for cultural diversity, internal multilingual bureaucracies and protection of minority languages, including in non-EU countries. One the other hand, there are complexities involved in synchronising these policies across multiple international programmes, representative offices and communication channels. Sometimes these inconsistencies are technical and understandable, but in sensitive contexts, such as in relation to the state of the Russian language in the former Soviet territories, one element of public opinion tends to associate them with discrimination.

The quoted comment stands out in comparison with other comments in the same feed. It received more positive responses from the audience, who can also like and comment on one another's comments. Not only was it the only comment in Russian, when all others were written in Romanian, but it was also more informative and discursively saturated. The other comments were either short phrases or sentence-long expressions of thanks. The moderator of the EURM account who published the promotion message also marked with likes some of the flattering comments, but neither did that nor replied in the case of the one containing criticism.

CONVERSATION WITH AUDIENCES

This discussion leads to the question of whether posts in different languages had different impacts on audiences. The example of the critical comment demonstrates digital diplomacy's capacity of conversation-generation and its relation to language issues. Setting the agenda only prepares and encourages conversations – another crucial aspect of digital diplomacy. According to Bjola and Jiang, 'informing is the prerequisite for interaction because real dialogue must be based on topic familiarity, shared understandings and common interests' (Bjola and Jiang 2015: 74).

On the whole, EURM has performed better in the task of conversation-generation. The probability of the EURM content engaging the audience to leave comments was significantly higher than that of the ERFRM content. Almost half of the EURM posts (46%) received at least one comment, whereas the majority of the ERFRM posts (80%) had no comments at all. The commenting results can be summarised as follows: when users commented on posts, EURM had on average 4.1 comments per post and a maximum of 25 comments, significantly higher than the average 1.7 and maximum 12 comments in the case of ERFRM. These are more than modest numbers for social media pages with thousands of followers, and they do not allow quantitative comparisons between the posts in different languages.

The linguistic preferences of the users were slightly more meaningful. Analysis of user likes shows that in the case of EURM, people did not discriminate significantly between the message languages. On average, the amount of likes per message was similar for posts in Russian and Romanian, and a little lower when both languages or English were used. In contrast, when ERFRM published its rare messages in Romanian, they received on average significantly fewer positive reactions (likes) than the messages in the Russian language. The most liked ERFRM post (2017a) in Romanian received seven likes. It linked to a news story on Moldovan media portal Publika.md, which reported on Moldovan President Igor Dodon's visit to Moscow shortly after his inauguration. This was the only post in Romanian of the nine ERFRM posts devoted to the visit and published that day, and it also had the lowest number of likes. All the posts about the event linked to external materials, including two press releases on the Kremlin's official website. The Russian embassy in Moldova neither expressed its own opinion nor commented on the visit with any original content. The event itself also signifies a major moment of agenda-setting and not conversation-generation for the Russian embassy – the daily output of nine posts exceeded more than twice the average weekly volume of posts on ERFRM during 2017. The users liked these posts on average more than they liked all the other ERFRM posts during the year. A similarly active day for the EU delegation, marked by seven posts on a single day, was the Christmas Charity Fair on 10 December 2017. The original photo and video updates of the event organised by the delegation included written texts in Romanian and resulted in lower than average levels of user likes.

However, the peaks of digital diplomacy activities were not the highest moments of user appreciation and feedback. The maximum amount of user reactions for a single post, the already mentioned 1,242 likes for EURM and 709 likes for ERFRM, help us understand what type of information, including language choices and implied target audiences, has the best chance of setting the agenda and generating conversations. Nations like to pride themselves on their achievements, especially when these are publicly recognised or emphasised by other nations. This is clearly seen in international communication when a nation rejoices in the flattering facts of having, for example, the world's best education system, fastest trains, strongest army or longest life expectancy. This gratifying effect is easy to see in the high rates of audience engagement in digital diplomacy messages.

A common history is one of Russia's key symbolic resources and instruments of soft power in the post-Soviet space (Forsberg and Smith 2016). For many nations in the region, there is still hardly anything more unifying emotionally than the memory of the Second World War, or Great Patriotic War (1941–5), and the Soviet Union's role in the victory. The symbolic strength of this historical event lies in its potential to feed the 'Great Power' image inside Russia and among much of the Russian-speaking diaspora abroad. The Soviet tradition of celebrating Victory Day (9 May) has enjoyed strong popular and governmental support across a majority of the former Soviet republics. Many of them recognise the official status of the holiday. In Moldova, and especially in its pro-Russian province of Transnistria, the holiday plays a crucial role in national self-identification (Șveț 2013). But commemorating the Second World War is also important for European identities. The end of the war in Europe is celebrated on 8 May, while 9 May marks Europe Day, relating to the beginning of post-war European integration.

In the case of the Russian embassy's Facebook activities, the users reacted most favourably to news that made Moldovans feel proud of their national symbols. This happened when ERFRM posted a link to a story and a video from a celebration ceremony of Victory Day in Moscow, where Moldovan President Igor Dodon stood next to Vladimir Putin, paying tribute to the war victims and accompanied by the sound of the Moldovan anthem. The story, from a Russian-language Moldovan news portal, proclaimed 'Unspeakable emotions for hundreds of thousands of citizens of the Republic of Moldova!' (ERFRM 2017c) and played a YouTube video taken from Russia's First Channel television broadcast of the event. Not only was this a moment of national pride and commemoration of Victory Day, but it was also a sign of recognition by the citizens of Russia as represented by the main Russian television channel.

For the EU's digital diplomacy on Facebook, it was a story highlighting the integration of the Moldovan economy in international markets that received more positive user reactions than any other story. It was a post devoted to the role of Moldovan workers in the global car industry. The added video in the post came with an interactive introduction: 'Did you know that the most famous European cars are based on electric cables produced in Moldova? Share this information with friends to show that Moldovans do make high-quality stuff!' (EURM 2017e). The message at once promoted European business – a company operating in Moldova (business diplomacy) – praised local employers and advanced the idea of economic integration. Symptomatically, the second and third most popular EURM posts also dealt with similar topics, showing how the EU and Moldova benefit from their economic relationships (EURM 2017c, 2017d). However, all of these most popular examples were video packages introduced in the Romanian language. Most interviews for these videos were also in Romanian. Although some interviewees spoke Russian, embedded Romanian subtitles ran throughout.

The two pages also had opposite strategies in drawing public attention to various issues. More than three-quarters of the EURM posts focused on the activities organised by the delegation inside Moldova, paying less attention to the work of the official EU institutions, EU foreign policy documents, and even less to external news media. The Facebook page of the Russian embassy (ERFRM) reported very few of its own activities – the most striking difference to EURM. Organising one's own offline activities and reporting about them is especially relevant for presence-expansion, as discussed below. For now, it is enough to mention that ERFRM mostly focused on the pro-Russian role of Igor Dodon, frequently referring to his official website and to news reports in the local Russian-language media (point.md, gagauzinfo.md, a-tv.md) and in some Russian state-run foreign media (Sputnik, Russian RT).

PRESENCE-EXPANSION

Effective digital diplomacy must also try to look beyond its established interest groups to expand its presence. An intuitive mechanism for that is to encourage social media users to share or repost the embassy stories:

> Presence expansion is measured via the levels of repost layers. The stronger the impact of a message, the greater the number of repost layers. Two or more repost layers suggest the influence of the message reaches beyond the immediate group of followers to a wider range. It is in this way that public diplomacy is able to expand its presence on social media. (Bjola and Holmes 2015: 208)

Achieving multiple repost layers, that is, ensuring a spread beyond the closest interest groups, may be a hard task when dealing with highly specialised content. The minimum requirement then is to start with the first step, when the interested community of followers decides to press the share button. In that respect, the Facebook page of the Russian embassy to Moldova (ERFRM) had only about one-quarter (27%) of its posts shared at least once. For the shared posts, the average value of shares was about 5 and the maximum value was 148. The posts in Romanian and Russian differed in that the latter were more likely to be shared, though the low number of posts in Romanian does not allow stronger conclusions about this relationship. The page of the European delegation (EURM) demonstrated significantly higher expansion capacity. Almost three-quarters (73%) of its posts were shared at least once, with 27 shares per post on average and a peak of 1,140 shares. The language of the posts did not have a significant effect on EURM presence-expansion.

Presence-expansion is also linked to the physical presence of the diplomats and their offline activities that can be publicised, discussed and shared on social media. This aspect indirectly influences the visibility of digital diplomacy, since Facebook is more likely to show original posts, such as status updates, and added photo and video material, than material linking to external websites (DeVito 2017). In digital diplomacy, original content typically tells about the embassy's own public work and the events it organises or participates in. Quite often, potential audience members also participate in these offline activities and feel more engaged to continue interacting online. Sharing of such content by the audience enables their social network contacts to also witness that work, and so potentially draws new followers in future. But Facebook also makes it easy for digital diplomats to simply borrow news and other content from various external sources, reducing their official social media pages to news aggregators and intermediaries. This second strategy helps in publishing more and faster, but does not help in improving presence-expansion. This approach instead facilitates presence-expansion of some selected sources, focusing solely on external agenda-setting.

This was exactly the difference I found between the Facebook pages of Russia's embassy (ERFRM) and the EU delegation (EURM) to Moldova. ERFRM outsourced 91% of its content, with the remaining 9% being original publications, containing announcements and photo reports of the embassy's own activities. EURM, in contrast, published most of its messages (73%) as original. The two virtually opposite strategies manifest, in the case of ERFRM, a mostly nominal, effortless, diffuse and monologic agenda-setting approach to digital diplomacy, and in the case of EURM, a more dedicated, resourceful, concentrated and dialogic presence-expansion.

The type of the original content, be it textual status update or photo or video attachments, played an important role in expanded dissemination. The followers of both Facebook pages liked all kinds of visual posts more often than text-based messages. But this difference was even more important for presence-expansion. Not only were the visual posts shared more frequently, but there was a significant difference between the visual formats. Posts with an attached video had an even greater chance of being shared than posts with photos, graphs and other still images.

Among its twenty-one original posts, the Russian embassy had no original video and published only eight posts with its own photographs – a publicity strategy which should have limited presence-expansion. The overreliance on external sources broadened the presence of these other sources within the community of ERFRM followers without encouraging further dissemination, due to the lower visibility of such posts. In terms of the language question, such a strategy, whether deliberate or due to a lack of interest in or resources for producing original content, can be considered as limiting its appeal to a group of active Russian speakers and consumers of selected media content.

Two-thirds of the 268 original Facebook posts by the European delegation contained attached photos. A little less than one-third of the original content was made up of video posts (interviews, reports, slideshow videos) – still a substantial workload of producing seventy-five video clips within a year. We have already discussed the balanced use of the Russian and Moldovan languages throughout the overall EURM output. This pattern, however, can be broken down by content type. The video posts tended to be preceded by textual descriptions in Romanian more often than Russian, and vice versa in the case of the posts with attached images. A thorough analysis of the multimedia use of language – voice-overs, interviews, written captions and pictures with texts – was not conducted here. A non-systematic observation revealed that EURM used Russian, Romanian, English and their combinations in a variety of ways, although in most of the video content Romanian appeared central, whereas Russian and English were secondary. This implies that on the level of content production and packaging there was more emphasis on the state language of Moldova, whereas Russian was used more on the level of content dissemination and communication.

CONCLUSIONS

This chapter has looked at how the EU's and Russia's digital diplomacy made use of the Russian language in the context of Moldova. The case is justified by the importance of language politics in this post-Soviet country, where part of the territory and a significant share of the population remain in a state of frozen conflict. It started more than thirty years ago from a sensitive language reform that undermined the Russian-speaking elites of Soviet Moldova (King 2000). It had important implications for nation-building and for Moldova's current international relations. It resonates today with the heightened level of confrontation and the rhetoric of sanctions between Russia and the West. The status of the Russian language raises questions concerning the future challenges to European integration processes in countries of the former Soviet Union, and in Moldova in particular.

This chapter began with the observation that the state language of Moldova is Romanian and that one-quarter of the Moldovan population are Russian speakers. For many others in Moldova, the Russian language is a lingua franca. Nevertheless, more than half of the country does not speak Russian at all (Aref'ev 2015: 33). The findings in this chapter show, however, how Russian dominates the digital diplomacy of both the EU and Russia. Facebook messages in Russian were also more likely to cause higher levels of audience reaction, significantly so in the case of the Russian embassy. These results indicate a disproportionate emphasis on engagement and relationship-building with Russian speakers, as opposed to with speakers of the state language. The EU delegation on Facebook displayed a more balanced approach, though there was also clearly a special interest in and a strategy directed towards being able to communicate in Russian. The results confirm previous research into the soft power resourcefulness of the Russian language in the region. Not included in this study was the question of other relevant digital diplomacy actors in Moldova. For example, the Romanian embassy also uses a Facebook page, analysis of which could have a corrective perspective on the language question and its politics.

A brief overview of the numbers of followers and the levels of their reactions to digital diplomacy pages on Facebook shows that the scale of such practices is low and at best limited to the most active core interest groups of no more than several thousand people. The commenting examples discussed in the chapter indicate that there are language-related tensions among the followers of these Facebook pages. The absence of Russian in the materials provided may trigger a critical response. The common Russian language is also linked to a common history, in particular the Second World War and Victory Day on 9 May – another important soft power resource for Russian foreign policy. History has played a lesser role in the EU's digital diplomacy in Moldova. A more successful EU narrative is that of economic relations and integration – showing the links between Moldovan workers and global markets.

Sourcing patterns in the use of Facebook by the European delegation and the Russian embassy in Moldova differed most strikingly. Whereas the European delegation invested substantially in the production of original multimedia content combining different languages (English, Romanian, Russian), the Russian embassy predominantly posted links to media materials, often to Russian state-run sources. This difference represents two opposite theoretical and normative models of (digital) public diplomacy. The Russian strategy is closer to the more traditional understanding of public diplomacy, with one-way communication channels, broadcasting principles, and the focus on high-level political elites and symbolic events. Even if this model can still be considered appropriate and efficient in certain situations, it makes more sense for much wider dissemination, with large mass audiences. The EU's strategy came closer to the theoretical model of the new public diplomacy, wherein diplomats are organisers of interaction rather than merely information transmitters. This model has its own limitations. In a highly fragmented world of instant global communication, 'practitioners of mediated diplomacy face the dilemma of crafting messages that work across vastly varying geographical and cultural boundaries' (Entman 2008: 99). The linguistic and thematic diversity of the EU delegation's diplomacy on Facebook may help in bridging disconnected communities, yet there remains the challenge of finding, metaphorically speaking, a common language.

NOTES

1. Translated from Russian by the author, Dmitry Yagodin.
2. Translated from Russian by the author, Dmitry Yagodin.

REFERENCES

Alexa (2021), 'Top sites in Moldova', <https://www.alexa.com/topsites/countries/MD> (last accessed 23 January 2021).
Alonso, A. and P. J. Oiarzabal (2010), *Diasporas in the New Media Age: Identity, Politics, and Community*, Reno, NV: University of Nevada Press.
Aref'ev, A. (2015), 'Russkii jazyk v mire: proshloe, nastoiashchee, budushchee', *Vestnik RAN* 84 (10), pp. 31–8.
Aref'ev, A. (2017), *Sovremennoe sostoianie i tendentsii rasprostraneniia russkogo iazyka v mire*, Moscow: Institut sotsial'no-politicheskikh issledovanii RAN.
Baltag, D. (2018), 'EU external representation post-Lisbon: The performance of EU diplomacy in Belarus, Moldova and Ukraine', *The Hague Journal of Diplomacy* 13 (1), pp. 75–96.
Baltag, D. and M. Smith (2015), 'EU and member state diplomacies in Moldova and Ukraine: Examining EU diplomatic performance post-Lisbon', *European Integration online Papers (EIoP)* 19 (1), pp. 1–25.
Billig, M. (1995), *Banal Nationalism*, London: Sage.
Bjola, C. (2015), 'Making sense of digital diplomacy', in C. Bjola and M. Holmes (eds), *Digital Diplomacy: Theory and Practice*, New York: Routledge, pp. 1–9.
Bjola, C. and M. Holmes (eds) (2015), *Digital Diplomacy: Theory and Practice*, New York: Routledge.
Bjola, C. and L. Jiang (2015), 'Social media and public diplomacy: A comparative analysis of the digital diplomatic strategies of the EU, US and Japan in China', in C. Bjola and M. Holmes (eds), *Digital Diplomacy: Theory and Practice*, New York: Routledge, pp. 71–88.
Blauvelt, T. K. (2013), 'Endurance of the Soviet imperial tongue: The Russian language in contemporary Georgia', *Central Asian Survey* 32 (2), pp. 189–209.
Boellstorff, T. (2010), *Coming of Age in Second Life: An Anthropologist Explores the Virtually Human*, Princeton, NJ: Princeton University Press.
Brinkerhoff, J. M. (2009), *Digital Diasporas: Identity and Transnational Engagement*, New York: Cambridge University Press.
Castells, M. (1996), *The Rise of the Network Society*, Malden, MA: Blackwell.
Castells, M. (2008), 'The new public sphere: Global civil society, communication networks, and global governance', *The ANNALS of the American Academy of Political and Social Science* 616 (1), pp. 78–93.
Ciscel, M. (2007), *The Language of the Moldovans: Romania, Russia, and Identity in an Ex-Soviet Republic*, Lanham, MD: Lexington Books.
Collins, N. and K. Bekenova (2017), 'Digital diplomacy of the European embassies in Kazakhstan', *EL-CSID Policy Brief* 2017 (3), September, <http://aei.pitt.edu/92496/1/119111_Policy_Brief_2017-3_HR_DEF[2].pdf> (last accessed 19 January 2021).
Cowan, G. and A. Arsenault (2008), 'Moving from monologue to dialogue to collaboration:

The three layers of public diplomacy', *The ANNALS of the American Academy of Political and Social Science* 616 (1), pp. 10–30.

DeVito, M. A. (2017) 'From editors to algorithms: A values-based approach to understanding story selection in the Facebook news feed', *Digital Journalism* 5 (6), pp. 753–73.

Dodon I. (2017), Facebook post, 27 September, <https://www.facebook.com/dodon.igor1/posts/1902642119976673> (last accessed 19 January 2021).

Embassy of Russia in the Republic of Moldova (2017a), Facebook post, 17 January, <https://www.facebook.com/rusembmoldova/posts/1307048532686786> (last accessed 19 January 2021).

Embassy of Russia in the Republic of Moldova (2017b), Facebook post, 26 March, <https://www.facebook.com/rusembmoldova/posts/1371283726263266> (last accessed 19 January 2021).

Embassy of Russia in the Republic of Moldova (2017c), Facebook post, 9 May, <https://www.facebook.com/790547397670238/posts/1421115641280074> (last accessed 19 January 2021).

Entman, R. M. (2008), 'Theorizing mediated public diplomacy: The U.S. case', *The International Journal of Press/Politics* 13 (2), pp. 87–102.

European Union in the Republic of Moldova (2017a), Facebook post, 10 January, <https://www.facebook.com/255840324431929_1623154887700459> (last accessed 19 January 2021).

European Union in the Republic of Moldova (2017b), Facebook post, 8 February, <https://www.facebook.com/255840324431929_1659757847373496> (last accessed 19 January 2021).

European Union in the Republic of Moldova (2017c), Facebook post, 14 May, <https://www.facebook.com/EUDelegationMoldova/videos/1771237786225501/> (last accessed 19 January 2021).

European Union in the Republic of Moldova (2017d), Facebook post, 21 May, <https://www.facebook.com/EUDelegationMoldova/videos/1779077228774890/> (last accessed 19 January 2021).

European Union in the Republic of Moldova (2017e), Facebook post, 25 June, <https://www.facebook.com/EUDelegationMoldova/videos/1819873891361890/> (last accessed 19 January 2021).

Fominykh, A. (2016), 'Russia's public diplomacy in Central Asia and the Caucasus: The role of the universities', *The Hague Journal of Diplomacy* 12 (1), pp. 56–85.

Forsberg, T. and H. Smith (2016), 'Russian cultural statecraft in the Eurasian space', *Problems of Post-Communism* 63 (3), pp. 129–34.

Gilboa, E. (2008), 'Searching for a theory of public diplomacy', *The ANNALS of the American Academy of Political and Social Science* 616 (1), pp. 55–77.

Gorham, M. (2011), 'Virtual rusophonia: Language policy as "soft power" in the new media age', *Digital Icons: Studies in Russian, Eurasian and Central European New Media* 5, pp. 23–48.

Hayden, C. (2012), *The Rhetoric of Soft Power: Public Diplomacy in Global Contexts*, Lanham, MD: Lexington Books.

Hill, C. (2010), 'Cheques and balances: The European Union's soft power strategy', in I. Parmar and M. Cox (eds), *Soft Power and US Foreign Policy: Theoretical, Historical and Contemporary Perspectives*, New York: Routledge, pp. 182–98.

Hill, W. H. (2012), *Russia, the Near Abroad, and the West: Lessons from the Moldova–Transdniestria Conflict*, Baltimore: Johns Hopkins University Press.

Hine, C. (2000), *Virtual Ethnography*, London: Sage.
Hyman, A. (1993), 'Russians outside Russia', *The World Today* 49 (11), pp. 205–8.
King, C. (2010), *The Moldovans: Romania, Russia, and the Politics of Culture*, Stanford, CA: Hoover Institution Press.
Kozinets, R. V. (2009), *Netnography: Doing Ethnographic Research Online*, London: Sage.
Laguerre, M. S. (2010), 'Digital diaspora: Definition and models', in A. Alonso and P. J. Oiarzabal (eds), *Diasporas in the New Media Age: Identity, Politics, and Community*, Reno, NV: University of Nevada Press, pp. 49–64.
Lai, H. and Y. Lu (2012), *China's Soft Power and International Relations*, New York: Routledge.
McCombs, M. E. and D. L. Shaw (1993), 'The evolution of agenda-setting research: Twenty-five years in the marketplace of ideas', *Journal of Communication* 43 (2), pp. 58–67.
McCombs, M. E., D. L. Shaw and D. H. Weaver (2014), 'New directions in agenda-setting theory and research', *Mass Communication and Society* 17 (6), pp. 781–802.
Mäkinen, S. (2016), 'In search of the status of an educational great power? Analysis of Russia's educational diplomacy discourse', *Problems of Post-Communism* 63 (3), pp. 183–96.
Manor, I. and E. Segev (2015), 'America's selfie: How the US portrays itself on its social media accounts', in C. Bjola and M. Holmes (eds), *Digital Diplomacy: Theory and Practice*, New York: Routledge, pp. 89–108.
Melissen, J. (2005), *The New Public Diplomacy: Soft Power in International Relations*, New York: Palgrave Macmillan.
Ministry of Foreign Affairs of the Russian Federation (2018), 'Social media', <http://www.mid.ru/en/press_service/social_accounts> (last accessed 19 January 2021).
Mkhoyan, A. (2017), 'Soft power, Russia and the former Soviet states: A case study of Russian language and education in Armenia', *International Journal of Cultural Policy* 23 (6), pp. 690–704.
Muth, S. (2014), 'Informal signs as expressions of multilingualism in Chisinau: How individuals shape the public space of a post-Soviet capital', *International Journal of the Sociology of Language* 228, pp. 29–53.
Nye, J. S. (2004), *Soft Power: The Means to Success in World Politics*, New York: Public Affairs.
Pavlenko, A. (2009), 'Language conflict in post-Soviet linguistic landscapes', *Journal of Slavic Linguistics* 17 (1–2), pp. 247–74.
Popescu, N. (2006), 'Russia's soft power ambitions', *CEPS Policy Brief* 115, October, Centre for European Policy Studies, <http://aei.pitt.edu/11715/1/1388.pdf> (last accessed 19 January 2021).
Prina, F. (2015), 'Linguistic justice, Soviet legacies and post-Soviet realpolitik: The ethnolinguistic cleavage in Moldova', *Ethnopolitics* 14 (1), pp. 52–71.
Rotaru, V. (2018), 'Forced attraction? How Russia is instrumentalizing its soft power sources in the "near abroad"', *Problems of Post-Communism* 65 (1), pp. 37–48.
Ryazanova-Clarke, L. (2014), 'Introduction: The Russian language, challenged by globalisation', in L. Ryazanova-Clarke (ed.), *The Russian Language Outside the Nation*, Edinburgh: Edinburgh University Press, pp. 1–30.
Saari, S. (2014), 'Russia's post-Orange Revolution strategies to increase its influence in former Soviet republics: Public diplomacy *po russkii*', *Europe-Asia Studies* 66 (1), pp. 50–66.

Samokhvalov, V. (2014), 'Russia, the near abroad and the West: Lessons from the Moldova–Transdniestria conflict', *Europe-Asia Studies* 66 (6), pp. 1021–2.

Seib, P. (2009), *Toward a New Public Diplomacy: Redirecting U.S. Foreign Policy*, New York: Palgrave Macmillan.

Sherr, J. (2013), *Hard Diplomacy and Soft Coercion: Russia's Influence Abroad*, London: Chatham House.

Silver, B. (1974), 'Social mobilization and the Russification of Soviet nationalities', *American Political Science Review* 68 (1), pp. 45–66.

Singh, J. P. (2015), 'The power of diplomacy: New meanings, and the methods for understanding digital diplomacy', C. Bjola and M. Holmes (eds), *Digital Diplomacy: Theory and Practice*, New York: Routledge, pp. 181–98.

Șveț, A. (2013), 'Staging the Transnistrian identity within the heritage of Soviet holidays', *History and Anthropology* 24 (1), pp. 98–116.

Thussu, D. K. (2013), *Communicating India's Soft Power: Buddha to Bollywood*, New York: Palgrave Macmillan.

Tsagarousianou, R. (2004), 'Rethinking the concept of diaspora: Mobility, connectivity and communication in a globalised world', *Westminster Papers in Communication and Culture* 1 (1), pp. 52–65.

Tsygankov, A. P. (2006), 'If not by tanks, then by banks? The role of soft power in Putin's foreign policy', *Europe-Asia Studies* 58 (7), pp. 1079–99.

van Dijck, J. (2013), *The Culture of Connectivity: A Critical History of Social Media*, New York: Oxford University Press.

Zaharna, R. S., A. Arsenault and A. Fisher (2013), *Relational, Networked, and Collaborative Approaches to Public Diplomacy: The Connective Mindshift*, New York: Routledge.

CHAPTER 7

Promoting Russian Higher Education

Sirke Mäkinen

INTRODUCTION

This chapter analyses how Russia, including Russian universities, promotes its higher education (hereafter also HE) abroad. First, I seek to answer whether Russian universities agree to the state-level approach of 'educational diplomacy', and what role the language plays in the promotion of Russian HE and the recruitment of international students. Second, I examine how Russian HE is received in the target countries of Russia's HE promotion and recruitment in the post-Soviet space and in the EU.

Russian state authorities have emphasised the importance of promoting Russian HE abroad, recruiting international students and taking active part in the global education market. On the basis of public diplomacy and international education literature, however, it has been argued that hitherto the main rationale for these actions has been political instead of economic, and therefore, that these activities could be placed under the label of educational diplomacy (see Mäkinen 2016: 184, 188–92). According to Hans de Wit (2002; see also Mäkinen 2016: 185), there are four main types of rationale for the internationalisation of higher education: political, economic, social/cultural and academic. Their importance varies, for example according to the level of actors and geographical regions or countries.

This chapter starts from the argument that at the state level the political rationale is closely linked with the language question, that is, the promotion of the Russian language abroad and the targeting of the promotion of Russian universities towards those 'markets' in which there are Russian-speaking audiences, and in which Russian HE is already well known and reasonably respected (Mäkinen 2016: 191). The economic rationale would rather suggest increasing the use of English as a medium of teaching, and therefore, reaching out also beyond the post-Soviet space (Mäkinen 2016: 183), which is certainly one of the goals advocated in the 'Development of the Export Potential of the Russian System of Education' project (Export Potential 2017).

According to this project, Russian universities should be able to attract more international students and to generate more income from the tuition fees of international students. Therefore, Russian universities should seek to provide more teaching and whole degree programmes imparted in foreign languages, and in particular in English.

However, in parallel, strengthening the position of the Russian language both within the Russian Federation, in its different federation subjects, and abroad has been one of the goals of the state in the 2000s. A government programme for the support of the Russian language in 2016–20 (Russian Language Programme n.d.) and the Concept of the State Support and Promotion of Russian Language Abroad (Concept of Promotion 2015) argue for strengthening the position of the Russian language both within the Russian Federation and abroad. Both are, at least indirectly, linked with education.

Analysing the reception of Russian HE abroad and examining its attractiveness in the global education market, I was guided by previous studies on how students make a choice to study abroad and what their motivations are for studying abroad. These have often been investigated with the help of the so-called push–pull model previously used in migration studies (see Altbach 1998; Lee 2017). Mazzarol and Soutar (2002: 82) explain 'push' factors as those operating within the source country, and 'pull' factors as those functioning within a host country. According to these authors, there are three stages in the decision-making process for studying abroad: the first involves the decision to study abroad; the second, the selection of the country; and the third, the choice of an educational unit. However, in more recent studies it has been argued that this is not necessarily the order of these stages, as, for example, the selection of the institution may precede that of the country and be seen as more important (Jiani 2017: 577). Mazzarol and Soutar (2002: 83) argue that in the decision to study abroad, push factors are crucial: such as, for example, 'lack of access to higher education' in the home country. As for the country selection, they list six factors: 'knowledge and awareness of the host country in the student's home country', including 'the reputation for quality and the recognition of its qualifications in the student's home country'; 'personal recommendations from parents, relatives and friends'; 'economic and social costs', such as tuition fees, living expenses, travel costs, crime, safety and racial discrimination; and finally 'environment', including physical conditions and lifestyles, geographical proximity and social links – that is, whether 'a student has family or friends living in the destination country and whether family and friends have studied there previously' (Mazzarol and Soutar 2002: 83).

Recent studies have, for example, addressed the personal decision-making process of degree-seeking students, factors influencing the choice of the destination country and institution (e.g. Fang and Wang 2014; Chen 2017; Lee 2017; Ahmad and Hussain 2017a, 2017b; Jiani 2017). These studies have been based on interviews and/or surveys of international students. As Chen (2017: 114–15) argues, micro-level factors, such as those mentioned above, have mainly been addressed, but in addition to this, meso-level factors (e.g. academic marketing) and macro-level factors (e.g. national marketing) should be taken into account when studying the factors affecting student mobility.

Unlike previous studies, this study is not based on student/graduate interviews or surveys, but the micro level will be touched upon indirectly, with the help of expert interviews. In addition, it addresses the meso and macro levels, by examining the promotion of Russia's higher education at the state and institutional level, and how these activities (if any) are perceived in the target countries. In addition, this empirical chapter analyses how the two elements being promoted, that of Russian education and that of Russian language, are intertwined. It should also be noted that in English-language literature the reception of Russia's higher education abroad, and the work of pull and push factors linked with it, is under-researched.

The remainder of the chapter is divided into five sections followed by a conclusion. First, the context – that is, Russia's position in the global education market – is briefly outlined. This is followed by a description of the data gathering. In the third and fourth sections, I discuss the findings of the study regarding the promotion of Russia's higher education abroad, that is, how the state and university actors represent it. Particular attention is paid to the role of language in promotion and recruitment. These sections touch upon the above-mentioned meso and macro levels, that is, promotion at the institutional and national level. Finally, the reception of Russia's higher education is discussed in four cases – Kazakhstan, Belarus, Germany and Finland – and again the role of the Russian language is given special attention. This represents the micro-level analysis, even though this study did not engage with the question through direct enquiries with students or graduates but through expert interviews. In this context, perceptions of meso- and macro-level activities are also discussed.

RUSSIAN HIGHER EDUCATION AND THE GLOBAL EDUCATION MARKET

Russian higher education has been in turmoil ever since the disintegration of the Soviet Union in December 1991. The economic crisis of the 1990s had a severe impact on the sector, and the 1990s saw also the so-called brain drain from the territory of the former Soviet Union and in particular from the Russian Federation to Western Europe and the United States in the field of sciences (Korobkov and Zaionchkovskaia 2012). Centralisation/privatisation, commercialisation and the adoption of 'European norms', that is, the Bologna process, characterised reforms of Russian HE in the 1990s and early 2000s (e.g. Gounko and Smale 2007a, 2007b). The economic slump and decentralisation led to side effects such as the intensification of corruption in higher education, including the selling of degrees. During the 2010s, there have been many more reforms in higher education, as in society as a whole. The trend turned from decentralisation towards recentralisation: for example, more state control over universities with the help of annual evaluation of universities and different funding projects such as the '5-100 Project' – a government-funded project which aims to bring five Russian universities into the top 100 in the leading global university rankings (ARWU, THE, QS) by 2020.

The university sector has also been restructured into four categories of universities, with Moscow State and St Petersburg State as leading national universities at the top, and below them national research universities, federal universities and regional 'flagship' (*opornye*) universities. In addition, there are twenty-one in the '5-100 Project' and thirty-nine so-called universities-exporters participating in the 'Development of the Export Potential of the Russian System of Education' project. They receive special funding in return for specific obligations emerging from that project. A hierarchy among the universities has since emerged.

A significant number of Russian universities and their branch campuses have faced either a closure or a merger in the 2010s. In January 2014 there were 567 state universities and 422 non-state universities, but in January 2018 there were just 484 state universities and only 81 non-state universities left. The number of branch campuses has also decreased almost by half (Kommersant 2018). In 2016, Russian higher education institutions (HEIs) had almost 4.8 million students, 296,200 of whom were 'foreign citizens' (Aref'ev 2017: 31). Tuition fees are paid by 60% of foreign students; the remainder study in 'budget places', that is, they do not pay for their tuition (Aref'ev 2017: 39, Table 2.2).

Although the Soviet Union had been one of the key recipient countries of foreign students, in the 1990s the situation changed. In the last whole academic year of the Soviet Union in 1990/1, the universities on the territory of the Russian Federative Socialist Republic accounted for 2.8 million HEI students, out of which 89,600 were foreign citizens – that is, 3.17% of the total. The same percentage was reached again only in 2012/13. At this time, 225,000 out of approximately 6 million students were foreigners, that is, the total number of university students had increased considerably (Pugach 2012: 35). During the Soviet period, engineering was the most popular field for foreign citizens, whereas since the 2000s the humanities, economics and business studies, medicine and health sciences have attracted the bulk of foreign students (e.g. Aref'ev 2017: 30, 131, Tables 1.6 and 2.5).

In the academic year 2015–16, Kazakhstan, China, Turkmenistan, Ukraine, Tajikistan, Uzbekistan, India, Azerbaijan, Belarus, Kyrgyzstan and Vietnam made up the top ten of the sending countries. More than one-third (36.9%) of international students came from the CIS (plus Abkhazia and South Ossetia) and less than one-fifth from Asian countries (16.5%). During the Soviet period, Mongolia, Vietnam, Afghanistan, Cuba, Bulgaria and Syria had been the top six countries of origin by percentages (Aref'ev 2017: 31, 40, 45).

DATA GATHERING AND ANALYSIS

Primary data for this chapter has been extracted from state-level documents and websites, expert interviews and media materials. Regarding Russia's promotion of higher education and the role of language, I have analysed the website of the Russian Federal Agency for the Commonwealth of Independent States Affairs, Compatriots Living Abroad, and International Humanitarian Cooperation (hereafter Rossotrudnichestvo), two separate promotion and recruitment websites of Russian HE, and media materials. I also conducted interviews in Russian universities and their branches in the CIS.

For the reception of Russian HE promotion abroad, I have selected two cases from the post-Soviet space, Belarus and Kazakhstan, and two cases from among the EU member states, Germany and Finland, and interviewed experts on the situation in these countries. The cases were chosen because of the numbers of students that they send to Russia. At the same time, they are different enough to be compared with one another in a meaningful way. Kazakhstan is the country that sends the biggest number of international students to Russian universities: 35,111 in the academic year 2015/16, according to Russian statistics (Aref'ev

2017: 40). Belarus sent 4,621 students. The historical orientation of the former republics of the USSR has frequently been quoted as being one of the main reasons for students from the CIS countries coming to study in Russia. These countries have been part of the Russian Empire/the Soviet Union, and the Russian language has served as a lingua franca. Moreover, it is less expensive to study in Russia than in many European or US HEIs (Nikitenko and Leont'eva 2015: 233). As we will see below, many of these pull factors are confirmed in the analysis of the expert interviews conducted in Kazakhstan and Belarus for this study. Among the EU member states, Germany is the country that sends the biggest number of students to Russia: 1,511 in 2015/16. These are most often exchange students. Finland ranks fifth as a country of origin among the EU countries, with 583 students, outnumbered by Italy, France and Latvia (Aref'ev 2017: 41–3). In the Finnish case, too, students are usually exchange students, that is, not degree-seeking students as in the cases of Kazakhstan and Belarus.

Eleven interviews concerning promotion and recruitment were conducted in Moscow universities and their branches from 2014 to 2018. Respondents included vice-rectors, deputy vice-rectors, deputy deans, heads or deputy heads of university branches abroad as well as heads of international affairs departments and heads of relevant research centres. The selected universities comprise some universities that are participants of the '5-100 Project' and some that are not, and some that are part of the thirty-nine universities with recognised export potential (Export Potential 2017). All but one university among my cases are state universities, and none of them is a sectoral university. There is a geographical bias regarding the universities, as all of their main campuses are located in Moscow, but the selected universities vary as to their respective statuses in the Russian HE hierarchy.

As for the perception of Russian higher education abroad, nineteen interviews were conducted from 2017 to 2018 with those working for government or private agencies dealing with international education. Further respondents were selected from researchers and administrators in the field of international education who were familiar with the role of Russian higher education in that particular 'target' country, and also from among Russia-based experts in the field of international education.

The interviews were semi-structured, and usually lasted between an hour and two hours. Fourteen interviews were conducted face-to-face, five by telephone or Skype and one by e-mail. All interviews were conducted in the post-Crimea period (the first ones in December 2014), and thus after the new Law on Education had come into force (2012). However, more than half of the interviews in Russia pre-dated the launch of the 'Development of the Export Potential of the Russian System of Education' project in 2017.

The interviewees are referred to neither by their names nor by their positions or specific affiliations in order to guarantee anonymity. Information is given regarding the type of affiliation, either a university (*Uni*) or a governmental or private agency (*Agency*). I used a partly different set of questions for those interviewed about the promotion of Russian education abroad, that is, those that are actively involved in it for a Russian university or agency. Such respondents are referred to as *Pro* in the embedded notes. Those interviewed about the reception of Russian education are referred to as *Rec*. As for the media data, materials were searched using the names of rectors of leading universities and ministers or deputy ministers responsible for Education and Science between 2007 and 2018. In references to public data, rectors and ministers are referred to by their names.

The interviews were analysed qualitatively by both inductive and deductive coding, that is, by searching for the themes that emerge from the data, but also coding them by the categories from the previous studies, that is, different rationales for internationalisation, and different pull and push factors.

PROMOTION OF RUSSIAN HIGHER EDUCATION ABROAD

State-level discourse and policy

In the state officials' discourse, the promotion of Russian HE abroad has been described with the term 'education export', denoting the recruitment of international students for degree programmes in Russian universities or their branches abroad. In 2010, a first draft of the Concept of Export of Educational Services of the Russian Federation for the Period of 2011–2020 (Concept of Education Export 2010) was published, but owing to changes that had taken place in Russian politics and the change of cadres in the Ministry of Education and Science, no implementation occurred (Pro-Uni-6-2017; Rec-Agency-2-2018). Finally, in 2017 a new project for education export was introduced under the title 'Development of the Export Potential of the Russian System of Education'. It formulates ambitious goals, such as attracting 310,000 foreign students in 2020, although in 2017 there were only 220,000 foreign students registered. By 2025 their number was to reach 710,000. However, according to an expert evaluation (Agency-2-2018), nobody takes these figures seriously.

These unrealistic figures are obviously meant to exert pressure on the universities to work harder.

With the new project comes no increase in the quota of tuition-free places for foreign citizens, which will remain limited to 15,000 places. EAEU citizens, however, may apply for budget places, that is, tuition-free education according to the same rules that apply to Russian citizens. According to the project, the number of those paying for their tuition is projected to increase from 135,000 in 2017 to 175,000 in 2020 and 405,000 in 2025. Revenue from tuition fees, according to the project, should rise from 85 million roubles to 135 million roubles in 2020 and to 373 million roubles in 2025. However, when launching this project in May 2017, Prime Minister Medvedev argued that the main goal of the export of education should not be earning money; rather, he cited the political rationale. Medvedev (2017) called it 'one of the strongest means of people-to-people communication, of broadening cultural contacts and attracting more talented people to the national economy who may stay in the country'.

These ambitious numbers would require a makeover of the available degree programmes in Russian HEIs. This includes offering more programmes in foreign languages, which the government document likewise describes as one of the ways to increase the number of international students and revenue generated from international education. One example would be an increase in distance education or online programmes in foreign languages. However, a 'two-track approach' is also discernible in this approach, as Russian HEIs are in parallel expected to attract more Russian speakers from other countries to come and study in Russia in Russian, including the so-called compatriots. This target group figures prominently also on the two other websites – the quota programme website Russia.study (Russia.study n.d.) and the Study in Russia website (Study in Russia n.d.).

Increasing the attraction of Russian HE cannot exclusively rely on the teaching of programmes in English, hence the project 'Export Potential 2017' argues also for amending legislation facilitating the entry and admission of foreigners and improving access to the labour market. As to the universities, they are called upon to develop their student services and other infrastructure. Russian HEIs are also supposed to invite more teachers from abroad, and at the same time 'safeguard the historical-cultural unity of those [compatriots] living in the near abroad' (Export Potential 2017[1]). Finally, they are expected to establish a specific scholarship programme for those among the foreign students who excel during their stay at a Russian university. The budget for the programme totals 4,972 million roubles (Export Potential 2017).

University-level discourse and policy

Ideas of educational diplomacy (see Mäkinen 2016) as developed on the state level are partly adopted at the university level. For example, one of the vice-rectors argued that education export will 'create . . . a group of people who are loyally attuned to that country . . . [and who] would understand the language of that country, [its] cultural-historical characteristics' (Pro-Uni-1-2014).[2] Another respondent proposed that 'if foreign partners learn to know [the university in question] and this experience is positive, then this is reflected in a positive image of the country' (Pro-Uni-2-2016).

However, the political rationale of educational diplomacy was not understood as the sole motive for the urge to promote Russian HE or recruit international students. As one of the interviewees put it, there are always 'commercial elements' (Pro-Uni-9-2016) or 'some kind of mercantile interest' linked to it, due to, among other things, the demographic problems that Russia is facing (Pro-Uni-4-2017). However, this 'commercial interest' has been difficult to realise for some universities, because their recruitment policies have to follow the so-called 'government order' (*goszakas*), that is:

> we teach students from those countries and fields which are priorities of our foreign policy and linked to the priorities of Russia in cooperation with many countries. But leading universities should also guarantee a certain quality of education [as far as the intake of students is concerned] . . . (Pro-Uni-9-2016)

Here the government order and the interests of HEIs are juxtaposed, that is, foreign policy interests and the interest of HEIs in quality assurance do not necessarily coincide. From the point of view of the universities, one should not emphasise the number of students, but their 'quality', and they should be recruited from those places where the best students are located. Here the respondent refers to the state quota system for tuition-free education, which prioritises the countries in the CIS (including the breakaway republics) and some Asian countries.

Sometimes universities display a very utilitarian view of the internationalisation of higher education, in particular as far as the recruitment of international students is concerned. It is perceived as an easy opportunity to rise in global university rankings, easier than increasing the amount of international publications and citations (Pro-Uni-6-2017). Accordingly, the reasons for promotion and recruitment of international students have to do with 'indicators in different indexes, rankings . . . Shanghai, THE have such criteria as the number of foreign students, foreign professors. So, in general, without a positive image, students do not come here and Russian education loses in these rankings' (Rec-Univ-5-2018).

State- and university-level practices

Russian HE is mainly promoted abroad by Rossotrudnichestvo and the Russian Centres for Science and Culture coordinated by it, and by the universities themselves. In 2009, an agreement on cooperation between Rossotrudnichestvo – an agency attached to the Ministry of Foreign Affairs – and the Ministry of Education and Science was signed. The agreement covered cooperation in international education and science, including the promotion of Russian science, education and language abroad, support for transfer to educational markets, assistance in recruitment of students to Russian universities, and relations with the foreign alumni of Russian universities. This cooperation has since been reinforced by the Concept for the Promotion of Russian Education with the Help of Rossotrudnichestvo Missions Abroad signed by Foreign Minister Lavrov in March 2014 (Concept-Rossotrudnichestvo 2014; see Mäkinen 2016).

There are two main websites for the promotion of Russian HE. One is titled Study in Russia (Study in Russia n.d.), the other Russia.study (Russia.study n.d.). The latter provides information about tuition-free education, that is, the quota programme of the Russian government. The application process for quota places is also organised by Rossotrudnichestvo through this website.

As to the Study in Russia website, it is available in Russian, English, French and Spanish. It can be searched for all study programmes available in Russian universities for international students on a tuition-paying basis. This includes the possibility to search for programmes taught in English. According to the website, in March 2018 there were 498 such programmes offered by Russian universities, some of them completely in English, some (usually at the PhD level) in a mixed form, that is, in both English and Russian. The English-language programmes were most often at the Master's level. These programmes were offered by twenty-four different universities all over the country, with the majority provided by the Russian University of Peoples' Friendship and the Moscow Higher School of Economics. The number of programmes and the universities providing them is quite modest compared with many other non-English-speaking European countries.

Another instrument for the promotion of Russian HE is participation in higher education study fairs or exhibitions. According to its website, Rossotrudnichestvo took part in study fairs or organised promotional events in China, India, Vietnam, Turkey, Kazakhstan, Moldova, Uzbekistan, Hungary, Mongolia, Romania, Czech Republic, Belgium, Slovenia, Greece, the United States and Sri Lanka in 2017/18. Twenty-five Russian HEIs participated in the China Education Expo in 2017, a key international education fair organised annually in Beijing (Rossotrudnichestvo 2017a). Russian universities and their faculties, or the new Association of Leading Universities, may also independently take part in education fairs, or submit materials for distribution through Rossotrudnichestvo (Pro-Uni-6-2017; Pro-Uni-1-2014; Rec-Uni-6-2018; Rec-Agency-2-2018).

Important agents in the promotion of Russian education are Russian schools abroad (Concept of Russian School 2015), and these function as a path to Russian HE. Rossotrudnichestvo's working plan for 2017 puts a lot of emphasis on the network of Russian schools, which it seeks to extend in other BRICS countries, Hungary, Egypt, Indonesia and Turkey, while supporting existing schools in the CIS countries (Rossotrudnichestvo 2017b). This chapter, however, focuses on higher education promotion as such and therefore the role of Russian schools remains to be studied elsewhere.

THE ROLE OF LANGUAGE IN THE PROMOTION OF RUSSIAN HIGHER EDUCATION

Both at the state level and the institutional level there are still two different views on the link between the promotion of Russian HE and the promotion of Russian language: those that argue that these two should go tightly together, and those who more actively advocate increasing teaching in English. Certainly, if the objective is to raise the number of international students in Russian universities considerably, the more realistic way would be to increase the number of courses and programmes taught in English or in other foreign languages. There is some potential to boost the number of Russian speakers, for example from Kazakhstan. As the majority of Kazakhstani students receive quota or budget places in Russia, this would serve the 'political' rationale more than the revenue-serving one.

State level

State authorities had already put strengthening the role of the Russian language on the agenda in the 2000s. According to statistics in a report on the Russian language at the turn of the twentieth to the twenty-first centuries (Aref'ev 2012), the share of those fluent in Russian was then diminishing even in the CIS countries, and less teaching was being offered in Russian in those countries. The figures given in this report called for an improvement in the position of the Russian language (see Mäkinen 2016: 191). A separate federal programme, 'Russian Language 2016–2020' (Russian Language Programme n.d.), was introduced for the protection and promotion of the Russian language. This programme calls for strengthening both the position of the Russian language as the federal language and its status in Russian regions. However, there are also goals relating to foreign countries and their educational systems: the Russian language as a language of international communication should be supported in order to increase the popularity and prestige of education in Russian. In particular, the programme aimed at stopping the decrease in the number of Russian schools and in the amount of Russian-language teaching in the CIS.

The goal of the 'Programme for the Promotion of the Russian Language and Education in Russian' is to 'popularise the Russian language in the world and increase the level of knowledge of Russian' and to create 'competitive positioning of open education in the Russian language and teaching of Russian in the global education space' (Pushkin Institute's Programme n.d.). There are many actors involved in the programme, such as Rossotrudnichestvo, the Russian World Foundation, and the International Association of Teachers of Russian Language and Literature, but the Pushkin State Institute of the Russian Language has been commissioned with its practical implementation. It has created an open education portal called 'Education in Russia' at www.pushkininstitute.ru and provides, for example, vocational training to teachers of Russian.

According to the Concept of the State Support and Promotion of Russian Language Abroad (Concept of Promotion 2015), the position of a given language abroad is one of the indicators of a state's influence in the world. Moreover, the Russian language is defined as 'one of the key instruments of promotion and implementation of the strategic foreign policy interests of the Russian Federation'. The state authorities are worried about the 'decrease in interest in the Russian language and its use in many countries and regions where a significant part of the population is of Russian origin' (*rodnye*) (Concept of Promotion 2015: 3).[3] The Concept sets out, for example, to safeguard and support compatriots in learning and using Russian, to facilitate their access to Russian-language education of good quality, to protect the Russian language as a language of inter-state and international communication within the CIS, and to support the study and teaching of Russian and the promotion of Russian science and education abroad (Concept of Promotion 2015: 4–6). In addition, the Concept supports the creation of Russian schools and pre-school education abroad. The Concept expects Russian embassies, Rossotrudnichestvo and the Russian Centres for Science and Culture, and branches of the Russian World abroad to implement the programme.

Another document, the Concept of Promotion of Russian Education with the Help of Rossotrudnichestvo Missions Abroad (Concept-Rossotrudnichestvo 2014: 6), emphasises the link between 'the promotion and strengthening of the position of Russian education and language' on the one hand and the 'strengthening of "soft power" and international prestige of Russia' on the other.

These documents clearly emphasise the political rationale for the recruitment of international students, and the focus on the territory of the CIS and Russian speakers elsewhere. The goals of the programmes are reiterated by leading authorities in the field of education. However, as then Minister of Education and Science Fursenko argued in 2010, Russia was only the second-best choice for many international students, that is, only those who could not afford to go to Europe or America came to Russia to study. According to Fursenko, making Russian HE more attractive would require the creation of a system of English-language education. Otherwise, 'we [Russia] will compete for students from the CIS: they know the language, they do not need good quality accommodation, they can get the visa easily' (Mel'nikova 2010).[4]

University level

Most of the teaching offered to international degree-seeking students from 2014 to 2017 was in Russian. As one of the university administrators reasoned, degree-seeking students would usually study in Russian, and only exchange students needed to be provided with courses in English; nonetheless, even his university offered a few programmes given entirely in English (Pro-Uni-6-2017). Hence, many universities stick to the Soviet tradition of enrolling non-Russian speakers in a preparatory faculty for one year, where they can learn Russian and acquire the ability to follow a degree programme taught in Russian.

Branch campuses of Russian universities are usually situated in the CIS countries and in the bordering regions in the Russian Federation, because there is a large demand for higher education in Russian and for Russian degrees. Hence, such demand is not necessarily created by Russia with the help of any active promotion measures at the macro level (Pro-Uni-6-2017; Pro-Uni-3-2014; Pro-Uni-4-2017). Moreover, some of these students plan on going to work in Russia after their graduation (Pro-Uni-7-2017). This is true not only for Russian speakers or those studying in branch campuses, as, for example, many Chinese students also want to find employment in Russia, which motivates them to learn Russian (Pro-Uni-8-2016). At the same time, my respondents acknowledged that many young people no longer possessed the necessary command of Russian to study in Russian. This was true even for the post-Soviet space in which Russian branch campuses are mainly located (Pro-Uni-3-2014).

Russian university actors also criticise the level of state support for the promotion of the Russian language abroad:

> if we look at how much Russia invests in the promotion of the Russian language abroad, then we see that it is many times, if not ten times, less in comparison with what France invests in the promotion of the French language or Germany and Spain in that of their national languages. (Pro-Uni-9-2016)

France is often taken as a comparison for Russia's poor funding for the promotion of the Russian language or public diplomacy as a whole. The former head of Rossotrudnichestvo, Konstantin Kosachev, has used this comparison, as well as the comparison with China and its Confucius Institutes, on several occasions (e.g. Kosachev 2012, 2013).

Changes will have to be drastic if the goals of the 'Export Potential' project are to be even partly reached. In 2014 and again in 2016, a representative of the central administration of one of the leading universities argued that 99% of their students studied in Russian, although the university is now among the thirty-nine universities earmarked to increase teaching in English to attract international students (Pro-Uni-1-2014).

Some administrators might also fear that if Russian universities turn to English-language education, they will lose part of their soft power. According to one respondent, language and understanding of a culture are strongly linked, and therefore, Russian universities may be afraid that they will not be able to teach international students to 'understand Russia' and its interests correctly if they change the language of tuition (Pro-Uni-10-2017).

There were those who saw the focus on teaching in Russian to international students as a problem, that is, according to them, it was not realistic to expect any increase in the numbers of international students if the teaching was given in Russian. In addition, these respondents assumed that the motivation to study in Russia followed a neoliberal logic: the economy and career prospects were the driving force for studying the Russian language and getting an education in Russian universities:

> it would be naïve in our cynical world to expect that for some ideological reasons ... other countries show us love and will learn Russian and get education in Russia. For real competition [in the higher education market] we need programmes in foreign languages. (Pro-Uni-9-2016; cf. Jiani 2017: 570 and the case of China)

In this logic the Russian language is something that might be learned when studying in Russia, but not primarily for educational purposes.

RECEPTION OF RUSSIAN HIGHER EDUCATION ABROAD AND THE ROLE OF LANGUAGE

Unsurprisingly, there are two different roles for the Russian language if we compare the cases of Belarus and Kazakhstan on the one hand, and Germany and Finland on the other. These differences concern also the promotion and recruitment of students in general, and the reasons why studying in Russia might be considered an attractive option. First of all, in the former Soviet republics, Russian HE is well known, there are traditions of studying in Russian HEIs, and the language is shared by many, that is, no specific promotion is required, even though there seem to be very active recruitment measures taking place, in particular in Kazakhstan. These findings confirm those of previous studies regarding the reasons for students' choices of particular destination countries (e.g. Mazzarol and Soutar 2002), that is, Russia's pull factors vis-à-vis Kazakhstan and Belarus are, in particular, knowledge and awareness of the country. Russian HE is thought of as being good in quality, geographically close and relatively cheap. Beyond that, personal recommendations and social links also play a role.

As for Germany and Finland, promotion of Russian HE is not really visible, and those who are interested are either Russian speakers or those German and Finnish citizens specifically studying Russia or the Russian language. We may safely assume that knowledge and awareness, social links and personal recommendations play a role in the case of Russian speakers. In the case of non-Russian speakers, geographical proximity and a willingness to study some specific programme not accessible to them in their home country, that is, a push factor, are of some importance.

As argued in previous literature, when thinking about the attractiveness and reception of Russian HE abroad, it is necessary to consider such push factors besides pull factors, that is, whether there is something specific that drives students of a particular country to study abroad, or perhaps at a Russian branch campus in that country. In the Belarusian and Kazakhstani cases, such push factors consist of the combination of tuition fees, the national school-leaving exam, and government policies which restrict access to certain fields of study, like the low number of budget places. Russia's ability to offer education free of charge or with lower tuition fees, and Russia's willingness to ignore the standards of the national school-leaving certificates are potential pull factors adding to the local push factors. This is true in particular for the Finnish and Belarusian cases due to the limited access to programmes in the humanities and social sciences in Belarus or in arts and medicine in Finland.

In both cases the language plays a significant role. In the Belarusian case, the Russian option offers study in the native tongue, that is, the role of the language is not visible but makes it a natural choice. In the Finnish case, language acquisition is a prerequisite for fulfilling one's educational or research interest. The situation in Kazakhstan resembles the Belarusian case, inasmuch as a Russian-speaking Kazakh or a Russian living in Northern Kazakhstan will certainly find studying in Russia a good option. Kazakhstani universities usually offer teaching in Russian, but more and more in Kazakh and English, too. This trilingual policy gives more opportunities to Kazakhstani pupils and students taking a decision on their place of study, and they can be interpreted as efforts to avoid dependence on Russia. The 'competition factor' is at play elsewhere as well: for example, in the case of Belarus, students may also choose to study in Russian at Polish or Lithuanian universities (Rec-Uni-5-2017). This is beyond the focus of this chapter, however.

Belarus and Kazakhstan

In the case of Kazakhstan, all my interviewees pointed to economic reasons, geographical proximity, familiarity with Russian HE and 'good propaganda' in the schools, as one put it (Rec-Uni-2-2017), as the pull factors attracting students to study in Russia. State-level arrangements benefit Russia too, as both countries are part of the Eurasian Economic Union, while Belarus and Russia still form a Union State. Large numbers of students from Belarus and Kazakhstan study without paying tuition fees, that is, they are either part of the quota system for foreign citizens or they have applied for budget places. There are also, however, negative pull factors, above all racism and security. For example, one interviewee mentions that 'attacks on Kazakhs in Moscow do not make studies in Russia as attractive' (Rec-Uni-1-2017). Another one confirms this: 'There is a lot of Russian nationalism, almost fascism there. Lots of students do not go there, especially to Moscow, because they are afraid for their security' (Rec-Uni-2-2017). There are also other negative pull factors, such as the methods of organising teaching and learning: for example, teacher- instead of student-centredness, or 'too much ideology in social sciences' (Rec-Uni-2-2017). Similar remarks about teaching in Russian HE were made by German and Finnish interviewees – Russian education is considered to be 'old-fashioned'. Other interviewees from Finland, Germany and Belarus also referred to the 'politicised nature' or 'indoctrination' present in the teaching of social sciences.

Russia's aggressive recruitment of Kazakhstani students in Northern Kazakhstan, close to the Russian border, worried Kazakhstani interviewees, too, as they claimed that this was severely felt by universities in Kazakhstan. One reason for the successful recruitment strategy was, according to my interviewees, the option not to take the combined Kazakhstani school-leaving and HE entrance exam, which is called the Unified National Test (UNT): 'I know that Russian universities conduct really aggressive international policies trying to attract students from Kazakhstan, especially in the regions which are on the border with Russia. Lots of students leave the country without even taking the UNT ...' (Rec-Uni-2-2017). Another argued that 'in Northern Kazakhstan it [Russia's provision of tuition-free education] is already a big problem and a big share [of pupils] leaves to study free of charge in Russia' (Rec-Uni-1-2017). A third referred to how Kazakhstani universities do not succeed in competition:

> Russia starts at a very early stage, when these prospective students are ninth- or tenth-grade students at schools ... [W]e started this year penetrating high schools, and we realised that we were too late ... because Russian universities have already been there ... targeting lyceums and gymnasiums where the best students are studying ... [T]here are also public schools, and their graduates are also leaving. Around 70% are leaving to Russia ... (Rec-Uni-3-2017)

The same interviewee mentions that 'this year we lost 40% of our enrolment' (Rec-Uni-3-2017). A fourth argued that 'they organise many visits from Russian universities and they start to enrol students somewhere in February–March. They are taking them in already, conducting examinations in schools, seeing the results and saying: you are enrolled in our university, come along!' (Rec-Uni-4-2017).

It is the northern regions whose students are interested in studying in Russian universities, while, as put by one of the interviewees, a representative of a branch campus, there is a 'language barrier' with the south (Pro-Uni-4-2017). However, according to the same interviewee, 'more than 90% speak Russian' in Kazakhstan (Rec-Uni-4-2017). The situation has started to change with the spread of English, however. 'As for the future, thanks to the trilingual policy, Russian HE may lose part of its attraction in Kazakhstan: more and more are fluent in English and therefore looking for other alternatives' (Rec-Uni-2-2017). As for Northern Kazakhstan, the geographical proximity factor also plays a huge role. 'It is much cheaper for them, closer to their cities, just Omsk is very close to the borderline and it is much better than going south' (Rec-Uni-2-2017).

Beyond this, many in Kazakhstan believe that '[education in] Russian is of better quality than that in English or Kazakh', since previously there have not been that many faculty members being able to teach in Kazakh. Therefore, many pupils from Kazakh-language schools continue their education in Russian in the universities (Rec-Uni-2-2017):

> In the 1990s, the majority of universities provided education in Russian; now the ratio is nearly fifty-fifty, and in addition, teaching is offered in English, for example at KIMEP, at the Kazakh-British technical university and at the Nazarbayev University. There are also forty-two to forty-four universities in Kazakhstan which provide their programmes in three languages. (Rec-Uni-2-2017)

As for Belarus, Russian universities can again rely on the knowledge and awareness factor as well as on social links and personal recommendations. Promotion of Russian HE is not really visible at the national level. Russian universities can rely on the tradition and reputation of Russian HE: 'pupils already know' (Rec-Uni-4-2017). Again, economic considerations are also a factor: 'When Russia developed quickly, it drew a lot of youth, students and teachers' (Rec-Uni-4-2017). In Belarus there are also strong push factors at play. Respondents argued that the state was only supporting those disciplines with budget places (i.e. tuition-free education) in which it saw a demand in the labour market, such as mathematics and IT. Students who are not interested in these fields or do not have the qualifications to study these subjects, and who cannot pay tuition fees in the fields that they would like to study, cannot therefore enter those fields in Belarus. 'Lawyers, economists, [students of] foreign languages – they go to Russia. In this context, Russia has a more liberal policy. And it is not always good' (Rec-Uni-4-2017). The interviewee refers here to branch campuses of Russian universities that have been opened in the Smolensk and Bryansk regions, that is, Belarusian students go to study in these branch campuses on the other side of the border.

Many universities based in Moscow, St Petersburg and even Saratov have opened branch campuses in these regions.

Finally, subjects not offered in Belarus also attract students to go to Russia: 'we don't have a literature institute here, for example, we don't have African studies and many other examples' (Rec-Uni-5-2017).

In terms of language, Russian is important not only in the case of Belarusian students going to study in Russia, but because Russia and Belarus are competitors in the same markets. Russian-speaking students from across the territory of the former Soviet Union also come to study in Belarus:

> they are coming here to study mainly because of the language. The language of instruction for the majority of programmes is Russian. So, you may go to some Russian institutions, but we compete with them in three dimensions: quality, price and security. There were examples of xenophobic stuff in Russia against foreign students as well ... (Rec-Uni-5-2017)

Security as a negative pull factor was thus mentioned in Belarus, too.

There has also been a less pleasant pull factor connected with Russian HE, and that is the selling of diplomas. In the wake of the evaluation of Russian universities and subsequent closure of some 'ineffective HEIs', and their branch campuses in particular, the situation may have improved to a certain extent: 'Some of them [referring to "money-stealers", those offering "distance education programmes", in particular in Smolensk] don't exist any more due to Russian authorities, finally' (Rec-Uni-5-2017). In addition, the legislation has been amended so that it is possible to close those HEIs which sell diplomas, as has been claimed by Vyacheslav Nikonov from United Russia, the head of the Duma Committee for Education (Nikonov 2016).

However, as in Kazakhstan, Russia is not the only choice for Belarusian students once the decision to study abroad has been made:

> When you compare what you can get of more or less the same quality in Copenhagen and in Moscow, for example, maybe Copenhagen is even cheaper than Moscow, and you are comparing what will be easier for you and your family, basing your decision on that ... (Rec-Uni-5-2017)

Some of the competitors also offer programmes in Russian, for example in Lithuania and Poland. 'Regardless of their hatred towards the Russian language – commerce makes miracles' (Rec-Uni-4-2017).

Finland and Germany

As for Finland and Germany, there are no nationwide knowledge and awareness factors benefiting Russian HE. For example, an interviewee from Finland argued that 'Finns know the Moscow State University and Saint Petersburg State University and that's it' (Rec-Uni-7-2018). In addition, it seems that the marketing of Russian HE is either not really visible to the Finnish-speaking or German-speaking public, or else is addressed to potential exchange students only. Due to tuition-free education in both countries, push factors do not exist, with the exception of some disciplines in the Finnish case.

In Finland, all respondents stressed that there is no visible promotion of Russian HE, except for a couple of individual initiatives by universities based in St Petersburg or Moscow. This may be different for Russian speakers, and especially for those who have relatives living in Russia. For them, the pull factors of social links and personal recommendations are likely to play a larger role. At the state level, the Russian Centre for Science and Culture is responsible for the promotion of Russian HE in Finland, but 'it is neither active, nor does there seem to be any modern marketing know-how . . . they do not use the language of the youth to communicate with the youth' (Rec-Agency-4-2017). The most active promoter of Russian education is the Finland–Russia Society, but their aim is promoting the study of the Russian language in Finnish schools and Russian-language courses in Russia (Rec-Agency-4-2017; Rec-Agency-5-2018). In particular, teachers and pupils at comprehensive and high schools are targeted (Rec-Agency-5-2018). On the Russian Centre for Science and Culture's website, the promotion of Russian HE is not present, except for one reference to quota places and scholarship programmes provided by the Russian government. It deserves to be mentioned that the Finnish National Board of Education is cooperating with the Centre by distributing information about such programmes on its website.

The only push factor from Finland to Russia and other countries is the high demand for subjects with highly competitive entrance regulations in Finland, such as medicine, dentistry or veterinary science (Rec-Agency-4-2017; Rec-Agency-5-2018; Rec-Agency-6-2018; Rec-Uni-7-2018; Rec-Uni-8-2018). Moreover, there are other competitive subjects in which the quality of Russian HE is appreciated in Finland, such as theatre, music and the visual arts (Rec-Agency-4-2017; Rec-Agency-5-2018; Rec-Agency-6-2018; Rec-Uni-7-2018; Rec-Uni-8-2018.). For a limited study-abroad period, business studies is a subject area attracting Finnish students due to the interest of Finnish companies in the Russian market. This applies also for law students and those interested in diplomatic careers, creating a willingness to study in Russia for a semester or two (Rec-Agency-4-2017; Rec-Agency-5-2018; Rec-Agency-6-2018; Rec-Uni-7-2018; Rec-Uni-8-2018). Finally, there are 'Russophiles' appreciating Russian culture, willing to study Russian language, literature and Russian studies in general (Rec-Agency-4-2017; Rec-Agency-5-2018; Rec-Agency-6-2018; Rec-Uni-7-2018; Rec-Uni-8-2018). This choice may be linked to career and employment considerations, too.

As for Germany, all German interviewees agreed that those interested in studying in Russia are to be found among those who study Russian language or Russian literature in Germany, or among those who have family roots in Russia or the territory of the former Soviet Union and who are Russian speakers. However, most German students take part in short-term exchanges or summer schools, from one to four weeks long (DAAD 2018; Rec-Uni-9-2018; Rec-Agency-7-2018; Rec-Uni-10-2018). By contrast, students from Finland more commonly embark on full semester exchanges. According to my respondents, hardly anyone from Germany aspires to study in Russia for a full degree programme. This is not surprising as there are no or very low tuition fees in Germany, admission is easy for the first-year courses and the quality of education is perceived to be very high, so there is no specific motivation to study abroad for Bachelor's degrees in general (Rec-Agency-7-2018; Rec-Uni-10-2018; Rec-Agency-8-2018). Thus, there is no such push factor from Germany or other European countries where tuition is free of charge for EU citizens. For the exceptions, that is, the disciplines that attract a few international students, there is a notable difference between Finland and Germany. German students are interested in mathematics, physics and other natural sciences and engineering, besides Russian language and literature. However, also in Finland all interviewees agreed that Russian universities are strong in natural sciences.

From a survey of Finnish students about studying abroad in Russia, we know the most common reasons for rejecting the Russian option. Lack of knowledge of Russian and Russia as a country ranked highest, with the latter obviously implying worries about security or the human rights situation. Those who had chosen Russia as a destination, at least temporarily, explained their choice with the aspiration to develop their knowledge of the Russian language and to learn about Russian culture, society and business, which they understand as strengthening and broadening their career prospects (Jänis-Isokangas 2017: 18–20). The results of the survey support the experts' point of view. Hence, one of the most pressing concerns was the bad reputation of Russian degree programmes and of the whole HE system, from corruption and lack of transparency to the diversity and fragmentation of the field, which supplements a generally negative image of Russia in Finland.

All of this suggests that the promotion of study in the Russian language seems to be more appropriate, as the few Germans and Finns who go to study in Russia for a whole degree programme accept Russian as the language of tuition. A good half of the students coming from Finland receive a Russian government scholarship and usually have a Russian background, that is, one of the parents is from Russia or a Russian speaker (Rec-Agency-4-2017). However, unlike their German peers, those with Russian roots are usually not interested in a full degree programme in Russia; they would rather study somewhere else in Europe (Rec-Agency-5-2018).

However, the language is important in that those students in Germany who have studied Russian at school are more open to the idea of studying in Russia: 'I am not sure if the Russian government realises this because I do not see much effort in investing in teaching Russian as a foreign language . . .' (Rec-Uni-9-2018). The situation is further complicated by the fact that those who have roots in Russia or in the post-Soviet space are not necessarily fluent in Russian either (Rec-Uni-10-2018).

In Germany, my respondents had noticed only some promotion of higher education by Russian universities themselves, usually addressed directly to universities and their students and promoting exchange studies or summer schools (Rec-Agency-7-2018; Rec-Uni-9-2018). This ties in with the DAAD's promotion of studies in Russia, for example within the framework of the 'Go East' programme, which again excludes full degree study in Russia (Rec-Uni-6-2018; Rec-Agency-7-2018; Rec-Uni-9-2018).

All interviewees in Finland and Germany agreed that the only way to increase the number of international students in Russian universities would be to offer more teaching in English. The numbers of those who study Russian abroad are too small. For the majority of students in Finland and Germany, English is the first foreign language and there is very little and ever-decreasing interest in studying any other language, let alone Russian. Russian is also perceived as too difficult a language to be learned during a one-year course in a preparatory faculty in Russia.

CONCLUSION

In the field of internationalisation of higher education, Russian universities have partly adopted the idea of educational diplomacy, and therefore the promotion of Russian HE is closely linked to the promotion of the Russian language abroad. The rationale for educating international students partly resides in the wish to familiarise international students with the 'true' Russia, who will in the future contribute to building good relations with Russia in their home countries.

The most common way of integrating international degree-seeking students has been the setting up of preparatory faculties for studying the Russian language, to prepare international students to its use as language of tuition. However, there is also dissatisfaction, at both state and institutional level, concerning the number and, sometimes, the quality of international students, or, in general, concerning the level of internationalisation of higher education and the revenue gained from international students. The project for the 'Development of the Export Potential of the Russian System of Education' tries to address some of these problems, one of the solutions being more teaching in English. Some universities are indeed interested in increasing teaching in English in order to attract more international students and faculty. Some of them might also see the opportunity for extracting extra government funding or for generating revenue from tuition fees. However, part of my Russian interviewees seem to be more worried about the possible loss of soft power opportunities if they should change from Russian to English as a language of tuition.

As for the perception of Russia's HE abroad and the role of the language of tuition in it, in my case studies students from Kazakhstan and Belarus encountered no obstacles, as their native tongue was usually Russian. It might even be argued that, in these cases, studies in Russia were not necessarily perceived as 'study abroad' or as part of an international and transnational education, but rather as some sort of 'borderline' case, between 'our own' and 'something foreign'. In both cases, push and pull factors were at play. In particular in the Kazakhstani case, meso-level promotion of Russian HE was quite active and sometimes perceived as 'aggressive' student recruitment by Russian universities. Pull factors for Belarusian and Kazakhstani students were easier access to higher education, lower prices and a greater variety of subject areas, some of which were not on offer in their home countries. Geographical proximity, knowledge and awareness of Russian HE and Russian universities were likewise responsible for the willingness to study in Russia.

In the cases of Finland and Germany, the wish to study the Russian language or the country as a whole played a key part in considering Russian HE. In Finland, the accessibility of disciplines not on offer in the country was an additional pull factor. For Russian speakers in both countries, more or less the same pull factors apply as in Belarus and

Kazakhstan. At least in the case of Germany, the idea of 'finding your roots', that is, identity-related reasons, also had a role to play.

Based on the interview data, it seems that macro-level promotion of Russian HE was invisible in all cases, while in particular in Kazakhstan the meso level seemed to be very active. Obviously, the running of two dedicated websites and some activities of the Russian Centres for Science and Culture went largely unnoticed. It remains to be seen whether Russia will devise more active measures at the national level during the implementation of the 'Development of the Export Potential of the Russian System of Education' project in the coming years.

NOTES

1. Translated from Russian by the author, Sirke Mäkinen.
2. All quotes from interviews in this chapter translated by the author, Sirke Mäkinen.
3. Translations from this and the following document by the author, Sirke Mäkinen.
4. Translated from Russian by the author, Sirke Mäkinen.

REFERENCES

Ahmad, Syed Zamberi and Matloub Hussain (2017a), 'An investigation of the factors determining student destination choice for higher education in the United Arab Emirates', *Studies in Higher Education* 42 (7), pp. 1324–43.

Ahmad, Syed Zamberi and Matloub Hussain (2017b), 'The analytic hierarchy process of the decision-making factors of African students in obtaining higher education in the United Arab Emirates', *Compare: A Journal of Comparative and International Education* 47 (2), pp. 163–76.

Altbach, Philip G. (1998), *Comparative Higher Education: Knowledge, the University, and Development*, Greenwich, CT: Ablex.

Aref'ev, Aleksandr Leonardovich (2012), *Russkii iazyk na rubezhe XX–XXI vekov*, Moscow: Ministerstvo obrazovaniia i nauki Rossiiskoi federatsii, Tsentr sotsiologicheskikh issledovanii, <http://www.isras.ru/files/File/Publication/russkij_yazyk.pdf> (last accessed 15 August 2015).

Aref'ev, Aleksandr Leonardovich (2017), *Eksport rossiiskikh obrazoval'nykh uslug. Statisticheskii sbornik*, Moscow: Ministerstvo obrazovaniya i nauki Rossiiskoi Federatsii, Tsentr sotsiologicheskikh issledovanii, <http://socioprognoz-u.1gb.ru/files/File/2017/Export_SB_7_%20496p.October.2017.pdf> (last accessed 16 March 2018).

Chen, Jun Mian (2017), 'Three levels of push–pull dynamics among Chinese international students' decision to study abroad in the Canadian context', *Journal of International Students* 7 (1), pp. 113–35.

Concept of Education Export (2010), *Kontseptsiia eksporta obrazovatel'nykh uslug Rossiiskoi Federatsii na period 2011–2020 gg*, (draft), <https://www.hse.ru/data/2011/01/18/1208078939/Concept_for_Exporting.pdf> (last accessed 15 January 2013).

Concept of Promotion (2015), *Kontseptsiia gosudarstvennoi podderzhki i prodvizheniya russkogo iazyka za rubezhom*, 3 November, <http://kremlin.ru/acts/news/50644> (last accessed 16 March 2018).
Concept-Rossotrudnichestvo (2014), *Kontseptsiia prodvizheniia rossiiskogo obrazovaniia na baze predstavitel'stv Rossotrudnichestva za rubezhom*, 27 March, <http://rs.gov.ru/sites/default/files/koncepciya_prodvizheniya_rossiyskogo_obrazovaniya_v_razdel_ekport_r o.pdf> (last accessed 20 October 2014).
Concept of Russian School (2015), *Kontseptsiia 'Russkaia shkola za rubezhom'*, 4 November, <http://kremlin.ru/acts/news/50643> (last accessed 9 December 2015).
DAAD (2018), *Länderstatistik 2017: Russische Föderation*, <https://www.daad.de/medien/der-daad/analysen-studien/bildungssystemanalyse/russland_daad_bsa.pdf> (last accessed 20 June 2018)
de Wit, Hans (2002), *Internationalization of Higher Education in the United States of America and Europe: A Historical, Comparative, and Conceptual Analysis*, Westport, CT: Greenwood Press.
Export Potential (2017), *Pasport prioritetnogo proekta 'Razvitie eskportnogo potentsiala rossiiskoi sistemy obrazovaniia'*, <https://минобрнауки.рф/%D0%BF%D1%80%D0%BE%D0%B5%D0%BA%D1%82%D1%8B/1355/%D1%84%D0%B0%D0%B9%D0%BB/9551/pasport_-_opublikovannyi.pdf> (last accessed 30 May 2017).
Fang, Wenhong and Shen Wang (2014), 'Chinese students' choice of transnational higher education in a globalized higher education market: A case study of W University', *Journal of Studies in International Education* 18 (5), pp. 475–94.
Gounko, Tatiana and William Smale (2007a), 'Russian higher education reforms: Shifting policy perspectives', *European Education* 39 (2), pp. 60–82.
Gounko, Tatiana and William Smale (2007b), 'Modernization of Russian higher education: Exploring paths of influence', *Compare* 37 (4), pp. 533–48.
Jänis-Isokangas, Ira (2017), *Korkeakouluyhteistyötä Venäjän kanssa. Arviointi CIMOn rahoittamista Venäjä- toiminnoista*, Opetushallitus, Raportit ja selvitykset 2017:3a, <https://www.oph.fi/download/182209_Korkeakouluyhteistyota_Venajan_kanssa.pdf> (last accessed 7 November 2018).
Jiani, M. A. (2017), 'Why and how international students choose Mainland China as a higher education study abroad destination', *Higher Education* 74, pp. 563–79.
Kommersant (2018), 'Polovina vuzov Rossii ne sdali zachet. Kachestvo', 27 March, <https://www.kommersant.ru/doc/3570555?query=%D0%B2%D1%8B%D1%81%D1%88%D0%B5%D0%B5%2 0%D0%BE%D0%B1%D1%80%D0%B0%D0%B7%D0%BE%D0%B2%D0%B0%D0%BD%D0%B8%D0%B5> (last accessed 29 March 2018).
Korobkov, Andrei V. and Zhanna A. Zaionchkovskaia (2012), 'Russian brain drain: Myths v. reality', *Communist and Post-Communist Studies* 45, pp. 327–41.
Kosachev, Konstantin (2012), 'Ot frankofonii k simfonii Russkogo mira', <http://blog.rs.gov.ru/node/12> (last accessed 19 December 2012).
Kosachev, Konstantin (2013), 'Konstantin Kosachev: Pora izbavit'sia ot fobii', *Rossiiskaia gazeta*, 6 September, <http://gorchakovfund.ru/news/8217> (last accessed 10 September 2013).
Lee, Se Woong (2017), 'Circulating East to East: Understanding the push–pull factors of Chinese students studying in Korea', *Journal of Studies in International Education* 21 (2), pp. 170–90.
Mäkinen, Sirke (2016), 'In search of the status of an educational great power? Analysis

of Russia's educational diplomacy discourse', *Problems of Post-Communism* 63 (3), pp. 183–96.

Mazzarol, Tim and Geoffrey N. Soutar (2002), '"Push–pull" factors influencing international student destination choice', *International Journal of Educational Management* 16 (2), pp. 82–90.

Medvedev, Dmitri (2017), *Razvitie eksporta obrazovaniia stanet dlia Rossii natsional'noi zadachei*, 30 May, <https://минобрнауки.рф/%D0%BF%D1%80%D0%B5% D1%81%D1%81-%D1%86%D0%B5%D0%BD%D1%82%D1%80/10123> (last accessed 21 February 2018).

Mel'nikova, Irina (2010), 'Uroki na zavtra. Kto vytashchit rossiiskie vuzy iz demograficheskoi yami', *Itogi*, 10 May.

Nikitenko, E. V. and E. O. Leont'eva (2015), 'Inostrannye studenty kak potentsial'nyi resurs rossiiskikh universitetov: est' li shans u dal'nevostochnykh vuzov?', *Vestnik TOGU* 37 (2), pp. 229–38.

Nikonov, Vyacheslav (2016), 'Nikonov: akkreditatsii lishaiutsia lish te vuzy, kotorye torguiut diplomami', *RIA Novosti*, 28 March.

Pugach, Viktoriya Fedorovna (2012), 'Mobile students in Russia's higher education', *Russian Education and Society* 54 (4), pp. 32–46.

Pushkin Institute's Programme (n.d.), *Programma prodvizheniia russkogo iazyka i obrazovaniia na russkom iazyke*, <http://www.pushkin.institute/programma/> (last accessed 7 November 2018).

Rossotrudnichestvo (2017a), *Predstavitel'stvo Rossotrudnichstva v Kitae prinialo uchastie v rabote krupneishei mezhdunarodnoi vystavki v Kitae China Edu*, 23 October, <http://rs.gov.ru/ru/news/18953?category_id=4> (last accessed 9 November 2018).

Rossotrudnichestvo (2017b), *Plan deiatel'nosti Rossotrudnichestva na 2017 god*, <http://rs.gov.ru/uploads/document/file/2071/План%202017.docx> (last accessed 7 November 2018).

Russian Language Programme (n.d.), *Federal"naia tselevaia programma 'Russkii iazyk' na 2016–2020 gody*, <https://минобрнауки.рф/%D0%BF%D1%80%D0%BE% D0%B5%D0%BA%D1%82%D1%8B/%D1%84%D1%86%D0%BF-%D1% 80%D1%83%D1%81%D1%81%D0%BA%D0%B8%D0%B9-%D1%8F%D0% B7%D1%8B%D0%BA> (last accessed 7 November 2018).

Russia.study (n.d.), *Ofitsial'nyi sait dlia otbora inostrannykh grazhdan na obuchenie v Rossii*, <https://russia.study/ru> (last accessed 7 November 2018).

Study in Russia (n.d.), *Sait Ministerstva Nauki i vysshego obrazovaniia Rossiiskoi Federatsii*, <http://www.studyinrussia.ru> (last accessed 7 November 2018).

CHAPTER 8

Stable or Variable Russian? Standardisation versus Pluricentrism

Ekaterina Protassova and Maria Yelenevskaya

INTRODUCTION

This chapter traces current trends in the development of the Russian language that testify to the intensification of centrifugal patterns. Since the emergence and evolution of language varieties is a dynamic process closely related to political and social changes, it is important to document different stages in the shaping of non-dominant language varieties. Relying on the theory of language pluricentricity, as developed by Clyne (1992), Clyne and Kipp (1999), Kachru (1992), Muhr (2012, 2013, 2015, 2016), Schneider (2018) and Schneider and Barron (2008), we look into the pluricentric features of the Russian language in the 'near' and 'far abroad'. In particular, we are interested in four interrelated issues:

- the legal status of Russian in the metropolis and in countries with sizeable Russian-speaking groups
- the attitude to multilingualism in societies where Russian speakers reside and its influence on the identity of individuals
- the distance between the dominant and Russian culture in the diasporic situation
- the experience of plurilingualism and the growing role of Russian as a lingua franca in diasporic groups.

Material for this chapter is drawn from the authors' long-term observation of Russian-speaking communities outside Russia. These observations are documented in our ethnographic diaries, photo archives, recorded interviews and written documents. We also keep track of the changes occurring in the Russian language in the diaspora by reading conventional and electronic media and online discussion forums. In addition, we analysed surveys conducted in different countries to reveal contexts in which the Russian language is used by respondents and their attitude to its maintenance.

In using these various sources, we seek to show that despite differences in the sociolinguistic situation in host countries, many of the changes Russian is undergoing in the diaspora are similar and allow for cross-country comparisons. Moreover, the rationale behind the study of these changes is the continued rejection of pluricentricity by speakers of the dominant variety, including educated elites, who are inclined to see deviations from what they consider the undisputable norm as contaminations (see Muhr 2012: 26–8, 33 on the monocentric and mono-normative view of the language).

WHAT IS 'NORMAL' IN THE RUSSIAN LANGUAGE?

A historical perspective on the norm of Russian takes us into the nineteenth century when the grammar of the contemporary language came to be taught at school. However, the actual imposition of the Russian norm took place later, when school textbooks were standardised under Soviet rule. The heterogeneity of the linguistic situation then was high and difficult to quantify (Restaneo 2017). In fact, the uniformity of the education system required that instructors were to teach the same material on the same day in all the regions of the huge country irrespective of the climate, local history, or contact languages and cultures. This was the situation with Russian taught as the first language. Speakers of other languages of the Russian Federation, for example Tatar, Chuvash and Nenets, and others learning Russian as a second language had to adhere to other standards and used different textbooks, which were equally uniform for each language community. Those who learned it in the national republics of the Soviet Union, that is, outside the Russian Federation, had to comply with still another standard. Moreover, the dialects spoken in Russia still differ from the so-called norm even more than regiolects that are part of everyday spoken language (e.g. Pozharitskaia 2005; Vaahtera 2009).

After the collapse of the Soviet Union, varieties of Russian in the CIS countries partly deviated from mainstream Russian and partly fossilised (Viaut and Moskvitcheva 2014). Mustajoki (2016) summarises the development of the standardisation of Russian, suggesting that the norm has never been uniform. As a matter of fact, the annual educational event 'Total Dictation' (*total'nyj diktant*), a Russian literacy test organised in Russian-speaking communities all around the world and aimed at promoting Russian literacy, proves that adherence to the norm is elusive. Yet there is a Department of Russian Linguistic Standards at the Vinogradov Russian Language Institute of the Russian Academy of Sciences in Moscow. Its head, Alexey Shmelev, claims that boosting the prestige of the Russian language and culture, as well as careful observation of the norm in the nation, aims to secure the high quality of the Russian language wherever it is used (Serov 2012).

The Federal Law of the Russian Federation No. 53, On the State Language of the Russian Federation, published on 7 June 2005, states that Russian must be used on all official occasions, for example when geographical names or road signs are written. In formal settings and in the national, regional and municipal media, only normative language can be accepted, and the norms are defined by the government; foreign words may only be used when no widely known current equivalent exists in the Russian language. When other languages of the country or foreign languages are used on the same occasion, texts must be identical in content and technical appearance to the text in Russian. These regulations do not affect trademarks, firm logos, or products designed for teaching languages.

This is a setback, reversing the linguistic tolerance of an earlier Law of the Russian Federation, No. 1807-I, About the Languages of the Peoples of the Russian Federation. Published on 25 October 1991, it states that languages are national property defended by the state. This concerned only the public sphere of language use. All languages of the RF were stated to be equal; all peoples and individuals could maintain and comprehensively develop their mother tongues, freely choose and use the language of communication, education and creative activities independently of their origins, social and property status, racial and national identity, gender, education, religion, or place of residence. National and regional media could use Russian or other languages; film production could be translated into other languages according to the interests of the population. The use of different languages was to follow similar principles in various sectors of the economy, like industry, communications and transport.

Russian government authorities monitor the linguistic situation in the nation (Artjomenko 2014; Bitkeeva and Mikhalchenko 2014; Bitkeeva 2015). State control, an increase in immigration to Russia, and the importance ascribed to relations with the Russophone diaspora encouraged researchers to analyse varieties of the Russian language as manifested in the speech of members of the returning diaspora, dubbed in Russian formal discourse 'compatriots' (see Chapters 1 and 9 in this volume). The research question common to many of these projects is whether these can be considered natives speakers of Russian. Notably, this term is not defined in the Language Law of 2005. The Federal Law No. 71-FZ, published on 20 April 2014, introduced several amendments facilitating the procedure of receiving Russian citizenship. Commonly referred to as Law on Native Speakers of the Russian Language (the official name of this legal act is On the Citizenship of the Russian Federation), it reduces the waiting time for native speakers of Russian from eight years to just one. In order to be considered a native speaker of Russian, a person has to be proficient in the language and use Russian on an everyday basis in the family and in cultural spheres; it is also required that this person or his or her direct ancestors permanently live or lived in the Russian Federation or in the territory which belonged to the Russian Empire or the USSR, and within the borders of the Russian Federation (Federal'nyi zakon 2014). Local committees are to evaluate the language proficiency of such candidates. Notably, the law does not specify whether there should be linguists among the experts assessing the interviewees. Anna Shevtsova (2017) interviewed more than 3,000 foreign citizens who claimed to be Russian speakers eligible for Russian citizenship on the basis of the requirements stipulated by the law. She comes to the conclusion that, in reality, full Russian proficiency is difficult to attain by applicants. Moreover, the term itself defies a clear and comprehensive definition.

While the Language Law adopted in 2005 stipulated the hegemony of Russian as the state language, it did not deal with the plurilinguistic situation in the country. The Internet resource openedu.ru offered a course 'Russian as the State Language of the Russian Federation', developed at the St Petersburg State University, but this is no longer available in 2021. This online course discussed the phenomenon of the state language from theoretical, historical and comparative perspectives. It targeted a wide audience, including civil servants, managers, students of different faculties and everybody interested in the state language policy. The syllabus dealt with the concept of norm and its complexity, but overlooked the issues related to non-dominant varieties and their norms.

As President Putin claimed in 2015,

> the preservation and development of the Russian language and the languages of all Russia's ethnic groups and nationalities[1] are of vital importance for ensuring harmony in interethnic relations and civic unity and for strengthening Russia's national sovereignty and integrity. [. . .] Russian is the country's state language, the language of interethnic communication. More than ninety-six per cent of our citizens speak Russian. It was the Russian language along with Russian culture that formed Russia as a single multi-ethnic civilisation,[2] for centuries maintaining intergenerational ties,

the continuity and mutual enrichment of various ethnic cultures. The ability to freely and properly use the Russian language opened up greater opportunities to representatives of all nationalities in terms of using their full potential, receiving education and achieving professional success. The state has to constantly improve the quality of the Russian language teaching of our children regardless of where they live or what type of school they attend. (Kremlin 2015)[3]

Teaching a pluricentric language to different audiences is a challenge which has been long experienced by teachers of English (Li 2017). The realities of the acquisition process differ depending on the context. In the past, second language acquisition targeted native-speaker proficiency and was oriented to monolingualism, ignoring the fact that many learners are bi- or multilingual and in their everyday activities they may need to use a non-dominant variety (Bolton 2018; Larsen-Freeman 2018). This monolingual bias is gradually being reconsidered. Experts recommend that educators should familiarise themselves with students' linguistic biographies, that is, their family background, contexts of encounters with the language being learned and other languages used on a day-to-day basis, and explore their linguistic attitudes. Educators should also take into account the type of community where the students live. Teachers should note and analyse cultural discrepancies that may divide communities as well as possible cultural and linguistic conflicts. These should be acknowledged in the curriculum and approached in actual teaching with sensitivity. Even if a student is brought up in a different culture, his or her educator should find out what sort of circumstances have shaped his or her linguistic identity. It is important to know how the student's proficiency in Russian differs from that in other languages. It is important to know how students choose different languages in different domains, and in which contexts the use of different language varieties may be the cause of misunderstandings and communicative failures.

Educators should therefore reflect on the roles of non-native and native language teachers. An instructor teaching his or her native language has the advantage of serving as a linguistic role model for his or her students but at the same time has to be sensitive to the cultural difference of the students, which may lead to breakdowns in communication. On the other hand, a non-native teacher, aware of his or her students' difficulties caused by interference with the students' mother tongue or dominant variety, may be proactive in helping students avoid many a language-learning pitfall. Nowhere does the learner's identity emerge as saliently as in their views on the language and the significance of their culture (Berry and Candi 2013). Aref'ev and Osipov (2018) look at the role of teachers of Russian in the contemporary world. They find that the number of Russian speakers, as well as the number of students interested in learning Russian, is in decline, which they perceive as dangerous for the 'destiny'[4] of Russian as a global language. Moreover, they find that the textbooks used to teach Russian as a heritage or foreign language do not meet present-day requirements and do not incorporate state-of-the-art methods, which further complicates the teachers' mission. They argue that the state should support developers of teaching materials and teachers, because if they fail, the role of Russian as the world language may further decline.

All the pluricentric varieties of Russian evolve their own lexis and idioms reflecting local realities, be they ethnic, administrative, religious, traditional, folkloric or something else. Localisms are routinely used in discourse in both informal and formal settings. Over vast territories, people speak oral varieties of Russian which differ from the centralised 'codified literal norm', as it is called. They barely write anything in Russian, and when they do, their written language reflects their oral habits. It is hard to find two individuals who mix Russian with other languages in the same way, and the frequency of the use of localisms to a large extent depends on the purpose of communication. Fieldwork gives ample evidence that laypeople often fail to note in what ways their speech deviates from the standard (Aboh 2015) and have trouble finding standard synonyms for regionalisms.

Many languages have evolved from dialects after countries' borders were redefined. The countries of the former Yugoslavia are a case in point. The situation with the Russian language is different. When symbolic borders between Soviet republics were transformed into national borders, Russian turned into the language of the 'other'. Essentially, it remained the same and there is no pressure within new states to change it. Nevertheless, it is changing, adapting to new realities. Studies by Külmoja (2002, 2016), Mustajoki and Protassova (2004), Mustajoki et al. (2010), Majorov (2013), Ryazanova-Clarke (2014), Yelenevskaya and Ovchinnikova (2015), Yelenevskaya and Protassova (2015), Baranova and Fedorova (2017), Muth (2017), Fedorova and Baranova (2018) and Mustajoki et al. (2019) demonstrate how the Russian language varies inside and outside Russia.

RUSSIAN IN THE DIASPORA

According to the Russian Academy of Sciences, 20,000 scholars left Russia in 2013, and by 2016 this number had more than doubled, reaching 44,000. Since 1990, the number of researchers in Russia has decreased by a factor of 2.7. Since 2000, the personnel involved in research has been shrinking annually by 1.3%, while in Europe and the USA there has been a 2–3% increase. During the same period, there has been a steady increase of 7–10% in the number of researchers in Brazil, China and South Korea. An article analysing this worrisome phenomenon quotes Russia's vice-premier, Dmitriy Rogozin, who refers to the brain drain as Russia's weakest point, since the country has invested generously in educating young talents and cannot afford to lose its intellectual elite. According to Rogozin, the best young people have left the country because they have not been given opportunities to realise ideas and discoveries born in their creative minds (Zvezdina 2018). It is the brain drain in science and technology that concerns Russian policymakers most. The emigration of social scientists and scholars in humanities is seldom discussed; yet it is researchers in these fields who have explored the new Russian-speaking diasporas, the maintenance of the Russian language and culture and the evolution of diasporic identities (Yelenevskaya and Fialkova 2009).

Puffer et al. (2018) claim that in Silicon Valley, well-educated, highly skilled and innovative Russian speakers make valuable contributions in various technological domains such as software development, social media, biotechnologies, medicine and others, yet remain virtually unknown. All of them have internalised the attitudes to knowledge and have absorbed the respect for science and research that ruled in the Soviet educational institutions – the very attitudes that shaped them professionally. Despite frequent incompatibility of requirements and skills (Remennick 2007), the fittest among émigré researchers and professionals have managed to compete in academia and high-tech industries and have found their niche in American society. For them, the post-Soviet developments destroyed many of the most important achievements of the Soviet period, and among them is the country's excellent educational system. On the one hand, these professionals have adjusted to the US work style; on the other hand, they are affected by Russian culture and continue to speak Russian at home, although they come from various places in the former Soviet Union (FSU).

Intellectuals are thus a growing group within the Russian diaspora. They pursue transnational lifestyles, maintaining professional ties and friendships with co-ethnics residing in different countries. Even those families that do not intend to return to their homeland see Russian-language maintenance by their children as a high-priority issue and turn to complementary educational institutions created by immigrants of the 1990s. Those who are located in Silicon Valley and near various American universities have accumulated valuable experience in teaching heritage speakers. Our visits to kindergartens and afternoon schools, and informal interviews, allow us to conclude that teachers and parents still share attitudes to education that evolved among the Russian intelligentsia. They are convinced that good teaching is not necessarily innovative; that what matters is that instructors are broadly educated, have expert knowledge of their subject and are dedicated to their profession. Moreover, they should be able to radiate authority but also love children (Kolesnikova 2012). More recently, a new generation of educators in the diaspora has begun to embrace different approaches. They view academic knowledge combined with creativity as the cornerstone of a good upbringing.[5] All lessons are taught by academics and technologists, experts in their field who did not study to be teachers but are able to transfer enthusiasm for their field to their pupils.

In the post-Soviet period, the geographical space in which Russian is spoken is shrinking. Mechkovskaia (2019) remarks that geographic and demographic factors in the CIS and Baltic countries testify to the deterioration of the situation for native speakers of Russian. Many Russian speakers are leaving the Caucasus and Central Asia for Russia, Ukraine, Belarus and other countries. The legal status of the Russian language has deteriorated across the territories of CIS. With the exception of Belarus and Eastern Ukraine, there has been a decline in the use of Russian in the mass media and educational programmes. In the 1990s, Russian was associated with the socialist past which newly formed independent states were eager to shed, allegedly returning to their traditional way of life before it was interrupted by the revolutions of 1917 or the onset of Russification. Moreover, across the post-Soviet space, as well as in other countries of the diaspora, the recent developments in Russia's foreign policy have adversely affected the number of new learners. What is more, in most CIS countries Russian has to compete with the advance of English, and in some areas with Chinese.

Outside the former Soviet space, Russian has received a new boost in Bulgaria (Ivanova 2018) and Greece (Kritsevskagia and Yanova 2019), where the descendants of the first wave of the White Emigration and the mixed families of the Soviet time encounter newcomers of the post-Soviet period. For those groups, the common language serves as a bridge for business and cultural interaction. In Slovenia, Russian is becoming more popular every year. It is taught in state schools, gymnasiums and universities and in private institutions. There is a steady increase in the number of Russian speakers settling in Cyprus, Montenegro and the Czech Republic. While after the demise of the Soviet Union the prestige of Russian-language teachers in the countries of the former Soviet bloc was as low as ever, and many had to retrain, today the need for people in service industries capable of working with Russian clients has created a new demand for teachers. Moreover, course requirements are markedly different from those that guided teaching in Soviet times. Demands for proficiency in the language of ideology have given way to demands for business Russian, which requires different language skills. This and a new interest in language contacts and intercultural communication made it necessary to launch scholarly periodicals dedicated to Russian studies, such as *Russkij kak inoslavjanskij, Sovremennoe izuchenie russkogo jazyka i russkoj kul'tury v inoslavjanskom okruzhenii*, published in Belgrade, Serbia, and *Bolgarskaja rusistika* in Sofia, Bulgaria.

In what follows, we give a more detailed description of the sociolinguistic situation in some of the countries of the 'near' and 'far abroad' where sizeable communities of Russian speakers reside and where regional varieties of Russian have developed and keep evolving.

Kazakhstan

The language situation and policy towards the Russian language in Kazakhstan is a model case of Russian as a pluricentric language. It has special functions, it is widely studied, and it has its own dictionary and textbooks that include specimens of the Russian language as it is used in Kazakhstan today (Smagulova 2008; Suleimenova 2013; Alisharieva et al. 2017). The speakers of Russian are mostly ethnic Kazakhs, and the world depicted by the language is the Kazakh world. According to Zinaida Sabitova and Akbota Alisharieva (2015), the most noticeable impact of the Kazakh language and culture on Russian is observed in the sociocultural, socio-political and household spheres as well as in the areas of proper names. The examples they offer include *akim* 'head of the local administration'; *zhuz* 'tribe'; *kamzol* 'woman's dress' – in the metropolis, the word is used for a male garment worn in former times; and *Ozkemen* 'Ust-Kamenogorsk' (Sabitova and Alisharieva 2015: 215).

Courses in Russian as a foreign language target the regional variety (incorporating words denoting typical Kazakhstani dishes, traditions and festivities, as well as politeness forms etc.), which is an implicit form of codification. The interrelations of the languages are tight in both directions. With the growing influence of the Kazakh language and relative distance from Russia, the language sometimes seems fossilised with some remnants from the Soviet era which are no longer used in the metropolis. The English influence usually comes through Russian as well, and most activities on social media occur in Russian while Kazakh dominates in the official and religious spheres. Younger generations increasingly speak Kazakh. The recent decision of ex-president Nazarbaev to introduce the Latin alphabet instead of Cyrillic reflects his intention to separate Kazakhstan from the Cyrillic-using world. However, Russian, rather than Kazakh, is used as a lingua franca in communication with other ethnic groups residing in Kazakhstan, for example Ukrainians, Uzbeks, Tatars and others. Moreover, the Kazakh diaspora, which is growing in Russia and abroad, also tends to use Russian for interethnic communication.

Estonia

In Estonia, many languages are used and heard without being identified as a factor influencing the intercultural reality of the eastern part of the country, which remains predominantly Russian-speaking. In our view, the goal of ensuring that all citizens of Europe are truly plurilingual can be attained by supporting their previous and current daily experiences of multilingualism. The research into Russian in Estonia tries to reflect upon old and recent mutual influences of the languages (Kostandi 2016, 2017; Verschik 2016, 2017).

The sociolinguistic change that has occurred in this part of Estonia since the disintegration of the USSR is evident to participants in the process and sharpens their language awareness. On the website journalist.delfi.ee, Internet users discuss 'Estonisms' (the word coined to denote Estonian borrowings in Russian as it is spoken in Estonia), and find that some speakers frequently use *kjul'movato*, derived from Estonian *külm* 'cold' with the addition of the Russian suffix '-то' (as in *plohovato*, *glupovato*), which is the counterpart of the native *holodnovato* 'coolish'. Discussants also reflect on the use of *koma* instead of *zapjataja* 'comma', *kaksikud* instead of *bliznecy* 'twins' and *lapselaps* instead of *vnuk, vnuchka* 'grandchild' because they sound 'interesting' (Ia zhurnalist 2018). Russian speakers also use Estonian *selge* when things are clear to them. For their part, Estonians have borrowed Russian curses and often end their telephone conversation with the Russian *davaj* – often replacing *poka* 'bye-bye' in informal conversations. The initial consonant is repeatedly changed davaj→*tafaaaj*, 'Estonifying' its pronunciation. Notably, ethnic mannerisms in pronunciation are then borrowed back into Russian.

One participant in the discussion suggests that *bussijaam* replaces *avtobusnaja ostanovka* 'bus stop' because it is shorter; another objects that they could say *avtovokzal* 'bus station'; still another discussant points out the difference of the terms and phenomena behind them: like *vokzal, jaam* is not just a stop but a station. Other popular borrowings from Estonian are words for 'licence, inhabitant, education (training), certificate'. Estonian words are regularly written under the influence of the Russian accent.

The popular joking phrase *Palju maksa banka vaksa* ('How much does a jar of blacking cost?') is a hotchpotch of Estonian and Russian words. Some Russian speakers resent overwhelming Estonification, which does not even leave their own first names intact, doubling the vowels: *Leena, Leera, Veera, Niina*. Moreover, feminine endings of their family names are dropped so that *Guseva* and *Tomina* turn into masculine *Gusev* and *Tomin*, which is an adjustment to the mainstream naming tradition imposed on the Russians in many countries.

Estonisms widely use diminutive, endearing and augmentative suffixes, turning *kaubamaja* 'shopping centre' into *kaubushka* and *leib* 'bread' into *leibushek*, which easily catches on due to its phonetic similarity with the Russian diminutive *khlebushek*. *Sybralishche* is an augmentative from *sõber* 'friend' and is modelled after its Russian counterpart *druzhishche*. Some of the foreign words well integrated into Russian are modified in adjusting to the forms used in Estonian. A case in point is 'identity', which is *identichnost'* in metropolitan Russian but *identitet* in Estonian (the same change we witness in Finnish Russian, German Russian, etc.). Likewise, *inventura* replaces *inventarizacija* 'inventory'. *Rabarbar* is used for 'rhubarb' instead of *reven'*. Some of the transformations are motivated by language economy, for example the noun phrase *byt'/javljat'sja kandidatom* 'be a candidate' is replaced by the verb *kandidirovat'*. In some cases, Estonisms deviate semantically from the native Estonian words: *palk* 'payment' has turned into *pal'ka* and is used instead of *zarplata* 'salary'. *Maksanut'* for 'pay, bribe' has a Russian suffix and negative connotations, while the Estonian source verb is neutral. The same word with the same morphological and semantic transformations is borrowed in St Petersburg Russian but from Finnish. Borrowings are seldom equivalent to the source words: they either narrow the meaning or shift it. Sometimes they obtain value-laden connotations absent in the source.

Discussants propose using (Russian) *Gosudarstvennoe Sobranie* for (Estonian) *Riigikogu*, although it is used in this form in the metropolitan Russian. In university students' slang, 'faculty' is not *fakul'tet* but *teduskond*. Code-mixing is an inseparable part of communication. The phrase *poluchit' õppelaen* combines Russian 'to get' with Estonian 'student loan'; *kupit' verivorstid* mixes Russian 'to buy' with Estonian 'blood sausage'; *mne nado zaplatit' riigilõiv v maksuamet* brings together Russian 'I have to pay' and Estonian 'taxes', Russian 'in' and Estonian 'the tax board', although the official name of the tax authority is *Maksu- ja tolliamet* 'Tax and Customs Board'. All these examples illustrate that bilinguals routinely use intrasentential code-mixing, and words from the contact languages are integrated into Russian speech with the help of native affixes. Thus, some of the Estonian nouns and adjectives are Russified and declined, for example Estonian *säästukaart* 'bonus card' turns into *säästukarta* (the Russian for 'card' is *karta*). When Russified, Estonian words are not recognised by Estonians – a well-known phenomenon when non-conventional pronunciation of a familiar word makes it opaque for listeners.

Semantic asymmetry between Russian and Estonian words also has a role in code-mixing and accounts for the disappearance of some native Russian words in everyday speech. The verb *myt'* 'wash' is used in Russian for washing dishes, floors and different objects, while *stirat'* is used for washing clothes and various textiles. In Estonian, only one word is used for both, so Russian speakers in Estonia use *myt'* in both cases.

Despite their own routine code-mixing, some of the Russian speakers in Estonia reveal puristic attitudes to language where borrowings from English are concerned. The adjective *kvalitetnyj* annoys them in Russian and in Estonian speech because it replaces Russian *kachestvennyj* and Estonian *hea*. Similarly, *perfektnyj* is ousting *sovershennyj* 'perfect', *korregirovat'* is used instead of the long-adopted loan word *korrektirovat'* 'to correct', and *intress* sounds like contamination. The capital of the country, Tallinn, is written with the double 'n' at the end, whereas in metropolitan Russian it is written with one. The euro cent is pronounced *sent* as in Estonian, not *tsent* as in Russian.

Russian speakers do not want to feel like second-class citizens in Estonia, and we see reflection of this sentiment in the coinage *estonozemel'cy* 'those on Estonian ground', which underscores that not all inhabitants are ethnic Estonians. Participants in the Internet discussions are sensitive to the ambivalence of their own ethnolinguistic situation. They share humiliating experiences related to their accent in Russian and lexical differences in their speech. When travelling to Russia, they are referred to as *estoshki* (a pejorative ethnonym). When they attend sport events, they are sometimes asked who they are rooting for. As in other bilingual communities, participants in Russian–Estonian language discussions sometimes mix scripts and sometimes transcribe the Estonian accent in Russian phrases. Some display imperialistic linguistic attitudes when they express admiration of the wealth of semantic and stylistic nuances in the 'Great Russian language' and its superiority over Estonian; others appreciate the beauty of Estonian. As is typical of folk linguists (Niedzielski and Preston 2000), Internet users reflect on the history of both languages, attempt etymological explanations and find numerous examples of mutual influence in both languages. They are aware that in other countries and in various regions of Russia, speakers of majority languages borrow from local languages, and they reflect on how it affects these languages. Some participants are bold enough to compete with Zamenhof's Esperanto and propose inventing a common international language.

Discussants believe that lexical borrowings are the 'upper layer of the language, representing realities of the local life'; however, the Estonian language also influences the deeper syntactic level: for example, multiple genitives in media headlines, or *Ja pozvonju tebe nazad* 'I'll call you back' instead of *Ja tebe perezvonju*, from Estonian *Ma helistan sulle tagasi*. Discussants mention calques: *Eto beret/voz'met vremja* 'It takes time' for *eto zanimaet vremja*; *dva goda obratno* 'two years ago' for *dva goda nazad*; *palochka pamjati* 'memory stick' for *fleshka*.

The issue of language use is a matter of concern among Russian speakers residing in different countries. Many sites devoted to Russian language maintenance abroad are transnational, and all of them recommend correcting wrong use of words, reading and writing extensively in Russian, and even coining new Russian terms to prevent penetration of foreign ones. At the same time, they often remark that Russian in the metropolis is deteriorating and English influence is overwhelming. Discussants also remark that one source of loan words is children's speech: coming home from day-care centres where they communicate with teachers and peers in the majority language, they code-switch all the time, and few parents resist it and instead echo the children, inserting Estonian words in their own speech. Bilingual families stimulate the mixed use of languages.

Research conducted within the framework of the 'Central Baltic Programme 2014–2020'[6] (PIM 2017) showed that most Russian-speaking Estonian parents of children aged 5–11 years were born in Estonia or migrated as children. Yet in their everyday life they continue using predominantly Russian. They assess their own and their children's linguistic skills as higher in Russian than in Estonian. They admit that their receptive skills (reading and listening comprehension) are better developed than their productive ones (speaking and writing). Only a small percentage of the respondents admitted having no command of Estonian. Some parents speak to the children's teachers and to their own friends in Estonian, and only about 18% speak Estonian only at work, while approximately 44% use both languages. They are reluctant to join in events held in Estonian and use information sources primarily in the language used at home. They are fairly satisfied with the language teaching but would like their children to be taught better Estonian. Most of the parents help their children with school homework in both languages and evaluate their help as more effective in Russian than in Estonian studies. About 70% have positive attitudes towards bilingual education (most of the children attend full or partial immersion groups or classes) and see the need to integrate into the majority.

Latvia

The website of the Latvian Bureau of Statistics does not provide any data about the ethnic composition of the country or use of languages (Central Statistical Bureau of Latvia 2021); however, according to Index Mundi, 25.2% of the total population of the country are ethnic Russians and 33.8% use Russian as a home language (Index Mundi 2020). Similar numbers are quoted by the website www.visitlatvia.lv.[7] Many of the Russian speakers want their children to maintain the Russian language and culture. Most of the young Latvian Russian speakers go to schools in which Russian is the main language of instruction, although some disciplines are taught bilingually and some only in Latvian.

Russian culture in the country is vibrant: mass media are diverse and active, and the Russian theatre in Riga regularly produces plays. In 2011, the festival 'Days of the Russian Culture' was launched and has since been held annually, turning into a popular event attracting large audiences (Malnach 2017). Yet, the milieu is not the same as in Russia, and the lexis reflects differences in local realities. Building, transportation, financial and trading firms and offices usually post advertising and information in two or three languages (Latvian, Russian and English), but the texts are often inaccurate and clumsy translations from Latvian. As a result, an imperfect linguistic landscape surrounds the young generation of Russian speakers. Given that the printed word enjoys authority, the linguistic landscape may create erroneous ideas about the language norm in heritage speakers. Aleksandrs Berdicevskis (2014) describes the deviations of the Russian language in Latvia from its counterpart in the metropolis. Ekaterina Protassova (2002, 2005) reveals the problems of Russian language maintenance and offers perspectives on multilingual education in Latvia.

According to Margarita Gavrilina (2018; here and further our examples come from her book), in formal settings the use of Latvian words is a prerequisite of effective communication with authorities: 'certificate, application, reference, head of department, head of a police department, kindergarten', as well as a multitude of banking and administrative terms. When a Latvian word sounds similar to its Russian equivalent, like Latvian *agentura* and Russian *agentstvo* 'agency', it is introduced in the function of the Latvian word, although the Russian *agentura* means 'undercover agents of police or secret service'. It is common to say *pojdem postradaem* 'let's go suffer/work'. This double entendre has a comic effect stemming from a phonetic similarity and semantic differences: Russian *stradat'* is to suffer while Latvian *stradāt* is to work – an instance of the inter-language word play enjoyed by every multilingual speech community. In Russian, some words acquire Latvian pronunciation features, for example *rehabilitacija* instead of *reabilitacija*, and *saiema* instead of *seim* 'parliament'. Colloquialisms with Latvian insertions are a common feature of speech: *O, eto mne daudz* 'Oh, it's too much for me'; *Nu i cik maksa?* 'How much does it cost?'; *poehat' na lauki* 'to go to the countryside'. Lots of expressions in everyday use are calqued from Latvian: *mne golova bolit* (dative instead of possessive) 'I have a headache'; *pjat' let obratno (pjat' let nazad)* 'five years ago'. Russian speakers sometimes confuse prefixes; for example, they say *vybrat' rebjonka iz detskogo sada* (instead of *zabrat'*) 'fetch the child from the day-care centre'.

Gavrilina (2018) claims that Latvian and Russian linguistic norms are superposed in bilingual proficiency and their verbal production deviates from the norms in both languages, whereas the Russian-language teachers demonstrate a monolingual bias and still want to obtain the 'old' Soviet norm. They do not always collaborate with the Latvian-language teachers. As a result, they ignore that one of the main aims of language learners today is to be functionally bilingual rather than to attain balanced bilingualism. Moreover, they disregard that competence in the second language does not duplicate the first language but complements it (Bolton 2018). Since the students do not have enough input in the Russian language, their vocabulary lacks academic terms, expressions of emotions and words denoting phenomena of Russian culture in different domains. If students come across an unfamiliar Russian word, they tend to stress the first syllable, which is typical of Latvian. When spelling international words, they omit double consonants if there is only one in Latvian, as in класс – *klase*, профессор – *profesors*. In Latvian, some verbs have negation as a part of the lexeme as in *negribu*; this causes pupils to join the Russian particle *ne* to a verb, which is not the norm in Russian. Russian composite adjectives such as *tjomno-sinij* 'dark blue' are conventionally hyphenated while they are separate words in Latvian: *tumši zils*. These differences in the rules make bilinguals' literacy unstable. Speakers frequently violate Russian politeness norms in favour of the Latvian ones. In writing, they use punctuation in accordance with the Latvian rules, for example they put a dot after the date before the name of a month. Furthermore, Gavrilina (2018) observes changes in the gender of nouns if they differ in the two languages.

Russian-speaking Latvian parents, it appears from respondents in the 'Central Baltic Programme 2014–2020' (PIM 2017), were mostly born in Latvia or moved there as little children. They use Russian in most situations and evaluate their oral skills rather highly, while written skills are assessed as middle to high. They evaluate their children's Russian proficiency as lower than their own. In family communication, Russian dominates; only a small percentage use some Latvian at home. Most of the children attend Russian-language or bilingual educational institutions. Children have more Latvian-speaking friends than their parents. Mass media enter homes in both languages. Respondents claim that they are attracted to social and cultural events organised in both languages, and that when they invite friends round, it does not matter which of the two languages they speak. Russian is perceived as the language of their community, identity, emotions and culture, while Latvian has a more pragmatic value. Parents are content with the Russian- and Latvian-language teaching but would prefer more hours of Russian in the curriculum. Parents assist their children in school homework. More than 50% of respondents approve of bilingual education while 17% are against it.

Finland

The situation regarding the Russian language in Finland is special in many respects. Russian has a long history and has gone through periods when its status was high but also very low. Unlike in most other countries with sizeable Russian-speaking groups, in Finland the state is actively involved in organising the life of the Russian-speaking community and funding its cultural and educational institutions (Baschmakoff and Leinonen 2001; Schenschin 2008; Viimaranta et al. 2017). According to Varjonen et al. (2017), by the end of 2017, 77,177 Russian speakers with different ethnic backgrounds lived in Finland (1.4% of the population). This does not include children born in bilingual families or those ethnic Finns who have the status of repatriates and who declared Finnish to be their mother tongue. There are diverse Russian cultural institutions: clubs, professional and amateur theatres, libraries, private radio and state-owned television studios, privately owned newspapers, literary magazines, Finland-based art exhibitions, literature for children and adults. There are day-care centres for young children, and at least six bilingual schools. Russian is also taught in Finnish schools as a foreign and as a home language. In the latter case, two hours per week of instruction starts in pre-school and continues through to the last grade, amounting to thirteen to fourteen years of study. At the end of the programme there is a state examination (Kettunen 2017).

Peculiarities of the Russian language in Finland (Protassova 2004, 2009) include borrowings, insertions, code-switching, adaptations and calques. We distinguish between the language of three groups: the historical minority, first-generation immigrants, and their children. Since immigration from Russia has been going on continuously since the early 1990s, the Russian language spoken by immigrants differs, depending on when they left the metropolis. Immigrants of the early 1990s have retained some Sovietisms in their speech but are also learning new colloquialisms and mannerisms from those who left Russia only recently. If immigration continues, 'fresh blood' will bring newer variants of the language. Common features distinguishing Russian in Finland include integration of the names of Finnish government institutions, administrative and cultural phenomena, as well as changes in word order and verb government. Speaking about the heritage Russian of the immigrants' children, it should be taken into account whether a specific speaker has studied Russian formally and for how long, whether he or she lives in an area of high concentration of co-ethnics, what languages his or her parents speak, how often he or she travels to Russia and to whom he or she speaks in Russian. For those in their teens, it matters whether they have had any training in translation, how many Russian-speaking friends they have, and so on. Some teenage bilinguals write naïve texts which are markedly different in terms of language use and forms of expression from essays written by their peers in Russia (Protassova 2008). Many bilinguals attain a high proficiency level in Russian, yet nobody is immune to specific mistakes and failures typical of heritage speakers. The errors are those caused by the difficulties of Russian grammar, which create problems for first-language speakers as well. In most cases these mistakes are aggravated by a weaker input. In addition, young speakers resort to transfers from the Finnish language to bridge gaps in their knowledge of Russian lexis and morphology. In such cases, children, and sometimes university students too, are engaged in guesswork, modelling Russian words after Finnish patterns.

The results of the 'Central Baltic Programme 2014–2020' (PIM 2017) for Finland show that in small and remote communities it is difficult to maintain Russian, whereas the capital and adjacent regions offer various services facilitating Russian language maintenance. Most of the respondents were born in Russia (76%), 12% came from Estonia, while only 3% were born in Finland. As in other participant countries, some Russian-speaking respondents were born in Ukraine, Belarus, the Baltic States or Central Asia. Yet almost all of them consider Russian to be their mother tongue; 66% of the partners of the respondents are also Russian speakers. Most of the respondents have lived in Finland since the 2000s (57%), about one-quarter (26%) immigrated in the 2010s, and 16% came in the 1990s. The level of education is generally high.

In their everyday communication, 78.2% use Russian. In 95% of cases, they use Russian when speaking to the children; but when speaking to their siblings, only 73% of the children use Russian, and 20% use Finnish and Russian. With their friends, 64.5% of the parents use Russian, and 30.8% two languages; among the children, the corresponding numbers are different: 50% use both languages, 30% use Finnish or Swedish, and 20% use Russian. Almost 90% use Finnish while speaking to their children's teachers. The language of the workplace is predominantly Finnish: 70% use it at work, about 22% use both Finnish and Russian, and 8% stick to Russian only. English is popular and is considered an asset. In terms of self-assessment, 92.6% consider their oral command of Russian to be excellent and 81% evaluate their written Russian as excellent.

Assessing their children's proficiency in Russian, only 60% consider their oral comprehension skills to be excellent. Another 60% of adults say that their oral comprehension of Finnish is good while their literacy skills are poorer. No less than 24% claim that their comprehension is excellent. About half of the participants rate their children's Finnish skills as poor, and only 20% evaluate their children's oral skills as excellent. The older the children, the more they outperform their parents born outside Finland in their Finnish proficiency. In the pre-school institutions and in primary schools, 70% of the children use the official languages, Finnish and/or Swedish, 28% use one of the official languages and Russian, and 2% use Russian only.

Entertainment, Internet-surfing and reading are done in different languages, in half of the cases in both Finnish and Russian, and in a third of the cases in Russian alone. The importance of Russian language maintenance is ascribed to better job opportunities for multilingual people; but at the same time, parents are convinced that Finnish is very important for their children's future. Russian culture has considerable value for the immigrants. Parents mostly help their children with homework in Russian but not in Finnish. Citizenship affects attitudes to language learning: those with dual citizenship value bilingualism more; 92% of the respondents are positive about bilingual education because of its cognitive importance. Parents are not very happy with the Russian-language teaching (one-third of the children do not study Russian formally at all) but they are quite satisfied with the Finnish-language teaching. Although the Finnish educational system is found attractive, some say they are nostalgic for the schools of their childhood.

Israel

Israel is a multilingual state. Despite the overwhelming hegemony of Hebrew, six languages are used institutionally and thirty-four in informal settings (Simons and Fennig 2018). Although Russian does not enjoy any officially recognised status, it has evolved into the third most spoken language of the country after Hebrew and Arabic and is spoken by 15% of the total population (9tv.co.il 2014). Moreover, as in other countries of the diaspora, it has become the lingua franca of émigrés from the countries of the former Soviet Union. Other speakers of Russian in Israel are guest workers, caregivers and builders. These are primarily from Moldova, which has an agreement with the Israeli government to grant its citizens work permits. Finally, there are Russophone Arabs and Druze, graduates of Soviet and post-Soviet universities and engineering schools.

Russian was integrated into the workings of state institutions in a slow and hesitant way, with the process lagging behind the adaptation of commercial enterprises, which quickly realised the benefits of serving thousands of new clients in their own language. In addition, many new immigrants of the 1990s, unable to find employment due to the saturation of the white-collar job market, started their own businesses in service industries catering to the needs of their co-ethnics. Many of these businesses rely on the use of language: conventional and electronic media, translation and legal services, pre-school and complementary education, and enterprises offering entertainment and leisure activities.

Widespread use of the Internet by government institutions and big service providers (banks, mobile communications companies, public transport services) has also contributed to an increase in the use of Russian in the public sphere. Most of the Internet sites of the ministries and municipalities have Russian-language sections (Yelenevskaya 2015; Yelenevskaya and Fialkova 2017).

The vitality of the Russian language in Israel is supported by several factors:

- There is a large number of speakers of different ages and different social groups. The small size of the country and high population density are favourable for communication and for the various activities of the immigrant community.
- Immigration from FSU countries is continuous. In 2014–16, more than 45,000 immigrated from Russia, Ukraine and Baltic countries (Khanin 2017).
- There is a multitude of mixed families and intergenerational households. Grandparents are actively involved in child-rearing and many are proponents of Russian language maintenance (Zbenovich 2016).
- Many Russian-speaking Israelis have dual citizenship and regularly travel to their native towns. Thanks to the abolition of visas with

Russia, Ukraine, Belorussia and Moldova, arranging these trips is also easy for Israelis who lack Russian citizenship.
- Russian-speaking Israelis have extensive transnational ties with friends and family, colleagues and business partners in the countries of the FSU, as well as in Canada, Germany, the US, and elsewhere. The language of transnational communication is Russian. Transnational ties have been mentioned as one of the more important contexts of Russian-language use by participants in the 'Verbal Association' project (Yelenevskaya and Ovchinnikova 2015) and as a motive for learning Russian by schoolchildren (Goriacheva 2017).

Despite numerous opportunities for speaking Russian, the question of whether members of the young generation need to maintain their heritage language frequently comes up in informal discussions and in the media. In April 2017, the Russian-language portal Newsru.co.il conducted a two-day online survey 'Russian Language in Israel', seeking to determine the level of Russian proficiency among the readers of the portal and their children. One of the questions invited 5,021 participants to choose their reasons for teaching their children Russian (more than one answer was possible). Here is the breakdown of the selected answers:

- an additional language cannot harm – 65%
- to facilitate communication with elderly family members – 29%
- to familiarise children with Russian culture – 27.5%
- to understand each other better – 24.5%
- to have children read the same books we used to read and are reading now – 19%
- there is no need to teach children living in Israel any Russian – 4%. (News.ru.co.il 2017)

These results may look very optimistic, but we have to take into account that the survey was conducted among readers of a Russian-language portal. Had it been conducted on a Hebrew-language site, the statistics may have been quite different.

Israelis, as speakers of different languages, are used to translanguaging, inserting words from Arabic and English, Yiddish and French into their speech. Russian speakers are no exception. The regiolect jokingly called *Ivrus* or *Hebrush* has incorporated a wide variety of words from Hebrew. As with loan words from other languages, the first to be inserted into speech denote objects, institutions and phenomena not found in Russia. New immigrants quickly learn such terms as *misrad a-pnim* 'Ministry of the Interior', *bituakh leumi* 'Institute of Social Security' and *lishkat avoda* 'labour exchange'. Notably, the last of these quickly turned into the diminutive and slightly pejorative *lishkatka*. Middle Eastern foods, such as *falafel*, *humus*, *tekhina* and *kube* have also become an integral part of the Russian–Israeli lexicon. Another group of words are names of occupations and professional terms. Job ads in Russian, which are an indispensable part of the linguistic landscape in many Israeli towns, are full of Russified Hebrew words, such as *shiputsnik* 'repair person', *ish kesher* 'liaison person', *metapelet* 'care worker', *mazkira* 'secretary', and many others. Together with borrowing work terminology, immigrants use Hebrew words denoting Jewish and Israeli holidays and various religious terms, mostly adapting them to familiar morphological patters by adding affixes, deriving new forms, and by adjusting pronunciation to the Russian phonetic system: *datishnik* (from *dati* 'a religious person'), *otmisaderit'* (from *lesader* 'make order'), *na nikayonakh* (declension and addition of plural to an uncountable noun) and others. There are also numerous cases of calques from Hebrew routinely used in informal and formal communication.

In the 'Russian Language in Israel' survey mentioned above, only 21% of the respondents said that their children born in Israel can read and write fluently in Russian. It can be hypothesised that with time, the number of heritage speakers unfamiliar with the norm accepted in the metropolis will increase and the Israeli version of the Russian language will continue its centrifugal development.

DISCUSSION AND CONCLUSION

The concept of pluricentric languages is closely related to the concepts of World Englishes, lingua franca, languages in contact (including pidgins and creoles), bilingualism, biculturalisim and hybrid/multiple identities. When we analyse diasporic communities, we should look into legislation in the migrants' home and host countries. We should take into account the distance between cultures, the attitudes of individual people and societies as a whole towards multilingualism. We should also consider whether each country under study has its own experience of plurilinguism and what its antecedents are.

Despite concerns about a decrease in the number of its speakers, Russian remains among the most widely used languages, as proven by the amount of material uploaded on the Internet, the number of sites where communication is conducted in Russian and the number of different software packages developed for it. Interactions in Russian occur all over the world between those who learned it as L1, L2, L3, and so on. For those who learned it as L2 or L3 and have a poor command of

English, Russian emerges as a better choice to be used as a lingua franca. For anyone who has ever lived in a Russian-speaking space, Russian is emotionally loaded with metaphors, associations and contexts.

In various historic periods – Ancient Rus', the Russian Empire, the USSR and the Eastern Bloc – the dissemination of Russian was triggered by wars; today it spreads thanks to soft power options. The motives that drive the spread of Russian language and culture may vary. They may be sincere or conceal a covert agenda. We should keep in mind that today, due to an increase in mobility, Russian, like many other languages, is spoken in more countries than ever, even in the absence of colonisation.

'World Russians' is not yet a widespread concept. Only recently have scholarly conferences in Russian studies started to probe this newly discovered diversity. And the motives are quite different from those behind the movement of World Englishes. The Russian authorities and members of the elite find it difficult to accept that whole language communities use the 'sacred' Russian in a non-standard form and, worse still, without permission. Nor does the use of unsanctioned forms lead them to suffer from an inferiority complex. In the way the authorities view language development and ecology, and in their perception of the speakers and their attitudes to language, centralisation tendencies remain as prevalent as in any sphere. Plurilingualism has a long history of debates behind it. A large variety of indigenous languages have developed pidgins in contact with Russian, and, unfortunately, they are only partially documented (Perekhval'skaya 2014). They were tolerated as an inevitable stage of learners' attempts to perfect their Russian, or as an exotic paradox on the way from illiteracy to full 'civilisation' in the Russian sense. In the Commonwealth of Independent States, the imperial and Soviet past has not been forgotten: local experts tend to say that they have managed to conserve 'pure' Russian without dialect influences and almost without anglicisms, which are a hallmark of Russian in the metropolis. In reality, however, they are more successful in preserving the Soviet approach to language and language use than Russia itself, and in teaching corroded Russian.

Localisation/regionalisation happens in any language community, helping people socialise in a specific time, in a specific workplace, and for interactions with specific groups. It shapes a variety of language under certain circumstances, such as climate, ethnicity, social, juridical and educational systems, and so on. Loan words stop being exoticisms when they form derivatives and are adapted to the rules of Russian grammar. Inside a country, the repertoire of localisation modes includes dialects; outside the country, under a different legislation system and under the influence of another dominant language, it inevitably triggers large-scale borrowing and calques. It is up to the local experts (politicians, linguists, activists) whether to declare officially that a new language variety has evolved and to create new textbooks, dictionaries, and so on, which reflect its specificity, or just to let it function and evolve (Schneider and Barron 2008; Trudgill 2011; Ayres-Bennett and Seijido 2013). Stabilisation of a new variety comes with new generations of speakers, along with identity shaping and changes in functions, and it involves pedagogical reforms. The sociolinguistics of globalisation has its say in this process, and the role of the Russian Federation and its cultural and economic influence in creating favourable conditions for letting new varieties flourish could be significant. Yet for the time being, its response to vibrant changes in the Russian language remains uncertain.

NOTES

1. Note that in modern Russian the term *natsional'nost'* means both nationality and ethnicity.
2. This term is widely used today in Russian political science, philosophy and anthropology, and also in the media (see Larina et al. 2017).
3. Translated from Russian by the authors, Ekaterina Protassova and Maria Yelenevskaya.
4. Although it may sound pathetic, the word 'destiny' is frequently used when the future of the Russian language and its status in the world are discussed.
5. See Russian Gymnasium at <https://www.russiangymnasium.com> (last accessed 15 April 2018).
6. The 'Central Baltic Programme 2014–2020' is a cross-border cooperation programme. It was launched to finance high-quality projects in Finland, Estonia, Latvia and Sweden and aims at collaborative solutions to common challenges. See <https://interreg.eu/programme/interreg-finland-estonia-latvia-sweden> (last accessed 18 September 2018).
7. <http://www.visitlatvia.lv/ru/jetnicheskij-sostav-naselenija-latvii> (last accessed 21 April 2018).

REFERENCES

9tv.co.il (2014), 'Russkii iazyk – tretii po raprostranennosti v Izraile', 9 February, <http://9tv.co.il/news/2014/02/09/168734.html> (last accessed 15 November 2017).
Aboh, Enoch O. (2015), *The Emergence of Hybrid Grammars*, Cambridge: Cambridge University Press.
Alisharieva, Akbota, Zhanar Ibrayeva and Ekaterina Protassova (2017), 'The Kazakhstani Russian: An outsider's perspective', *Ab Imperio* 4, pp. 231–63.
Aref'ev, Aleksandr L. and Gennadij V. Osipov (2018), *Sotsiologiia iazyka. Russkii iazyk. Sovremennoe sostoianie i tendentsii rasprostraneniia v mire*, 2nd edn, Moscow: Iurait.

Artjomenko, Olga I. (ed.) (2014), *Forum pedagogicheskogo masterstva*, Moscow: Institute of the National Problems of Education.

Ayres-Bennett, Wendy and Magali Seijido (eds) (2013), *Bon usage et variation sociolinguistique: perspectives diachroniques et traditions nationales*, Lyon: ENS.

Baranova, Vlada V. and Kapitolina S. Fedorova (2017), '(Ne)vidimost' i (vne)nakhodimost': Trudovye migranty i iazykovoi landshaft Sankt-Peterburga', *Gorodskie issledovaniia i praktiki* 2 (1), pp. 103–21.

Baschmakoff, Natalia and Marja Leinonen (2001), *Russian Life in Finland 1917–1939: A Local and Oral History*, Studia Slavica Finlandensia, Vol. 18, Helsinki: Institute for Russian and East European Studies.

Berdicevskis, Aleksandrs (2014), 'Predictors of pluricentricity: Lexical divergences between Latvian Russian and Russian Russian', in Lara Ryazanova-Clarke (ed.), *The Russian Language Outside the Nation*, Edinburgh: Edinburgh University Press, pp. 225–45.

Berry, Theodorea R. and Matthew R. Candi (2013), 'Cultural identity and education: A critical race perspective', *Educational Foundations* 27 (3–4), pp. 43–64.

Bitkeeva, Aisa N. (ed.) (2015), *Iazykovaia politika v kontekste sovremennykh iazykovykh protsessov*, Moscow: Azbukovnik.

Bitkeeva, Aisa N. and Vida Y. Mikhalchenko (2014), *Language Policy and Language Conflicts in Contemporary World*, Moscow: Institute of Linguistics of the Russian Academy of Sciences, Research Center on Ethnic and Language Relations.

Bolton, Kingsley (2018), 'World Englishes and second language acquisition', *World Englishes* 37, pp. 5–18.

Central Statistical Bureau of Latvia (2021), 'Search all themes', <https://www.csb.gov.lv/en/statistics/search?keyword=language&publication_date%5Bmin%5D=&publication_date%5Bmax%5D=> (last accessed 25 January 2021).

Clyne, Michael (ed.) (1992), *Pluricentric Languages: Differing Norms in Different Nations*, Berlin/New York: Mouton de Gruyter.

Clyne, Michael and Sandra Kipp (1999), *Pluricentric Languages in an Immigrant Context: Spanish, Arabic and Chinese*, New York: Mouton de Gruyter.

Federal'nyi zakon (2014), 'Federal'nyi zakon ot 20 aprelia 2014 g. N 71-FZ "O vnesenii izmenenii v Federal'nyi zakon 'O grazhdanstve Rossiiskoi Federatsii' i otdel'nye zakonodatel'nye akty Rossiiskoi Federatsii"', *Rossiiskaia Gazeta*, 23 April, <https://www.rg.ru/2014/04/23/grazhdanstvo-dok.html> (last accessed 20 April 2018).

Fedorova, Kapitolina S. and Vlada V. Baranova (2018), 'Moscow: Diversity in disguise', in Dick Smakman and Patrick Heinrich (eds), *Urban Sociolinguistics: The City as a Linguistic Process and Experience*, London: Routledge, pp. 220–36.

Gavrilina, Margarita (2018), *Izuchenie russkogo (rodnogo, pervogo) iazyka v shkolakh Latvii*, Riga: Mācību grāmata.

Goriacheva, Svetlana (2017) 'Zachem rebionku uchit' russkii iazyk esli on ne zhivet v Rossii', *Letopis'*, <http://ruskaljetopis.hr/info.phtml?c=9&id=47> (last accessed 20 January 2021).

Index Mundi (2020), 'Latvia demographics profile', <https://www.indexmundi.com/latvia/demographics_profile.html> (last accessed 20 January 2021).

Ivanova, Nelya (2018), 'Russkie i russkii iazyk v Bolgarii: iazykovaia sreda i dvuiazychnoe obrazovanie', in Ahti Nikunlassi and Ekaterina Protassova (eds), *Mnogoiazychie i sem'ia*, Berlin: Retorika, pp. 26–36.

Ia zhurnalist (2018), 'Obsudim: Kakie ėstomimy vas razdrazhaiut?', <http://journal

ist.delfi.ee/news/news/obsudim-kakie-estonizmy-vas-razdrazhayut?id=36016109& com=1&reg=0&no=0&s=1> (last accessed 30 April 2018).
Kachru, Braj B. (ed.) (1992), *The Other Tongue: English Across Cultures*, 2nd edn, Urbana, IL: University of Illinois Press.
Kettunen, Irma (2017), *Venäjän kielen opiskelu Suomessa*, Helsinki: Cultura-säätiö.
Khanin, Zeev (2017), 'Novaia alia iz SNG i Baltii: shtrikhi k portretu', <http://9tv. co.il/news/2017/02/03/238306.html> (last accessed 20 January 2021).
Kolesnikova, Elena M. (2012), 'Obraz professional'nogo uchitel'skogo soobshchestva v britanskikh i rossiiskikh SMI', *Vestnik Instituta sotsiologii* 6, pp. 253–77.
Kostandi, Elizaveta I. (2016), 'Metiazykovoi diskurs diaspory: invariant i varianty', *W poszukiwaniu tożsamości językowej*, Tom I. Gdansk: Wydawnictwo Uniwersytetu Gdańskiego, pp. 244–53.
Kostandi, Elizaveta I. (2017), 'Teksty bilingva: "svoe" i "chuzhoe"', *Acta Slavica Estonica* 7, pp. 78–88.
Kremlin (2015), 'Joint meeting of Council for Interethnic Relations and Council for the Russian Language', 19 May, <http://en.kremlin.ru/events/president/news/49491> (last accessed 20 January 2021).
Kritsevskagia, Eugenia and Elisaveta Yanova (2019), 'Rossiia-Gretsiia: krutye virazhi "dvoinoi" emigratsii', in Iulia Men'shikova and Ekaterina Protassova (eds), *Mnogoiazychie i obrazovanie*, Berlin: Retorika, pp. 28–43.
Külmoja, Irina P. (ed.) (2002), *Problemy jazyka diaspory*, Trudy po russkoi i slavianskoi filologii, Lingvistika, Novaia seriia 6, Tartu: Tartu Ülikooli Kirjastus.
Külmoja, Irina P. (ed.) (2016), *Svoe – chuzhoe v iazyke i rechi*, Acta Slavica Estonica VIII, Tartu: Tartu Ülikooli Kirjastus.
Larina, Tatiana, Arto Mustajoki and Ekaterina Protassova (2017), 'Dimensions of Russian culture and mind', in Arto Mustajoki and Katja Lehtisaari (eds), *Philosophical and Cultural Interpretations of Russian Modernisation*, New York: Routledge, pp. 7–19.
Larsen-Freeman, Diane (2018), 'Second language acquisition, WE, and language as a complex adaptive system (CAS)', *World Englishes* 37, pp. 80–92.
Li, Guofang (2017), 'Preparing culturally and linguistically competent teachers for English as an international language education', *TESOL Journal* 8 (2), pp. 250–76.
Maiorov, Aleksandr P. (ed.) (2013), *Regional'nye varianty natsiona'nogo iazyka*, Ulan-Ude: Ministerstvo obrazovaniia i nauki Respubliki Buriatiia.
Malnach, Aleksandr (2017), 'VII Dni Russkoi kul'tury v Latvii oznamenovalis' vypuskom marki v pamiat' I.N. Zavoloko', *Baltnews*, 23 May, <https://lv.baltnews. com/news/20170523/1019840067.html> (last accessed 25 January 2021).
Mechkovskaia, Nina B. (2019), 'Russkii iazyk v postsovetskoe vremia: chto sokrashchaet i chto rasshiriaet obshchenie po-russki?', in Ahti Nikunlassi and Ekaterina Protassova (eds), *Russian Language in the Multilingual World*, Helsinki: University of Helsinki, pp. 226–39.
Muhr, Rudolf (2012), 'Linguistic dominance and non-dominance in pluricentric languages: A typology', in Rudolf Muhr (ed.), *Non-Dominant Varieties of Pluricentric Languages: Getting the Picture. In Memory of Michael Clyne*, Frankfurt am Main: Peter Lang, pp. 23–48.
Muhr, Rudolf (2013), 'Codifying linguistic standards in non-dominant varieties of pluricentric languages adopting dominant or native norms?', in Rudolf Muhr, Carla Amorós Negre, Carmen Fernández Juncal, Klaus Zimmermann, Emilio Prieto and Natividad Hernández (eds), *Exploring Linguistic Standards in Non-Dominant Varieties of Pluricentric Languages*, Frankfurt am Main: Peter Lang, pp. 11–44.

Muhr, Rudolf (2015), 'Manufacturing linguistic dominance in pluricentric languages and beyond', in Rudolf Muhr and Dawn Marley (eds), *Pluricentric Languages: New Perspectives in Theory and Description*, Vienna: Peter Lang, pp. 13–54.

Muhr, Rudolf (2016), 'The state of the art of research on pluricentric languages: Where we were and where we are now', in Rudolf Muhr, Kelen E. Fonyuy, Zeinab Ibrahim and Corey Miller (eds), *Pluricentric Languages and Non-Dominant Varieties Worldwide, vol. 1: Pluricentric Languages Across Continents – Features and Usage*, Vienna: Peter Lang, pp. 13–37.

Mustajoki, Arto (2016), 'Challenges in the standardisation of contemporary Russian', in Ingrid Tieken-Boon van Ostade and Carol Percy (eds), *Prescription and Tradition in Language: Establishing Standards Across Time and Space*, Bristol: Multilingual Matters, pp. 288–302.

Mustajoki, Arto and Ekaterina Protassova (eds) (2004), *Russkoiazychnyi chelovek v inoiazychnom okruzhenii*, Helsinki: University of Helsinki.

Mustajoki, Arto, Ekaterina Protassova and Nikolai Vakhtin (2010), 'Russkie iazyki', in Arto Mustajoki, Ekaterina Protassova and Nikolai Vakhtin (eds), *Instrumentarium of Linguistics: Sociolinguistic Approaches to Non-Standard Russian*, Helsinki: University of Helsinki.

Mustajoki, Arto, Ekaterina Protassova and Maria Yelenevskaya (eds) (2019), *The Soft Power of the Russian Language: Pluricentricity, Politics and Policies*, London: Routledge.

Muth, Sebastian (ed.) (2017), *Commodification of Russian*, special issue of *Russian Journal of Linguistics* 21 (3), pp. 463–675.

News.ru.co.il (2017), 'Russkii iazyk v Izraile. Itogi oprosa NEWSru.co.il', 12 April, <http://newsru.co.il/israel/12apr2017/russian_opros_111.html> (last accessed 28 April 2018).

Niedzielski, Nancy A. and Dennis R. Preston (2000), *Folk Linguistics*, Trends in Linguistics: Studies and Monographs, vol. 122, Berlin: De Gruyter.

Perekhval'skaia, Elena V. (2014), *Issledovaniia po russkim pidzhinam*, Berlin: Directmedia.

PIM (2017), *Development of Parent Involvement Models for Bilingual Pre- and Primary School – PIM Project*, Central Baltic Interreg Project, University of Tartu Narva College, <https://www.narva.ut.ee/en/pim-project> (last accessed 20 January 2021).

Pozharitskaia, Sof'ja K. (2005), *Russkaia dialektologiia*, Moscow: Akademicheskii proekt.

Protassova, Ekaterina (2002), 'Latvian bilingual education: Towards a new approach', *Intercultural Education* 4, pp. 439–49.

Protassova, Ekaterina (2004), *Fennorossy: zhizn' i upotreblenie iayzka*, St Petersburg: Zlatoust.

Protassova, Ekaterina (2005), 'The situation of the Russian minorities in Latvia and Finland – a comparison', in Sture Ureland (ed.), *Integration of European Language Research*, Berlin: Logos, pp. 158–70.

Protassova, Ekaterina (2008), 'Teaching Russian as a heritage language in Finland', *Heritage Language Journal* 5 (2), pp. 127–52.

Protassova, Ekaterina (2009), 'Russian as a lesser used language in Finland', in, Bert Cornillie, José Lambert and Pierre Swiggers (eds), *Linguistic Identities, Language Shift and Language Policy in Europe*, Leuven: Peeters, pp. 167–84.

Puffer, Sheila M., Daniel J. McCarthy and Daniel M. Satinsky (2018), *Hammer and Silicon: The Soviet Diaspora in the US Innovation Economy – Immigration, Innovation, Institutions, Imprinting, and Identity*, Cambridge: Cambridge University Press.

Remennick, Larissa (2007), *Russian Jews on Three Continents: Identity, Integration and Conflict*, New Brunswick, NJ/London: Transaction.
Restaneo, Pietro (2017), 'Governing the word: Antonio Gramsci and Soviet linguistics on language policy', *Language History* 60 (2), pp. 95–111.
Ryazanova-Clarke, Lara (ed.) (2014), *The Russian Language Outside the Nation*, Edinburgh: Edinburgh University Press.
Sabitova, Z. and A. Alisharieva (2015), 'The Russian language in Kazakhstan: Status and functions', *Russian Journal of Communication* 7 (2), pp. 213–17.
Schenschin, Veronica (2008), *Venäläiset ja venäläinen kulttuuri Suomessa*, Helsinki: University of Helsinki.
Schneider, Edgar W. (2018), 'World Englishes', in Mark Aronoff (ed.), *Oxford Research Encyclopedia of Linguistics*, <https://doi.org/10.1093/acrefore/9780199384655.013.270> (last accessed 20 January 2021).
Schneider, Klaus P. and Anne Barron (eds) (2008), *Variational Pragmatics: A Focus on Regional Varieties in Pluricentric Languages*, Amsterdam: John Benjamins.
Serov, Boris (2012), 'Aleksei Shmelev: Chtoby podderzhivat' russkii iazyk za rubezhom, nuzhno stavit' realistichnye zadachi', Russkiy Mir, Informatsionnyi portal, 23 March, <https://russkiymir.ru/publications/88035/> (last accessed 20 January 2021).
Shevtsova, Anna A. (2017), 'Determining whether migrants who formerly resided in Russia are native speakers of the Russian language', *Rodnoy yazyk* 2 (7), pp. 45–53.
Simons, Gary F. and Charles D. Fennig (eds) (2018), *Ethnologue: Languages of the World*, 21st edn, Dallas, TX: SIL International, <https://www.ethnologue.com> (last accessed 20 January 2021).
Smagulova, Juldyz (2008), 'Language policies of Kazakhization and their influence on language attitudes and use', in Aneta Pavlenko (ed.), *Multilingualism in Post-Soviet Countries*, Bristol: Multilingual Matters, pp. 166–201.
Suleimenova, Eleonora D. (2013), 'O vozmozhnosti diversifikatsii russkogo iazyka v Kazakhstane', in Eleonora D. Suleimenova (ed.), *Kazakhstanskaia lingvistika na rubezhe vekov: docendo discimus*, Astana: Foliant, pp. 70–93.
Trudgill, Peter (2011), *Sociolinguistic Typology: Social Determinants of Linguistic Complexity*, Oxford: Oxford University Press.
Vaahtera, Jouni (2009), *Evoliutsiia sistemy glasnykh fonem v nekotorykh russkikh govorakh Vologodskoi oblasti*, Helsinki: University of Helsinki.
Varjonen, Sirkku, Aleksandr Zamiatin and Marina Rinas (2017), *Suomen venäjänkieliset: tässä ja nyt. Tilastot, tutkimukset, järjestökentän kartoitus*, Helsinki: Cultura-säätiö.
Verschik, Anna (2016), 'Mixed copying in blogs: Evidence from Estonian–Russian language contacts', *Journal of Language Contact* 9 (1), pp. 186–209.
Verschik, Anna (2017), 'Metalinguistic comments and multilingual awareness: Estonian–Russian language contacts in blogs', *Applied Linguistics Review*, <https://doi.org/10.1515/applirev-2017-0049> (last accessed 20 January 2021).
Viaut, Alain and Svetlana Moskvitcheva (eds) (2014), *Catégorisation des langues minoritaires en Russie et dans l'espace post-soviétiques*, Bordeaux-Pessac: Maison des sciences de l'homme d'Aquitaine.
Viimaranta, Hannes, Ekaterina Protassova and Arto Mustajoki (2017), 'Aspects of commodification of Russian in Finland', *Russian Journal of Linguistics* 21 (3), pp. 620–34.
Yelenevskaya, Maria (2015), 'An immigrant language in a multilingual state: Status competition', *Russian Journal of Communication* 7 (2), pp. 193–207.
Yelenevskaya, Maria and Larisa Fialkova (2009), 'The case of ex-Soviet scientists', in Eliezer Ben-Rafael and Yitzhak Sternberg, with Judit Bokser Liwerant and Yosef

Gorny (eds), *Transnationalism: Diasporas and the Advent of a New (Dis)order*, International Comparative Social Studies 19, Leiden/Boston: Brill, pp. 613–35.

Yelenevskaya, Maria and Larisa Fialkova (2017), 'Linguistic landscape and what it tells us about the integration of the Russian language into Israeli economy', *Russian Journal of Linguistics* 21 (3), pp. 557–86.

Yelenevskaya, Maria and Irina Ovchinnikova (2015), 'Russkoiazychnye assotsiatsii izrail'tian kak otrazhenie izmenenii v iazyke i kul'ture', *Voprosy psykholingvistiki* 2, pp. 226–41.

Yelenevskaya, Maria and Ekaterina Protassova (2015), 'Global Russian: Between decline and revitalization', *Russian Journal of Communication* 7 (2), pp. 139–49.

Zbenovich, Claudia (2016), 'Cross-cultural communication in Russian-speaking families in Israel: Language practices of the second generation', *Russian Journal of Linguistics* 3, pp. 103–16.

Zvezdina, Polina (2018), 'V RAN zaiavili o vozrosshei v dva raza za tri goda "utechke mozgov"', *RBK*, 31 March, <https://www.rbc.ru/society/29/03/2018/5abcc9f59a7947e576977387> (last accessed 20 January 2021).

CHAPTER 9

The Russian World in Perspective: Comparing Russian Culture and Language Promotion with British, German and French Practices

Christian Noack

INTRODUCTION

The emergence of new cultural diplomacy institutions in Russia has elicited substantial scholarly attention in the context of the public and academic debates about Russia's use of soft power. One of the central questions is whether the Russian Federation has indeed substantially modernised its arsenal of cultural diplomacy, or whether it merely fell back on tried and tested Soviet practices after a hiatus of more than a decade. Famously, Joseph Nye took part in the debate, criticising what he saw as the shortcomings of China's and Russia's approaches to soft power, namely the strong role of the state and the lack of engagement of civil society in Russia's and China's contemporary cultural diplomacy (Nye 2013).

Occasionally, the Russian institutions, the Russian World Foundation (Fond Russkii Mir) created in 2007, and the Federal Agency for the Commonwealth of Independent States Affairs, Compatriots Living Abroad, and International Humanitarian Cooperation (Rossotrudnichestvo), established in 2008, have been compared with Western or Chinese organisations dealing with foreign cultural policy (Wilson 2015; Pashaeva 2016). Following Patricia Goff's suggestions, such comparison should distinguish between 'the official cultural diplomacy framework policies' defined by governments and the 'cultural diplomacy efforts' aimed at their implementation. While the former are 'more enduring, more consistent over time and space' (and much better documented), the latter often appear to be 'contingent, ad hoc, the product of individual creativity' (Goff 2013: 13).

Given that the implementation of language promotion is central to this volume, a concluding comparative chapter on Russian and Western practices should obviously help to put the findings of case studies from the preceding chapters into a broader perspective without abandoning the focus on the language promotion practices. Owing to the geographical and thematical scope of these practices, such a task almost amounts to squaring the circle. For the following comparison, I have sought a compromise solution. First, I examine the institutional arrangements, the funding and the geographic spread of the institutions promoting language and culture. Second, I take a look at the discursive framing of language promotion, comparing the answers given on the websites of the Russian and Western institutes against the rhetorical question of why one should study the promoted language. On the one hand, I am interested in the degree to which the learning of the foreign language is couched in terms of cultural enrichment or utilitarian gains. On the other hand, I discuss whether or not the process of language learning is treated as a unidirectional process, or whether it is rather portrayed as a key element in a broader cultural exchange. In the third section, I consider the practical services that the institutions offer to language learners and teachers. My examination of this question focuses on offerings available through the central websites of the institutions, in particular the access to online teaching and learning materials. In the last part, I briefly review cognate activities, in fields such as teacher training or the support for language learning in the educational systems of the host states.

INSTITUTIONAL SET-UP

With the collapse of the USSR, much of the Soviet infrastructure of cultural diplomacy was disbanded. Some institutions continued to lead a shadowy existence on the margins of Russia's new governmental apparatus. One important example would be the former Union of Soviet Societies of Friendship and Cultural Relations with Foreign Countries, now called Centre for International Scientific and Cultural Cooperation. Initially attached to the Government of the Russian Federation, it was moved to the Foreign Ministry in 2002.

An institutional rebuilding began in earnest only during Putin's second term, 2004–8. The political context was shaped by Russia's economic recovery, the perception of Western encroachment upon Russia's self-defined zone of influence in the 'near abroad', and the rise of a political discourse about the fate of the Russian-speaking 'compatriots' outside the borders of the Russian Federation. At the same time, a process of 'indigenisation' of the concept of 'soft power' could be observed in political and academic discourses, demanding that Russia be provided with the means to 'wield its own soft power to balance and – where necessary – oppose the American effort' (Osipova 2016: 346–7).

When the Kremlin began to rebuild its cultural diplomacy arsenal, it did indeed partly fall back on reviving old Soviet institutions, but it also partly emulated international best practice in the field. Within a single year, the Russian Federation created two institutions that would become active in the field of external culture and language promotion. In June 2007, Putin signed a decree establishing a private foundation, Russkii Mir. In September 2008, interim president Medvedev authorised the creation of the Federal Agency for the Commonwealth of Independent States Affairs, Compatriots Living Abroad, and International Humanitarian Cooperation (Rossotrudnichestvo). Russkii Mir was conceived as a public charity, ostensibly styled according to Western models. Rossotrudnichestvo, by contrast, is a state agency under the control of the Foreign Ministry and sees itself as a direct successor to the earlier Soviet All-Union Society for Cultural Relations with Foreign Countries (VOKS), created in 1925 and remodelled into the above-mentioned Union of Soviet Societies of Friendship and Cultural Relations in 1958 (Gould-Davies 2003).

The mission statement of the Russkii Mir Foundation defines the promotion of language and culture as its core duty. Pointing to two of the three possible translations of the Russian word *mir* ('peace, 'world' and 'community'), the Foundation's website reiterates one of the basic principles of cultural diplomacy, namely the 'promotion of peace and understanding in the world by supporting, enhancing and encouraging the appreciation of Russian language, heritage and culture'. As to the teaching of the Russian language 'within Russia [!] and abroad', the target groups are defined as 'new learners of the language and [. . .] those who already know and love Russian and wish to recapture or maintain their fluency' (Russkii Mir 2020a).

Of course, the mission statement also refers to the third translation of *mir*, 'community', identified here with the 'Russian community abroad', which the Foundation wishes to 'reconnect' with its homeland, through 'cultural and social programs, exchanges and assistance in relocation'. The website also aims to explain the collocation 'Russian World', which is described as 'the largest diaspora population the world has ever known' and said to comprise not only ethnic Russians, but also 'millions of people who have chosen the Russian language as their subject of study, those who have developed an appreciation for Russia and its cultural heritage' (Russkii Mir 2020a). At this juncture, the Foundation refers to the political discourses on the 'Russian World' and 'compatriots living abroad', although it was Rossotrudnichestvo that had explicitly been commissioned to look after the latter group. As the state agency's long official name already suggests, the government assigned two other tasks to it that had been largely irrelevant in the Yeltsin years, but had risen in importance under Putin. These were, first, improving political relations with what remained of the Commonwealth of Independent States, and, second, managing Russia's re-emergence as a donor in international development policies.

As to the promotion of language and culture, there is indeed significant overlap in the duties allotted to the Russkii Mir Foundation and Rossotrudnichestvo. The state agency, too, defines 'preserving the cultural heritage, promoting the Russian culture and language and educational and scientific cooperation' as part of its tasks. Rossotrudnichestvo has taken over or reopened the former Soviet 'Centres of Science and Culture'. According to Rossotrudnichestvo's website, such centres currently operate in 62 states. Moreover, 24 representatives of the agency are attached to Russian Embassies in 21 other countries (Rossotrudnichestvo 2020a). The Russkii Mir Foundation, for its part, is supposed to promote Russian language and culture through 'Russian Centres' and smaller 'Russian Cabinets' created in collaboration with host institutions abroad, mostly universities and libraries. Many of the smaller cabinets in the West are also run by Russian expat organisations. The Russkii Mir website lists 102 centres and 106 cabinets, which indicates a slight decrease since 2018, when the annual report counted 112 centres (Russkii Mir 2019a: 20; 2020b).[1]

There is also no clear-cut division of tasks between the two institutions as far as language promotion is concerned. Rossotrudnichestvo has been commissioned to implement the successive federal target programmes titled 'The Russian Language' since 2008. The state agency also bears responsibility for the current 2016–20 cycle. In 2015, the programme's ambitious goals were set as 'improving the conditions for teaching, learning and promoting the Russian language, Russian culture and Russian-language schooling in other countries'. The programme aims at raising by a factor of ten the number of qualified language teachers and translators, the quality and quantity of available online materials, and finally the number of schools abroad receiving direct assistance from the Russian Federation. For the realisation of these ambitious aims, the government designated 7.6 billion roubles for five years, the equivalent of just under 100 million euro (Government of the Russian Federation 2015; see also the section on language promotion below). All of this suggests a conscious, albeit ambiguous division of activities in the field of language and culture promotion between a public charity and a state agency. The former is responsible for contact with, and the co-funding of, Russian language-related partner institutions abroad, while the latter engages in the promotion of language and culture through its own networks of branches attached to the Russian embassies. In 2007, the newly designated director of Russkii Mir, Viacheslav Nikonov, described the Foundation as having been created

> on the principle of state–private partnership. Some of the funds will come from the state, but I hope not the bulk of it. [. . .] There are far more limitations on the use of state funding [than with respect to private funding]; there are strict guidelines on where it may go or not go. In this specific area, which involves broad international network activities, it would of course be easier to operate with private funding. (Nikonov 2007)

In international comparison, the closest resemblance to this arrangement can be found in France. On the one hand, the promotion of French culture and language is carried out by the Alliances Françaises, a network of decentralised non-governmental organisations, often emerging as a result of local initiatives abroad and largely self-funded. On the other hand, the Instituts Français, state agencies attached to French embassies abroad and paid and staffed by the Ministry of Foreign Affairs, likewise engage in culture and language promotion. This is not to say that the system of the Alliances Françaises would have been totally independent of state influence since their creation in the 1880s. The initiators were celebrated French intellectuals of the time, acting against the backdrop of a broad public perception that French diplomatic and cultural influence was decreasing after the defeat at the hands of Prussia. Only late in the interwar period, in 1936, reacting to both National Socialist and Soviet propaganda, did the French Foreign Ministry create its first office for cultural diplomacy (Paschalidis 2009: 278–80).

The double structure of state-run Instituts Français and non-governmental Alliances Françaises expanded during the Cold War. The French government started to worry about the efficiency and the visibility of France's external cultural policies not long before the post-1989 era of 'cultural capitalism' (Paschalidis 2009) and has recently tried to realign the system. The largely independent Alliances were subordinated to the Fondation des Alliances Françaises, created in Paris in 2007. A little later, in 2010, the Instituts Français were subordinated under a new central agency by the same name, tasked to coordinate language and culture promotion between the Alliances, the Instituts and a couple of other state and public agencies. With this institutional rearrangement, the aims of culture and language promotion changed, too, as will be discussed in more detail below. Suffice to say here that, besides enhancing international 'recognition', French language and culture promotion was increasingly linked, as in other Western countries, to the aim of promoting the French higher education system and the country's cultural industries (Steinkamp 2009; Ahearne 2018). As of today, the hoped-for streamlining of French cultural diplomacy has not been fully realised. Attempts to merge the governmental and public institutions have made some progress, yet the fusion meets protracted resistance, in particular from the French and oversees Alliances (Guerrin 2018; Eschapasse 2019; Robert 2019; Institut Français 2019).

Returning to the new Russian structures, Rossotrudnichestvo, in its subordination to the Foreign Ministry and in its institutional integration into the system of Russian diplomatic representations abroad, is indeed reminiscent of the French Instituts. Unlike its French counterparts, the state agency neither directly supervises the Russkii Mir Foundation, nor possesses the degree of independence from the Russian Foreign Ministry that the French Instituts enjoy. Russkii Mir, for its part, seems to be modelled on 'para-public entities' (Goff 2013: 13), such as the British Council or the German Goethe-Institut. The Foundation is governed by a director and small management board, under the supervision of a board of trustees, which comprises academics and above all politicians, including the Minister of Foreign Affairs, some business people and a representative of the Russian Orthodox Church (Russkii Mir 2020c, 2020d). The British Council's leadership team is likewise controlled by a board of trustees, on which politicians, businessmen and cultural administrators are represented (British Council 2020a).

As a public association (*Verein*), the Goethe-Institut is led by a director and a smaller steering committee consisting of six members, either academics or business people. Both the British and the German institutions rely on the recommendations of several specialist advisory boards, which do not seem to exist for Russkii Mir. The Foundation's website lacks detailed information concerning its inner administration or its connections with the Ministry of Foreign Affairs. The British Council and the Goethe-Institut both provide on their websites the relevant statutes and further documentation regarding their working relationships with the governments and, in the British case, the parliament (British Council 2020b; Goethe-Institut 2020a). The British Foreign and Commonwealth Office delegates culture and language promotion to independent agencies, of which the British Council is only one, and one increasingly losing influence (Bell 2016: 76–7). Creating 'friendly knowledge and mutual understanding' and 'promoting British education and education cooperation', and finally selling courses in the English language as the key resource for this, the British Council is intended to support and complement 'diplomatic, commercial and development efforts' (quoted in Martens and Marshall 2003: 267).

In the German case, the collaboration has been formalised in a series of framework agreements (*Rahmenverträge*) between the government and the Goethe-Institut, the last of which was concluded in 2004. Although the German Foreign Ministry is responsible for regulating foreign cultural policies, it delegates this task to a public association (Goethe-Institut 2020b). The Goethe-Institut's website describes the 'promotion of German language', 'international cultural cooperation' and 'intercultural dialogue' as its main tasks, but also hopes to 'create a comprehensive image of Germany' (Goethe-Institut 2020c).

FINANCIAL ENDOWMENT

While the British and the German institutions make considerable efforts to display their 'arm's-length' distance from the state, there is less determination noticeable in the case of Russkii Mir. It is very difficult, for example, to find information about the Foundation's budgets and the share of public funding in them. The Foundation invites donations, but does not record them on the website. All 'partners' listed on the website are state institutions (Russkii Mir 2020e). To be sure, Russkii Mir, in contrast to Rossotrudnichestvo, publishes annual reports on its websites, as do all Western institutions discussed in this chapter. However, Russkii Mir's annual reports do not contain information on funding either (Russkii Mir 2019a). There are only scattered references to the amount of money available to the Foundation. According to newspaper articles, the budget allocated to the Russkii Mir Foundation by the Ministry of Education and Science of the Russian Federation amounted to 500 million roubles in 2013 and just 427.5 million roubles in 2015, worth 11 million euro in 2013 and only 5.7 million euro in 2015 (Wilson 2015: 1192; Mkhoyan 2017: 693). Rossotrudnichestvo's budgets are also undisclosed. Several sources indicate that it stood at 2.5 or 2.19 billion roubles in 2013 (roughly 60 and 52 million euro, respectively). It should have more than trebled until 2020, but due to Russia's economic troubles in the 2010s it has likely been decreasing since, as have the budgets of foreign language media outlets (Osipova 2016: 351–2; Wilson 2015: 1192).

All of this is small change when compared with the funding of the

Western institutions. Their annual budgets keep growing, albeit not exclusively through state funding. Taking 2015 as a point of comparison, the Goethe-Institut received 236.6 million euro from the Ministry of Foreign Affairs. The British Council had a total income of 864.3 million pounds (or roughly 1 billion euro) for the 2013–14 academic year. The Alliances Françaises collected 1.59 million euro from the French Ministry of Foreign Affairs in 2014; their own income for the same year amounted to 203 million euro (Mkhoyan 2017: 693). By 2017–18, for which we have no data for the Russian institutions, the British Council had a budget of 1.3 billion euro, the Goethe-Institut 366 million euro, the Alliances Françaises 212 million euro and the Institut Français 33 million euro. State share in funding amounted to 89% for the Institut Français, 65% for the Goethe-Institut, 14.3% for the British Council and merely 4% for the Alliances Françaises. In turn, this means that the branches of the British Council earned a staggering 800 million euro (or 60%) of their funds by selling services such as language courses and exams. Moreover, the British Council received another 335 million euro (or 25.7%) in donations. The Alliances Françaises earned 195 million euro, and donations amounted to 8.5 million euro (4%). For the Goethe-Institut, the figures are 90 million euro of generated income (24%) and 12 million euro in donations (3%). The lion's share of income generated by the British, German and French institutions themselves comes from the sale of language instruction and certification of language skills (British Council 2019: 80–130; Goethe-Institut 2018: 126–28; Fondation des Alliances Françaises 2018a: 90–101; 2018b; Institut Français 2019: 88–9).

That there is a growing market for courses and certificates even in languages other than English has dawned on Russian experts and politicians as well (Medvedev 2012), yet we have no data and little evidence that Russkii Mir and Rossotrudnichestvo are aiming to capitalise on this. This lack of initiative seems even more puzzling as British and French external culture and language promotion is explicitly seeking to prepare the ground for expanding the commercial scope of the culture industries. As far as we can deduce from the media use of Russian speakers abroad, this would represent a significant opportunity for Russia as well, which remains largely untapped as of yet (see Chapters 3 and 5 in this volume).

GEOGRAPHY

The relatively modest funds clearly restrict the scope of activities of the Russian institutions in geographic terms, too. Judging by the numbers reported on the websites and in Russkii Mir's annual reports, both organisations managed to create an impressive network of Centres and Cabinets within a decade. This has certainly been easier for Rossotrudnichestvo, due to its larger budgets and its institutional integration with the Russian diplomatic representations abroad. In many cases, Centres for Science and Culture were still existing or were recreated by the cultural divisions of the embassies. The state agency lists 85 branches abroad on its website, of which more than 70 are attached to the embassies in capital cities. The only country hosting several branches across the country is India, with 5 representations. States such as Poland, Egypt, the USA and Brazil count 2 branches each. In terms of geographic spread, the largest number of Russian Centres for Science and Culture operate in Europe and Asia (28 each), followed by 16 in the post-Soviet space, including Russia. Notably, there are no representations in the Baltic States. Rossotrudnichestvo is comparatively underrepresented in Africa and the two Americas, with just 20 branches in total, which also sheds light on the priorities of Russia's development aid (Wilson 2015: 1184–5).

Although comparatively underfinanced, Russkii Mir, too, managed to set up a quite impressive network of Centres and Cabinets. The website lists 100 Centres and 114 Cabinets in 2020 (Russkii Mir 2020f, 2020g). The degree to which these institutions depend on Russian subsidies is unclear, however. In the case of Centres at Western universities, Russkii Mir largely contributes by sending books or language teachers or sponsoring guest lectures; the brunt of the costs is borne by the local host institutions, who as a rule were dealing with Russia prior to Russkii Mir's engagement (Oostra 2019: 25–6). Cabinets are by definition relatively small 'corners', bookshelves stacked with literature and media in the Russian language, donated by the Foundation. The scope of activities of Centres in and outside the former Soviet space also seems to be fairly limited, when compared with the offerings of the Western institutions (see Chapters 1–3 in this volume). Russkii Mir's news section on its website and in its annual reports presents a mix of public lectures, short-term training, summer schools, workshops and commemorative events. The number of taught language courses was about 250 in total in 2018 (Russkii Mir 2019a: 21–30).

The geographical focus of Russkii Mir's activities clearly lies in Europe, which counts 48 Centres and 44 Cabinets, followed by the post-Soviet space with 24 Centres and 25 Cabinets. It is worth mentioning that, unlike Rossotrudnichestvo, Russkii Mir is cooperating with host organisations in Lithuania and Estonia (1 Centre and 2 Cabinets each). Besides universities, the partners are schools and associations of the Russian-speaking minorities. In the case of Moldova (4 Centres and 12

Cabinets), many representations work in internationally non-recognised Transnistria. In Europe, particularly high numbers of branches can be found in Slavic-speaking countries such as Bulgaria (5 Centres and 9 Cabinets). With 21 Centres and 25 Cabinets, Asia is another area of focus; here the brunt of representations can be found in former communist allies such as Mongolia or Vietnam. Interestingly, there are no Russkii Mir representations in India, perhaps due to the strong presence of Rossotrudnichestvo. Again, Africa and the two Americas are clearly underrepresented, with just 7 Centres (none in Africa) and 19 Cabinets. Oceania is a complete blind spot for both Rossotrudnichestvo and Russkii Mir (Russkii Mir 2020f, 2020g; Rossotrudnichestvo 2020c).

The professed programmatic focus of the Russian institutions on the 'near abroad' is thus not explicitly mirrored by the geography of branches. There are several possible explanations for this. First, the number of existing branches does not necessarily reflect the scope and intensity of activity in a given country. Second, a number of representations have been closed down in Ukraine since 2014, with only a few remaining in the self-declared People's Republics of Donetsk and Luhansk. Third, the quest for mutual recognition and the principle of reciprocity (Ahearne 2018: 696–7) seems to have channelled quite a few resources to Europe, where there is not only a large number of independent states that have been running their own cultural institutes since 1989 (Paschalidis 2009: 284), but also a growing proportion of Russian-speaking minorities, organising themselves in expat associations and seeking collaboration predominantly with Russkii Mir. That said, a closer look at the geography of Centres and Cabinets in the former Soviet space shows that Russia's culture and language promotion through Russkii Mir and Rossotrudnichestvo rarely ventures beyond the larger cities and the areas densely settled by ethnic Russians, that is, areas populated by those Russophones that Moscow considers to be 'compatriots'.

In comparison with the European institutions, Russia's selective geographical focus does not particularly stand out, except for in its focus on the Russian-speaking diaspora. All of the British, German and French cultural institutions run between one-quarter and one-third of their branches in Europe. In relative terms, the geographical spread of the British Council's and the Goethe-Institut's offices is quite similar. The former runs 48 branches in Europe and another 11 in the post-Soviet space, out of 176 in total. The latter has 151 branch offices in total, of which 55 are located in Europe, and likewise 11 in the post-Soviet space. Due to its colonial past, Britain is better represented in Asia (66 against 42 German branches) and Africa (34 and 21, respectively). The Americas and Oceania play a lesser role, with 17 British Council and 22 Goethe-

Institut branches. The state-run French institutes display a similar global distribution (Europe 77, post-Soviet space 9, Asia 53), except for their strong presence in Africa (61 branches), which corresponds to the declared ambitions of the French to develop *francophonie* above all in this demographically fast-growing world region. Only the network of the Alliances Françaises shows a significantly diverging picture, being more evenly spread across the world regions. Of 832 branches, more than 200 Alliances are based in Europe, some 30 in the post-Soviet space, around 70 in Asia, 39 in Oceania, 110 in Africa, 112 in North America and an astounding 181 in Latin America. This suggests that the bottom-up principle underlying the development of the Alliances and their relative independence from state funding created a network which reflects demand *sur place* much more than the state-run or largely state-financed networks, which seem to reflect political imperatives and geo-strategic considerations to a much larger degree (British Council 2020c; Goethe-Institut 2020d; Institut Français 2020a; Fondation des Alliances Françaises 2018a).

FRAMING LANGUAGE PROMOTION

Language promotion and, through the tool of language, the facilitation of cultural exchange, has formed the backbone of cultural diplomacy since its 'invention' in the age of nationalism. According to the rationale of cultural diplomacy, good relations between societies or states are rooted in mutual understanding and recognition. As a rule, cultures and languages are fundamental and distinctive for different societies, hence language and education represent the most significant entry points into another culture. Culture and education can thus draw people closer together and accentuate commonalities or facilitate mutual recognition, even if cultures seem poles apart or even strongly adversarial (Goff 2013: 2–3; Ahearne 2018: 696–7). The promotion of language and culture is thus central to the work all of the institutions described here, and represents the main point of comparison in this chapter. It is, however, applied in different forms and practised in various combinations with other activities, which can only be summarily described and contrasted in this section.

In a narrow sense, language promotion comprises the teaching of the language, the issuing of language certificates, and the provision of teaching and reading materials in the target language. With the exception of language test certificates, the Russian and all other institutions discussed here engage in these activities. The only broadly recognised

Russian test, TORFL/TRKI, is the intellectual property of Herzen University. It can only be taken at larger Russian universities, or at selected contracted partner institutions abroad, but not in Russkii Mir's or Rossotrudnichestvo's branches (Russia.study 2020). Beyond direct language tuition, institutions active in the field of cultural diplomacy usually aim at improving the teaching of their respective language abroad, either through teacher training or by supporting teaching in the education system of the host country through the provision of didactic material and textbooks. In both cases, the physical representation of the institutes in the host countries has an important role to play, providing classrooms and libraries for students from the host countries. Some organisations offer temporary placements for language instructors and teaching assistants, too. Again, most of these resources are offered by both the Russian institutions and their Western European equivalents.

Further related services are in connection with the preparation and admission of foreign students to the higher education systems of Britain, Germany and France, including the provision of study grants. As Chapter 7 in this book extensively discusses Russian activities in that field, it is sufficient to say here that the institutes under discussion fulfil different roles, very often in cooperation with other state-run agencies that bear the principal responsibility for foreign student recruitment. The British Council, for example, actively seeks to recruit international students for British higher education institutions. Since 2016, the British Council has also been the main organiser of the global 'Study UK' campaign that promotes the UK as the first-choice study destination for international students.[2] The UK's universities are primarily targeting 'growth markets' in Asia, in states such as China, India, Indonesia, Malaysia, Thailand and Turkey (British Council 2020i; Cai 2019: 56).

In the French and German cases, the language promotion institutions are not directly charged with foreign student recruitment. The French Instituts and Alliances and the German Goethe-Institut clearly conceive of their language teaching as an important channel for attracting foreign students to France and Germany, though, and closely collaborate with the bodies in charge, Campus France and the German Academic Exchange Service. In particular, France has seen a 'major concerted legislative and budgetary endeavour over the last fifteen years to merge grandes écoles, universities and other higher education institutes' to make its 'complex, idiosyncratic and fragmented' higher education system more attractive to foreigners. As in the Russian case, the use of English as a language of tuition, which was actually legally banned before 2013, is making only slow inroads (Ahearne 2018: 705).

WHY STUDY RUSSIAN, ENGLISH, GERMAN OR FRENCH?

All institutions discussed here assume that learning the language they represent is attractive per se, as it provides the gateway to a different culture. The international reputation of one's language is frequently emphasised, sometimes more strongly than the practical advantages that command of that language offers. As a rule, the target audience is conceived as 'non-native speakers', for whom specifically designed teaching and learning methods and materials are suggested. Native speakers abroad, that is, diaspora groups and expats, are targeted only by the Russian institutions. During the interwar period, the Goethe-Institut's institutional forerunner, the Akademie zur Wissenschaftlichen Erforschung und Pflege des Deutschtums or, for short, the Deutsche Akademie, created in 1925, was also very active in this field. After the Second World War, this politically tainted task was taken over by another private association, the Verein für Deutsche Kulturbeziehungen im Ausland, which was dissolved only as late as 2019 (Michels 2005).

The connections between Britain and France and their former colonies, in which English and French are still used as second languages, falls somewhere between these poles. Relationships between the former metropolises and the colonies are recast in less one-sided ways than in the Russian case, even though French language promotion targets francophone countries in particular with the aim of buttressing the international importance of the French language.

Russkii Mir and Rossotrudnichestvo emphasise the aim of promoting the Russian language outside the Russian Federations, referring both to its significance as part of a shared cultural 'world heritage', and, as already mentioned, to Russia's responsibility for the ethnic Russians or Russian-speaking diaspora. Russkii Mir refers on its website to reconnecting 'the Russian community abroad to its homeland, forging new and stronger links through cultural and social programmes, exchanges and assistance in relocation' (Russkii Mir 2020a), with the latter actually being a task assigned to Rossotrudnichestvo. The state agency's website, in turn, delivers a large amount of statistical data relating to the Russian language's position as a world language – from being the sixth most spoken language in the world after English, Chinese, Hindi, Spanish and Arabic, to functioning as the second most frequently used language on the Internet. In terms of numbers, Rossotrudnichestvo claims that some 273 million people in the world speak Russian, 146 million of them living in the Russian Federation and no fewer than 127 million outside its borders (Rossotrudnichestvo 2020b). These numbers seem fairly accurate: other sources quote 260 million Russian speakers as of 2010, some 50 million fewer than in 1990 (Aref'ev and Sheregi 2014: 19).

In the quest for international recognition, both websites link the transnational 'value' of the Russian language to its role as the carrier of Russian high culture in general and Russian classical literature in particular. Russkii Mir features five lines from Anna Akhmatova's patriotic poem *Muzhestvo* ('Courage'), evoking the 'great Russian word' as the mediator of Russianness between generations (Russkii Mir 2020a). Rossotrudnichestvo's website is more detailed on the accomplishments of Russian literature, listing many Russian authors as well as composers of classical music, artists and filmmakers in the past and present (Rossotrudnichestvo 2020d). Against this backdrop, learning the Russian language either appears as an inherited, patriotic duty, or is motivated by the desire to gain access to one of the world's most acclaimed high cultures. There is comparatively little space on either website devoted to pragmatic motives for acquiring Russian. Russkii Mir refers to its historic function as a lingua franca in Eurasia (Russkii Mir 2020a). Rossotrudnichestvo, by contrast, notes its status as one of the United Nation's working languages and lists post-Soviet states in which it still functions as an official language or a language of instruction in the educational system. The state agency also concedes that 'many people learn [the] Russian language with a practical goal to study and work in Russia' and that Russian-speaking people 'can communicate with Russian business partners or work in a Russian company abroad' (Rossotrudnichestvo 2020b).

Of course, neither references to the global status of the language promoted nor to its function as the carrier of a commonly recognised high culture are absent from the online presences of the Western institutions. As a rule, however, they are mitigated with references to diversity and dialogue between cultures. With English as the dominant world language, the British Council's self-presentation does not dwell extensively on possible reasons for partners or clients to study English. It is simply said to 'unlock a whole new world of opportunities'. This motive is taken up again when parents across the globe are advised to give their child 'the gift of the world's most widely spoken language' by booking courses for children at a British Council branch (British Council 2020d). The British Council, too, underlines the role of language acquisition in cultural diplomacy, claiming to contribute to the creation of 'friendly knowledge and understanding between the people of the UK and other countries' (British Council 2020e).

The German and French institutions, by contrast, have developed different strategies for 'selling' their language to their respective audiences. 'We promote knowledge of the German language abroad', states the Goethe-Institut's website, 'and foster international cultural cooperation. We convey a comprehensive image of Germany by providing information about cultural, social and political life in our nation' (Goethe-Institut 2020e). Among 'ten reasons to learn German', the Goethe-Institut's website lists at least six that are more or less career-oriented. They include learning the language of your German business partner, the possibility of a global career with German under one's belt, employment in tourist industries catering for German travellers, and career opportunities in science, research or communication in Germany (Goethe-Institut 2020f).

Not entirely voluntarily, French language promotion has possibly undergone the most significant changes in recent years, in terms of both structure and philosophy. The Institut Français, in its new role as the body responsible for the coordination of French external cultural politics, promotes 'French and plurilingualism', accepting the predominance of English and attempting to carve out a niche for the French language. In its 2019 annual report, the Institut Français presented this new rationale under the header 'et en plus, je parle français':

> The Institut Français aims to promote, in an offensive and innovative manner, a renewed image of the French language [. . .] To achieve this objective and break with the traditional image of the French language, glamorous and romantic, the new campaign [. . .] conveys the idea of French as the language of employment, innovation, digital technology, the business world and *Francophonie*. This campaign also highlights the multilingualism and the complementarity of the French language compared with English. (Institut Français 2019: 36)

In other words, the future of global French is seen as being one of several languages learned and used in parallel, in particular in francophone Africa. Quickly growing populations in that continent will soon represent the largest share of French speakers worldwide. As in the case of the fusion of the Alliances with the Institute, this is clearly a political vision, imposed top down by the centralised French administration. It remains to be seen whether the decentralised system of Alliances will smoothly accept the top-down redefinition of their tasks. After all, a perceived need *sur place* and local initiatives have been at the roots of many of the hundreds of Alliances worldwide.

TEACHING AND LEARNING SUPPORT

What can teachers and learners of Russian actually expect from the new Russian institutions? And how does this relate to the established practices of their British, German and French peers? Conventionally, the language promotion institutes organised and continue to organise language courses in their representations across the globe. So do Russkii Mir and Rossotrudnichesvo with their Centres and Cabinets. As discussed above, their networks are, however, much less extensive and are geographically concentrated in Europe, the former Soviet space and some former communist allies in Asia. According to their web presentations, both agencies target non-native speakers across the globe, as well as heritage speakers and their children in the near abroad. There are only occasional hints in the news section of Russkii Mir's website, however, that the focus on these heritage speakers and learners has informed new didactic approaches (Russkii Mir 2010, 2019b). In general, Russian is taught with established methods developed either for a 'foreign language audience' or for native speakers in Russia (Oostra 2019: 26-7).

Beyond that, there is little generic information about specific offerings for adults, adolescents or children. Language learners are referred to the individual offerings at the nearest branches in their countries. The Foundation's Centres and Cabinets at foreign partner institutions, as well as the state agency's Russian Centres for Science and Culture, offer Russian-language library and database resources, although not for remote access. Language courses on the spot are open to individuals and groups, and tailored to different age groups, to schoolchildren, students or to professionals. Language learners will find specific courses preparing them for language exams, too (Russkii Mir 2020h). Information about prices for the language courses or examinations are absent from the central websites.

By comparison with their Western European peers, both institutions have very little to say about teacher training, although this is also listed as one of the fields of activity. In its 'education' section, however, Russkii Mir advertises the 'Russkii Mir professor program' offering placements for Russian-language instructors in educational institutions abroad. Possibly the grants can also be used for the training of foreign teachers in Russia (Russkii Mir 2020i). Rossotrudnichestvo features no dedicated section for teacher training on its own websites. Courses for Russian teachers in the 'near' and 'far abroad' are regularly mentioned in the news section, however. Such courses are organised by Russian pedagogical universities and held in the Russian Centres for Science and Culture.

As a rule, they last a few days and the number of participants is fairly small (Rossotrudnichestvo 2019a, 2019b).

According to the 2015 presidential decree regarding Russian schools abroad, accessible on its website, Rossotrudnichestvo develops and implements a policy of supporting Russian language schools abroad together with the Ministry of Foreign Affairs and the Ministry of Science and Higher Education of the Russian Federation (Rossotrudnichestvo 2020e). The document suggests both direct support and the provision of online study materials for schools registering with Rossotrudnichestvo. It neither sets geographical or quantitative aims, nor contains any reference to the financial sums involved (Kremlin 2015). Due to the lack of annual reports, there is very little evidence about the implementation process; again, only occasional reports in the news section of Rossotrudnichestvo's website provide scattered evidence for the type of schools involved and the concrete support schools have received. Such information is also lacking on the Internet portal 'Sistema podderzhki russkikh shkol' ('Support System for Russian Schools').[3] Instead, this website offers links to the databases of commercial enterprises selling Russian teaching material and textbooks, such as LitRes.[4]

Given the fact that both Russian institutions are building or rebuilding a network, the lack of online resources for people living beyond the scope of the Centres, which are usually located in capital cities or urban agglomerations, is perhaps most surprising. Russkii Mir offers a few links, for example to Russian-language child-friendly websites and to a list of 100 literary works canonical for Russian schoolchildren (Russkii Mir 2020j). The link to an 'online beginner's class for the study of Russian as a foreign language, including two basic courses with supplemental language learning materials', did not work when access was attempted repeatedly in the spring of 2020. If the Foundation's writing and translation grants have helped to produce new textbooks, there is neither explicit reference to them, nor links to publishers where they could be purchased. The publication of bilingual books for the children of expats is occasionally announced in the news section, however (Russkii Mir 2020k). Rossotrudnichestvo, in a 2014 report on its activities during the federal target programme for the Russian language since 2008, claimed to have sponsored the development of 53 textbooks on literature and culture, 44 manuals on grammar and 17 textbooks designed specifically for the children of compatriots (Oostra 2019: 33). Although the agency is responsible for the current successor programme, there is no detailed information about the deliverables on its website.

This is in stark contrast to the broad array of services offered by the websites of the British Council, the Goethe-Institut, and the Alliances

Françaises and Institut Français. Every single one of them offers much more detail on different target groups, using the European language self-assessment grid (CEFR) system to indicate the level of language knowledge required or attained in a certain course. Obviously, a lot of teaching and learning is still organised physically in the branches of these institutions across the globe, and the website offers search engines for finding the best offerings in the local area. With the exception of the Goethe-Institut, no detailed information on tuition fees for courses and exams is provided, obviously due to extreme differences between regions. The websites leave the visitor in no doubt, however, that most of these services are commercial. All these institutions also offer paid online courses, again tailored to different audiences and age groups (British Council 2020f; Goethe-Institut 2020g; Fondation des Alliances Françaises 2018a; Institut Français 2019).

The websites recommend selected, commercially produced textbooks, with links to the publishers or traders where these can be acquired. Beyond that, all institutions provide online teaching aids and materials for free. Often these are collections of published or literary materials with thematic focuses, accompanied by didactic suggestions. Beyond introductions to the politics, culture and society of Britain, Germany or France, such collections often focus on the practice of intercultural contacts and learning (British Council 2020g; Goethe-Institut 2020h).

Like their Russian counterparts, the British Council and the French Instituts are also supposed to support the teaching of English and French respectively in their host countries. The Goethe-Institut, by contrast, is not directly involved in improving language teaching in the schools of the host countries. This task is assigned to another federal state body, the Zentralstelle für das Auslandsschulwesen.

The British Council does not just look after the quality of teaching of English abroad, but also in the UK itself. With a view to increasing future student exchange or intake, it is supporting some countries in improving the level of English teaching on a bilateral basis, promoting, for example, the study of English in China and the study of Mandarin in Britain.[5] In response to the global use of English, the British Council has also teamed up with commercial companies such as Microsoft to improve the quality and use of IT in education, for example in Africa (Cai 2019: 48). As for France, the Institut Français offers grants for innovative projects in the teaching of the French language abroad, of which 37 were funded with some 280,000 euro in 2019. Beyond that, in 2018 the French Foreign Ministry commissioned the Institut with the implementation of the project 'IFclasse – le français de l'enseignement', aimed at improving the French skills of teachers working primarily in French-speaking

Africa. Finally, the Institut is realising the ambitious project of creating a global professional network for French teachers, 'IFprofs'. Launched in 2018 with the aim of pooling pedagogical and methodological resources at a global level, it encourages teachers to exchange best practice among themselves and provides the Institut with a large pool of potential clients for its own teacher training. Already by 2019, IFprofs counted no fewer than 31,000 members from 76 countries (Institut Français 2019: 37–8).

ON- AND OFFLINE LIBRARY SERVICES

Media repositories and libraries are established instruments in culture promotion abroad, and Russkii Mir's Centres and Cabinets could be said to be built around physical libraries, providing 'access to a broad range of learning materials and popular science information from Russia'. They offer, first, fictional and non-fictional literature, textbooks, reference books and dictionaries and a selection of books for children. Second, they stock classic Soviet and contemporary Russian films, audiobooks, plays and multimedia (language) learning programmes. Finally, they offer online access to Russian databases. The use of all these materials requires physical attendance (Russkii Mir 2020g, 2020h).

Such libraries are less important for the usually better equipped Centres of Science and Culture, which comprise exhibition spaces, conference halls, theatres and cinemas, and so on. There is no generic description of the Centres on Rossotrudnichestvo's website. To find out about the cultural and linguistic offerings, the websites of the local branches must be referred to, whose addresses are listed on the central website (Rossotrudnichestvo 2020f). A cursory browse through a couple of these websites suggests that, likewise, many of the activities taking place at Rossotrudnichestvo's branches require physical attendance. Neither Rossotrudnichestvo nor Russkii Mir seem to engage directly in the creation of online libraries and media centres.

To be sure, the system of Western cultural promotion also anticipates physical attendance for its language courses, as described above, and offers physical library space with comparable materials and aims. The Goethe-Institut alone runs 96 libraries with some 800,000 titles (Goethe-Institut 2020i). In times of tighter budgets, such physical libraries have become financial liabilities, however, and that may be one of the reasons that the well-entrenched institutions are far ahead of their newly founded Russian peers in terms of online services. The British Council's online library offers a large collection of fictional and non-fictional e-books and periodicals; however, full access requires membership (British Council

2020h). The Goethe-Institut, for its part, offers a broad range of German-language e-books, periodicals and visual media, in total 19,000 items, for free in its media centre, 'Onleihe' (Goethe-Institut 2020j). The French 'Culturethèque' is perhaps the most ambitious of the online media centre projects. It offers access to 190,000 electronic documents. According to its website, Culturethèque has more than 250,000 users in 110 different countries. Access is free of charge for people registered with the Institut Français or Alliances Françaises (Culturethèque 2020). By comparison, the Russian institutions merely provide links to online libraries outside their jurisdiction.

CONCLUSION

A new chapter in Russia's cultural diplomacy, or old wine in new bottles? In terms of the institutional set-up, the Russkii Mir Foundation is clearly emulating established international models of public corporations taking over foreign cultural policy tasks, as seen in the British Council and the German Goethe-Institut. At the same time, in terms of tasks assigned and financial endowment, Russkii Mir is clearly dwarfed by the state agency Rossotrudnichestvo. For the state agency, however, while the promotion of language and culture is important, it is not its only task. Perhaps this imbalance between public corporation and state agency is indeed a sign of a deep-seated distrust of public participation in Russian politics. In international comparison it is not unique, though. Centralised France also has a long history of exploiting state agencies and public associations in parallel when it comes to promoting language and culture. At the same time, the French example illustrates the problems of coordination and international visibility that this approach entails. With the latter ranking high among the aims of Russia's foreign cultural policy, the future of the arrangement remains to be seen.

As far as the practice of promoting culture and language is concerned, the comparison highlighted four substantial differences between the work of the Western agencies and their Russian counterparts. First, a lack of transparency as far as funding and the reporting of activities are concerned. Russkii Mir as a public charity publishes annual reports, and both the Foundation and Rossotrudnichestvo run a broad and multilingual web presence. Nonetheless, judging the scope, seriousness and efficiency of their work in international comparison is difficult due to the selectivity and narrowness of the information.

Second, and closely related, the Russian institutions conceive of the promotion of language and culture as a largely unidirectional undertaking. Their presentation of Russian language and culture in an international environment is mainly geared at convincing others of the status and value of Russian language and culture. By comparison with their Western peers, both institutions provide fairly little room for dialogue or exchange, not to mention integration into a multicultural environment. The question of ownership and of the acceptance of different rules and standards strongly sets the Russian practice apart from those of the other countries discussed in this chapter. It is precisely a multifaceted and pluralistic understanding of culture which is lacking in Russia's language and culture promotion. Russian culture is understood in an essentialist way, and there seems to be a widely shared consensus among Russia's political and cultural elites that a unified and 'indivisible' Russian culture and language should lie at the basis of the Federation's cultural diplomacy, which is thus subordinated to domestic priorities stemming from the unfinished process of nation building (Ryazanova-Clarke 2017: 446, 450).

Third, the actual methods of language promotion follow established routines, both in terms of how language and learning are conceived, and in terms of a very slow inclusion of online or hybrid learning formats. While this requires further, case study-based research on the work of Russian Centres on the spot, in general both the content and availability of online resources lag substantially behind those of the Western agencies. This may be partly due to the lack of funding. At the same time, Russkii Mir's annual reports, the case studies in the other chapters of this volume, and policy documents and speeches by Russian leaders suggest a continuing reliance on an 'old-school' understanding of the task and on the quantitative rather than qualitative measurement of the Russian institutions' efficiency (Medvedev 2012).

Fourth, and perhaps most important, none of the Western agencies targets expats and diaspora groups. Both Russia's and China's institutions do, and that is an important explanation for their rather conservative approach to multiculturality and plurilingualism. The promotion of language and culture is, in the Chinese and Russian cases, aimed at reintegrating large collectives beyond the borders of the states. Both projects rely on language and culture conceived as unitary and state-controlled.

That said, taking a historical look at the emergence and development of language and culture promotion of the European powers helps to put Nye's ideas about soft power into perspective. Nye developed his concept by discussing the correlations between different types of power in what would be called the 'American century', that is, from a position of political, economic and military strength. European powers, by contrast, reverted to cultural diplomacy when they perceived a loss of strength and prestige in times of real or perceived crisis. The French reacted to their defeat in the war against Prussia in 1870–1. The Germans built up an aggressive 'defence' of German cultural and linguistic influence in Eastern Europe after their territorial losses in the wake of the First World War. The British, finally, embarked on cultural diplomacy in the 1930s to counter German and Soviet influences in Europe and the Near East. The geopolitical and security arguments that they used at the time are not too far a cry from current Russian discourses on applying soft power with the aim of stabilising Russia's cultural and linguistic dominance in the former Soviet space.

NOTES

1. All translations from Russian, French and German language sources in this chapter by the author, Christian Noack.
2. <https://study-uk.britishcouncil.org/> (last accessed 29 June 2020).
3. <https://russchools.org> (last accessed 29 June 2020).
4. <https://rs.litres.ru/> (last accessed 29 June 2020).
5. See <https://www.britishcouncil.org/education/schools/support-for-languages> (last accessed 29 June 2020).

REFERENCES

Ahearne, Jeremy (2018), 'International recognition regimes and the projection of France', *International Journal of Cultural Policy* 24 (6), pp. 696–709.
Aref'ev, Aleksandr Leonardovich and Frants Edmundovich Sheregi (2014), *Inostrannye studenty v Rossiiskikh vuzakh*, Moscow: Ministry of Education and Science of the Russian Federation, Centre for Sociological Research, <http://www.socioprognoz.ru/files/File/2014/full.pdf> (last accessed 20 May 2020).
Bell, Emma (2016), 'Soft power and corporate imperialism: Maintaining British influence', *Race & Class* 57 (4), pp. 75–86.
British Council (2019), 'Annual report and accounts 2018–19', <https://www.britishcouncil.org/about-us/how-we-work/corporate-reports/annual-report-2018-19> (last accessed 20 May 2020).
British Council (2020a), 'Board of Trustees', <https://www.britishcouncil.org/about-us/how-we-are-run/board-trustees> (last accessed 15 December 2019).
British Council (2020b), 'How we work', <https://www.britishcouncil.org/about-us/how-we-work> (last accessed 15 December 2019).
British Council (2020c), 'Contact your local British Council office', <https://www.britishcouncil.org/contact/local-office> (last accessed 29 May 2020).
British Council (2020d), 'Learn English', <https://www.britishcouncil.org/english> (last accessed 20 February 2020).
British Council (2020e), 'About us', <https://britishcouncil.org/about-us> (last accessed 20 February 2020).

British Council (2020f), 'Learn English online', <https://www.britishcouncil.org/english/learn-online> (last accessed 20 February 2020).
British Council (2020g), 'Find classroom resources', <https://www.britishcouncil.org/school-resources/find> (last accessed 20 May 2020).
British Council (2020h), 'Search through our digital library collection', <https://library.britishcouncil.org/> (last accessed 20 May 2020).
British Council (2020i), 'Study UK', <https://www.britishcouncil.org/education/ihe/what-we-do/study-uk-campaign> (last accessed 20 May 2020).
Cai, Liexu (2019), 'A comparative study of the Confucius Institute in the United Kingdom and the British Council in China', *Citizenship, Social and Economics Education* 18 (1), pp. 44–63.
Culturethèque (2020), 'Institut Français: Culturethèque', <https://www.culturetheque.com/EXPLOITATION/NLD/culturetheque.aspx> (last accessed 29 May 2020).
Eschapasse, Baudouin (2019), 'Révolution culturelle à l'Alliance Française', *Le Point International*, 6 February, <https://www.lepoint.fr/monde/revolution-culturelle-a-l-alliance-francaise-06-02-2019-2291862_24.php#> (last accessed 19 May 2020).
Fondation des Alliances Françaises (2018a), 'Rapport d'activité 2018', <https://www.google.com/url?sa=t&rct=j&q=&esrc=s&source=web&cd=&cad=rja&uact=8&ved=2ahUKEwjnoPnR9OrpAhUR26QKHbW8CcMQFjABegQIAhAB&url=https%3A%2F%2Fwww.fondation-alliancefr.org%2F%3Fcat%3D1066&usg=AOvVaw3a2TQvIW8JP9JVVNN7X_Vs> (last accessed 20 May 2020).
Fondation des Alliances Françaises (2018b), 'Les Alliances dans le monde. Affiche', <https://www.fondation-alliancefr.org/wp-content/medias/DATA2018/HautPage-Affiche-2018.pdf> (last accessed 29 May 2020).
Goethe-Institut (2018), 'Jahrbuch 2017/18', <https://www.google.com/url?sa=t&rct=j&q=&esrc=s&source=web&cd=&ved=2ahUKEwib3on-8-rpAhWLLewKHR55D-JwQFjAAegQIBhAB&url=http%3A%2F%2Fwww.goethe.de%2Fresources%2Ffiles%2Fpdf180%2Fgi_jahrbuch_17_18_web_doppelseiten1.pdf&usg=AOvVaw1a_fC9zJY65jxdNkGQ0PRF> (last accessed 20 May 2020).
Goethe-Institut (2020a), 'Vereinssatzung', <http://www.goethe.de/resources/files/pdf166/vereinssatzung-de.pdf> (last accessed 15 December 2019).
Goethe-Institut (2020b), 'Basic agreement', <http://www.goethe.de/resources/files/pdf165/rahmenvertrag_engl_300kt18.pdf> (last accessed 15 December 2019).
Goethe-Institut (2020c), 'Responsibilities', <https://www.goethe.de/en/uun/auf.html> (last accessed 15 December 2019).
Goethe-Institut (2020d), 'Standorte', <https://www.goethe.de/de/wwt.html> (last accessed 29 May 2020).
Goethe-Institut (2020e), 'Organisation', <https://www.goethe.de/en/uun/org.html> (last accessed 20 May 2020).
Goethe-Institut (2020f), 'Warum Deutsch lernen?', <https://www.goethe.de/en/spr/wdl.html> (last accessed 20 February 2020).
Goethe-Institut (2020g), 'Deutsch online', <https://www.goethe.de/de/spr/kup/kur/doln.html> (last accessed 20 February 2020).
Goethe-Institut (2020h), 'Konzepte und Materialien', <https://www.goethe.de/de/spr/unt/kum.html> (last accessed 20 May 2020).
Goethe Institut (2020i), 'Zukunft Bibliotheken', <https://www.goethe.de/de/kul/bib.html> (last accessed 20 May 2020).
Goethe Institut (2020j), 'Über 100 deutsche Filme online ansehen', <https://www.goethe.de/de/kul/bib/ser/fio.html> (last accessed 20 May 2020).

Goff, Patricia M. (2013), 'Cultural diplomacy', in Andrew F. Cooper, Jorge Heine and Ramesh Thakur (eds), *The Oxford Handbook of Modern Diplomacy*, Oxford Handbooks Online, <https://www.oxfordhandbooks.com/view/10.1093/oxfordhb/9780199588862.001.0001/oxfordhb-9780199588862-e-24> (last accessed 20 May 2020).

Gould-Davies, Nigel (2003), 'The logic of Soviet cultural diplomacy', *Diplomatic History* 27 (2), pp. 193–214.

Government of the Russian Federation (2015), 'The Russian Language Federal Targeted Programme for 2016–2020', 20 May, <http://government.ru/en/docs/18169/> (last accessed 20 May 2020).

Guerrin, Michel (2018), 'Francophonie ou cacophonie?', *Le Monde*, 26 January, <https://search.proquest.com/docview/1991106466?accountid=1725> (last accessed 19 May 2020).

Institut Français (2019), 'Rapport d'activités 2019', <https://www.if.institutfrancais.com/sites/default/files/medias/documents/if_ra_2019.pdf> (last accessed 20 May 2020).

Institut Français (2020a), 'La culture française dans le monde', <https://www.if.institutfrancais.com/fr/dans-le-monde/liste/lieux> (last accessed 29 May 2020).

Kremlin (2015), 'Kontseptsiia "Russkaia shkola za rubezhem"', <http://www.kremlin.ru/acts/news/50643> (last accessed 31 March 2020).

Martens, Kerstin and Sanen Marshall (2003), 'International organisations and foreign cultural policy: A comparative analysis of the British Council, the Alliance Française and the Goethe-Institute', *Transnational Associations* 4, pp. 261–72.

Medvedev, Dmitry (2012), 'President Dmitry Medvedev speaking at a meeting of the heads of foreign offices of the Federal Agency for the Commonwealth of Independent States, Compatriots Living Abroad, and International Cultural Cooperation (Rossotrudnichestvo)', Government of the Russian Federation, 3 September, <http://archive.government.ru/eng/stens/20531/> (last accessed 29 January 2018).

Michels, Eckard (2005), *Von der Deutschen Akademie zum Goethe-Institut: Sprach- und auswärtige Kulturpolitik 1923–1960*, Munich: Oldenbourg.

Mkhoyan, Anna (2017), 'Soft power, Russia and the former Soviet states: A case study of Russian language and education in Armenia', *International Journal of Cultural Policy* 23 (6), pp. 690–704.

Nikonov, Vyacheslav (2007), 'Delivering the Russian language to the world', *Moscow News* 2007 (32), 16 August, <https://web.archive.org/web/20091109085145/http://www.mnweekly.ru/national/20070816/55268005.html> (last accessed 30 January 2018).

Nye, Joseph (2013), 'What Russia and China don't get about soft power', <https://foreignpolicy.com/2013/04/29/what-china-and-russia-dont-get-about-soft-power/> (last accessed 20 February 2019).

Oostra, Sjoerd (2019), *A Russian World? On the Inner Workings of Russian Cultural-Linguistic Institutes and Their Effectiveness as Vehicles of Soft Power*, MA thesis, University of Amsterdam Graduate School of the Humanities.

Osipova, Yelena (2016), 'Indigenizing soft power in Russia', in Naren Chitty, Li Ji, Gary D. Rawnsley and Craig Hayden (eds), *The Routledge Handbook of Soft Power*, London: Routledge, pp. 346–57.

Paschalidis, Gregory (2009), 'Exporting national culture: Histories of cultural institutes abroad', *International Journal of Cultural Politics* 15 (3), pp. 275–89.

Pashaeva, Giulshan (2016), 'Mirovye iazyki kak sostavnaia chast' publichnoi diplomatii', SAM Kommentarii 16, Baku: Centr Strategicheskikh Issledovanii pri Prezidente Azerbajdzhanskoi Respubliki.

Robert, Martine (2019), 'Les grands chantiers de l'Institut Français', <https://www.lesechos.fr/industrie-services/services-conseils/les-grands-chantiers-de-linstitut-francais-960822> (last accessed 19 May 2020).

Rossotrudnichestvo (2019a), 'Povyshenie kvalifikatsii v Moskve i Sankt-Peterburge dlia rusistov iz Armenii', <http://www.rs.gov.ru/ru/news/51269> (last accessed 31 March 2020).

Rossotrudnichestvo (2019b), 'Kursy povysheniia kvalifikatsii dlia uchitelei-rusistov startovali v Rossiiskom kul'turno-informatsionnom tsentre v Sofii', <https://gov.ru/ru/news/58672> (last accessed 31 March 2020).

Rossotrudnichestvo (2020a), 'About Rossotrudnichestvo', <http://rs-gov.ru/en/about> (last accessed 2 April 2020).

Rossotrudnichestvo (2020b), 'Strengthening the position of the Russian language', <http://rs.gov.ru/en/activities/9> (last accessed 2 April 2020).

Rossotrudnichestvo (2020c), 'Contacts', <http://rs.gov.ru/en/contacts> (last accessed 22 May 2020).

Rossotrudnichestvo (2020d), 'Popularization of Russian culture in the world', <http://rs.gov.ru/en/activities/2> (last accessed 20 May 2020).

Rossotrudnichestvo (2020e), 'Education and science', <http://rs.gov.ru/en/activities/10> (last accessed 29 May 2020).

Rossotrudnichestvo (2020f), 'Predstavitel'stva v mire', <http://rs.gov.ru/ru/contacts/inworld> (last accessed 20 May 2020).

Russia.study (2020), 'Russian language certification', <https://russia.study/en/public-material/ru-lang-certification> (last accessed 20 May 2020)

Russkii Mir (2010), 'First Russian textbook for Russian-language children in Estonia', <https://russkiymir.ru/en/news/136013/> (last accessed 20 February 2020).

Russkii Mir (2019a), 'Otchet o deiatel'nosti fonda "Russkii Mir" v 2018 god', <https://russkiymir.ru/events/docs/Report_2018.pdf> (last accessed 20 May 2020).

Russkii Mir (2019b), 'Russian textbook for bilingual kids to be presented in UK', <https://russkiymir.ru/en/news/251400/> (last accessed 20 February 2020).

Russkii Mir (2020a), 'About Russkii Mir Foundation', <https://russkiymir.ru/en/fund/> (last accessed 2 April 2020).

Russkii Mir (2020b), 'Katalog Ves' Russkii Mir 2020', <https://russkiymir.ru/catalogue/catalog.php?country=-1&category=50&set_filter=%CF%EE%EA%E0%E7%E0%F2%FC> (last accessed 20 May 2020).

Russkii Mir (2020c), 'Management Board', <https://russkiymir.ru/en/fund/management-board.php> (last accessed 1 February 2020).

Russkii Mir (2020d), 'Board of Trustees', <https://russkiymir.ru/en/fund/board-of-trustees/> (last accessed 1 February 2020).

Russkii Mir (2020e), 'Partnery', <https://russkiymir.ru/fund/partners/> (last accessed 20 May 2020).

Russkii Mir (2020f), 'Katalog russkikh tsentrov', <https://russkiymir.ru/rucenter/catalogue.php> (last accessed 22 May 2020).

Russkii Mir (2020g), 'Chto takoe kabinet?', <https://russkiymir.ru/rucenter/cabinet.php> (last accessed 22 May 2020).

Russkii Mir (2020h), 'Russian Center – definition and mission', <https://russkiymir.ru/en/rucenter/what-is.php> (last accessed 20 May 2020).

Russkii Mir (2020i), 'Education', <https://ruskiymir.ru/en/education/> (last accessed 20 May 2020).
Russkii Mir (2020j), 'Biblioteka knig i multimediinyi izdanii', <https://russkiymir.ru/education2/library/> (last accessed 31 March 2020).
Russkii Mir (2020k), 'Uchebniki dlia detei-bilingvov, a takzhe ikh roditelei', <https://russkiymir.ru/publications/273229/?sphrase_id=1018719> (last accessed 20 April 2020).
Ryazanova-Clarke, Lara (2017), 'From commodification to weaponization: The Russian language as "pride" and "profit" in Russia's transnational discourses', *International Journal of Bilingual Education and Bilingualism* 20 (4), pp. 443–56.
Steinkamp, Volker (2009), *Die auswärtige Kulturpolitik als Instrument der französischen Außenpolitik*, Berlin: DGAPAnalyse Frankreich 5.
Wilson, Jeanne L. (2015), 'Soft power: A comparison of discourse and practice in Russia and China', *Europe-Asia Studies* 67 (8), pp. 1171–202.

Index

Abkhazia, 21, 38, 141, 165
Academy of Sciences (Belarus), 60
Academy of Sciences (Russia), 189, 192
AfD see Alternative für Deutschland
Africa, 106, 223–5, 229, 232–3
Aleksei II (Patriarch of Moscow), 28–9
All-Union Society for Cultural Relations with Foreign Countries, 217
Alma-Ata *see* Almaty
Almaty, 70, 71, 73, 76, 80, 81, 84–5, 86–7
Alternative für Deutschland (AfD), 120–1, 131–2, 133, 135
Arabic *see* Arabic language
Arabic language, 205, 206, 227
Armenia, 111, 141
Asia, 84, 165, 169, 223–5, 226, 230
  Central, 12, 68, 71–2, 80–7, 194, 203
Astana, 82, 85
Azerbaijan, 99, 141, 165

Baltic countries *see* Baltic states
Baltic region *see* Baltic states
Baltic states, 13, 27, 85, 93, 109, 111, 112, 123, 194, 203, 205, 223
Belarus, 1, 6, 7, 9, 11, 12, 45–67, 93, 111, 144, 163, 165–6, 175, 176–7, 178–9, 183, 194, 203
  language, 45–63
  (national) identity, 12, 53, 60, 62–3
  nationalism, 49, 55, 57
Belarusians, 12, 45–67, 68
  students, 179, 183

Belarusian Language Society (Tavarystva Belaruskai Movy, TBM), 46, 50, 56
Belarusian National Front (Belaruski Narodny Front, BNF), 46, 57
Belarusian-Russian mixed speech (BRMS), 12, 52–3, 62–3
Belgium, 171
Berlin, 120, 121, 125, 132
biculturalism, 207
bilingualism, 8, 12, 25, 83, 88–9n.5, 113, 204, 207
  asymmetric, 7–9
  balanced, 8, 201
  Belarus, 47, 55
  Central Asia, 71
  Kazakhstan, 75
  official, 21, 25
  Ukraine, 25–6
borrowings, 196–9, 202, 207, 209
Bourdieu, Pierre, 19–20
Brest, 48
British Council, 220–1, 222, 224, 225, 226, 228, 231–3, 234
British Foreign and Commonwealth Office, 220
Bulgaria, 165, 194, 195, 224

calques, 199, 202, 207, 209
censuses
  Belarus, 51–2, 62
  Ireland, 93
  Kazakhstan, 72–3
  Soviet, 25, 45

Central Baltic Programme, 199, 201, 203, 209n.6
Centre for International Scientific and Cultural Cooperation (Russia), 216–17
children
  Belarus, 47, 62
  books, 233
  English language courses, 228
  Kazakhstan, 74, 76
  of heritage speakers in the near abroad, 230–1
  of Russian speakers outside the Russian Federation, 98, 100, 122, 129–30, 191, 193–4, 199–207
  Russia, 231
China, 4, 79, 83–4, 165, 171, 174–5, 193, 215, 226, 232, 235
Chinese *see* Chinese language
Chinese language, 84, 99, 117n.8, 194, 227, 232
Chisinau, 141, 149
CIS, 1, 3, 5–6, 22, 25, 48, 83, 86, 121, 165–6, 169, 171–3, 188, 194, 208, 215, 217, 218
citizenship, 9–10, 99, 114
  Azerbaijani, 99
  Belarusian, 53, 58
  dual, 204, 205
  Finnish, 204
  German, 122
  Russian, 9, 24, 190, 206
civilization, 4, 6, 23, 29, 122, 208; *see also* Russian World
  Orthodox, 38
  polyethnic, 2, 190
  Russian, 31, 38
  Soviet, 71
codes, 12, 21, 59, 85, 94
code-mixing, 197–8
code-switching, 99, 199, 202
Cold War, 219
colloquialisms, 201, 203
colonialism, 224
colonisation, 70–1, 208
colour revolutions, 3, 5, 23, 27–8, 39
Commonwealth of Independent States *see* CIS
communication, 7, 74, 75, 78, 82, 83, 93, 97, 112, 122, 127, 149, 155, 168, 189, 191, 192, 197, 200, 205, 229

channels, 149
everyday, 36, 88n.2, 203
formal/informal, 207
global, 156
horizontal, 143
intercultural, 76, 195
interethnic, 25, 46, 77, 141, 146, 149, 190, 196
international, 20, 98, 151, 172, 206
mass, 143
means of, 28, 58, 78, 81, 126, 139, 142
medial, 3
one-way, 143, 156
online, 125, 143
oral, 13, 63
platforms, 144
technologies *see* communication: means of
theory, 147
tools *see* communication: means of
within the family, 89n.20, 124, 202, 206
communities
  bilingual, 198
  diasporic, 104, 207
  ethnic, 94–6, 101, 106, 190, 193, 196, 203, 205
  imagined, 12
compatriots, 1, 2, 6, 9–15, 24–5, 35, 39, 48, 56, 62, 69–71, 83, 87, 93, 165, 168, 172, 189, 215–18, 224, 231
Concept of the State Support and Promotion of the Russian Language Abroad (2015), 162, 172
conflicts, 19, 23, 33–4, 37–8, 45, 49, 57, 59, 98, 138, 142, 155; *see also* Ukrainian crisis
Confucius Institutes, 84, 174, 215, 235
Coordinating Council of Russian Compatriots, 48, 93
cosmopolitanism, 60, 130
Council of Ministers, Russia, 24
creole, 207
Crimea, 6, 23, 26–7, 30, 32–3, 48, 57, 59, 62, 166
Cuba, 165
cultural diplomacy, 1–2, 3, 4, 14, 215, 216–17, 219, 202, 225–6, 228, 234–6; *see also* public diplomacy, soft power

culture, 1, 2, 5, 6, 8, 15, 19, 20, 24, 26, 35, 46, 54, 56, 81, 84, 98, 105, 113, 115, 129, 134–5, 142, 174, 188, 191, 207, 216–17, 225, 227, 233, 234, 235
  Belarusian, 46, 50, 53–4
  dialogue between, 228
  global, 72, 84
  high, 15–16, 60, 71, 228
  industries, 222
  Irish, 98
  Kazakh, 88, 195
  pluralistic understanding of, 235
  popular, 16, 141
  Russian, 1–3, 4, 7, 8–10, 13–16, 19, 26–7, 30, 35, 38, 48, 53, 56, 69–71, 78, 80–3, 86, 88, 98, 101, 116, 181, 187, 189, 190–1, 193, 200–2, 204, 206, 208, 215, 217, 219, 224, 231, 235
  Russophone, 82
  Soviet, 26–7
  Ukrainian, 38
  Western promotion of, 15, 219–22
Culturethèque, 234
Customs Union, 3
Cyprus, 194
Cyrillic script, 88n.4, 102, 140, 196
Czech Republic, 171, 194

Delegation of the European Union to the Republic of Moldova (EURM), 145–50, 153–5
de-Russification, 140
Development of the Export Potential of the Russian System of Education Project, 162, 164, 167, 170, 183–4
dialects, 12, 139, 208
diaspora, 9, 95, 97, 104, 106–7, 113, 115, 143, 189, 217, 227, 235
  'beached', 9, 16
  Chinese, 105
  Russian (speaking), 95, 103–4, 106, 112, 116, 122, 124, 142, 151, 189, 224, 227
  scattered, 144
diversity, 5, 6, 95, 101, 114, 144, 149, 156, 182, 208, 228
Dnipro, 32, 36–7
Dodon, Igor, 139, 145–6, 152

domains (of language use), 46, 59, 80, 191, 193, 201
Donbas, 26, 32, 33, 34, 38, 48, 57, 59, 62
Donetsk, 25, 26, 27, 30, 32, 35, 224
Dublin, 96–7, 102
Duma Committee for Education (Russia), 179

education, 5, 6, 25, 50, 72, 80, 121, 122, 132, 151, 176, 181, 188, 189, 191, 193, 194, 196, 203, 208, 216, 225–6, 228, 230, 232
  Belarusian higher, 46, 50
  Belarusian system of, 47, 50, 54, 59, 69
  bilingual, 199, 202, 204
  British, 221, 226
  complementary institutions of, 193, 205
  diplomacy, 161, 169, 182
  distant, 168, 178
  English language, 173–4
  fairs, 170–1
  Finnish system of, 204
  French system of higher, 220, 226
  global market, 161–3
  higher, 103, 126, 148, 162, 173, 183
  Indian initiatives in Central Asia, 83–4
  internationalisation of, 14, 161, 166, 168–9, 182–3
  Irish system of, 117n.8
  Kazakh higher, 86
  Kazakh system of, 72, 74, 88–9n.5, 178
  multilingual, 200
  promotion of abroad, 141, 148–9, 161–84, 218
  reform in Moldova, 145
  Russian higher, 14, 164–5, 170
  Russian language outside Russia, 74, 80, 87, 202
  Russian system of, 14, 15, 16, 76, 87, 177, 188, 193
  secondary, 34, 72, 74
  tuition-free, 168–9, 170, 176, 177, 178
Egypt, 171, 223
Embassy of the Russian Federation to Moldova (ERFRM), 145–8, 150–4
emigration, 93, 121–2, 193, 194
empire, 6, 49, 63, 71, 111
English *see* English language

English language, 14, 56, 182, 191 194, 208, 222, 227, 232
   as a medium for teaching, 162, 168, 183, 226
   Belarus, 176
   Estonia, 198–9
   Finland, 200
   Germany, 127
   global, 207–8, 228–9
   Ireland, 93–4, 98–9, 102–3
   Israel, 206
   Kazakhstan, 72, 75–6, 79, 82, 178, 195
   Latvia, 200
   Moldova, 141, 144, 148–50, 155–6
   Russian higher education, 162, 170–1, 173–4
   world *see* English language: global
entertainment, 13, 50, 125–6, 204–5
Esperanto, 199
Estonia, 111, 196, 198–9, 203, 223
Estonian language, 196–200
ethnicity, 6, 24, 71, 115–16, 192, 208; *see also* ethnic communities
   Belarusian, 51–2
   Estonian, 198
   Finnish, 202
   German, 123
   Jewish, 123
   Kazakh, 74, 80, 87, 195
   Kyrgyz, 80
   non-Russian, 8, 74, 83
   'Old Russian', 55
   Russian, 8, 12, 35, 51–3, 62, 70–1, 73, 81, 83, 85, 101, 103, 140, 200, 271, 224, 227
   Russo-Irish, 116
   titular, 69–71, 73, 75
   Uzbek, 80
EU *see* European Union
Eurasia, 2, 113
Eurasian Economic Union, 3, 5, 7, 68, 73, 176
eurasianism, 1
European Union, 7, 13, 108, 116, 123, 126, 134, 138–9, 140, 144–5, 147–9, 151–2, 154–6, 161, 165–6, 181
expats, 227, 231, 235

Facebook, 145–9, 151–6
Family, 78, 81, 88n.5, 96–7, 101, 105, 123–4, 163, 179, 181, 190–1, 202, 206
   bilingual, 199, 202
   histories, 108
'far abroad', 11, 13, 15, 187, 195, 230
Federal Agency for the Commonwealth of Independent States Affairs, Compatriots Living Abroad, and International Humanitarian Cooperation see Rossotrudnichestvo
Federal Ministry of the Interior (Germany), 132–3
Federal Target Programme 'The Russian Language' (Russia), 218, 231
Fond Russkii Mir see Russian World Foundation
former Soviet Space, 2, 3, 5, 13, 15, 16, 39, 179, 180, 193–4, 205, 223, 224, 230, 236
France, 166, 174, 219, 226, 227, 232, 234
French *see* French language
French language, 56, 170, 174, 206, 220, 227, 229, 232
Fursenko, Andrei, 173

geopolitics, 1–2, 6, 73, 84, 87, 98, 142, 236
Georgia, 3, 4, 85, 93, 111, 141
Germany, 1, 4, 13, 16, 120–36, 163, 165–6, 174, 175–6, 180–2, 183, 184, 221, 226, 229, 232
globalisation, 6, 75, 84, 209
Greece, 171, 194
Gromyko, Aleksei, 21, 23

Hebrew *see* Hebrew Language
Hebrew Language, 204–7
heritage, 5, 7, 8, 48, 60, 82, 95, 97–8, 101, 105, 203, 217–18, 227
   language, 98, 100, 114, 192, 206
   speakers, 194, 200, 203, 207, 230
Homel, 48
Horlivka, 35
human rights, 5, 51, 128–30, 134, 181
Hungary, 171

identity, 4, 7, 26–7, 39, 50, 69, 81, 99, 105, 108–9, 113, 115–16, 144, 184, 187, 197, 209

INDEX 245

Belarusian, 12, 45, 48
  collective, 11, 107–8, 115
  diasporic, 116, 193,
  ethnic, 53, 81, 94, 99, 139; *see also* ethnicity
  hybrid, 109, 207
  language preference and, 10–11, 13, 15, 16, 33, 51, 61–3, 98, 101–2, 108, 112, 115–16, 191, 202
  Moldovan, 139
  multiple, 207
  national, 13, 45, 53, 61–3, 94, 99, 189
  Russian, 19, 70, 140
  Ukrainian, 26, 28, 39
imposition, 20, 188
India, 82, 83, 111, 165, 171, 223, 224, 226
Indonesia, 171, 226
insertion, 201, 202
integration, 4, 5, 7, 71, 97, 98, 105, 121, 123–4, 129–31, 139, 152, 220, 223, 235
  Belarusian-Russian, 49
  EU, 140, 145
  European, 151, 155–6
  of the former Soviet space, 1, 3, 7, 76, 85
internationalisation, 14, 167
  of education, 14, 161, 169, 182, 183
internet, 35, 50, 76, 84, 85, 127, 133–4, 142, 143, 190, 196, 198, 204–5, 207
  Russian (language), 50, 144, 227, 231
Irish Gaelic, 98–100
Israel, 14, 16, 116
  Russian language in, 204–7

Jews, 13, 106
  Germany, 16
  Soviet, 122

Kazakh *see* Kazakh language
Kazakh language, 12, 69–74, 76–81, 83, 88, 88n.2, 88n.4, 88n.5, 176, 178, 195–6
Kazakhstan, 1, 7, 11, 12, 21, 22, 122–3, 129–30, 163, 165–6, 171, 183–4
  perception of Russian higher education, 175–8
  Russian language, 68–88, 195–6
Kazakhstanis, 12, 80–2, 84, 86–8, 171, 176–7, 183, 195
Kharkiv, 29, 30, 32

Kherson, 26, 32
Kievan Rus', 28, 29, 55, 208
Kirill (Patriarch of Moscow), 22, 23, 29, 33–3
Kivalov-Kolesnichenko law (Ukraine), 30, 33; *see also* language: law
Kremlin, 4, 15, 28, 33, 39, 112, 217
Kryvyi Rih, 32
Kyiv, 28, 29, 32, 33, 35, 38, 141
Kyrgyzstan, 21, 71, 77, 80, 82–3, 87, 123, 165

language
  bilingual proficiency, 205
  certificates, 222, 225
  contacts, 195
  exams, 222, 230, 232
  law, 73, 190; *see also* Kivalov-Kolesnichenko law
  minority, 8–9, 148–9
  monocentric, 61, 188
  of tuition, 25, 174, 182–3, 226
  preference, 10, 47, 123, 124
  regional, 30
  rights, 30
  titular, 8, 14, 52, 69, 71–2, 76, 109, 114, 140
Latin alphabet *see* Latin script
Latin America, 225
Latin script, 88n.4, 140, 196
Latvia, 21, 101, 103, 107–13, 166
  Russian language, 200–2
Latvian *see* Latvian language
Latvian language, 93, 200–2
Lavrov, Sergey, 4, 170
lexicon, 24, 60, 207
libraries, 76, 84–5, 96–7, 202, 218, 226, 233–4
lingua franca, 1, 7, 8, 72, 98, 140, 144, 155, 166, 187, 196, 205, 207–8, 228
Lithuania, 93, 107–8, 110–12, 141, 176, 179, 223
loanwords, 198, 199, 206, 208
Luhansk, 26, 27, 30, 32, 35, 224
Lukashenka, Aliaksandr, 11, 12, 45, 47, 48–9, 50, 54, 56, 57–9, 61, 62

Mahilu, 48
Maidan, 12, 27, 34, 39

Mandarin *see* Chinese language
media, 3, 13, 50, 72, 86, 143, 146, 150, 152, 154, 156, 165, 167, 189, 199, 206, 221, 222, 232, 234; *see also* communication: means of, social media
   consumption of Russian speakers in Germany, 120–35
   digital, 50, 144, 187, 205
   electronic *see* media: digital
   mass, 60, 141, 147, 194, 200, 202
   Russian (language), 1, 13, 16, 31, 49, 57, 61, 86, 120, 124–6, 127–8, 133–5, 141, 146, 223
Medvedev, Dmitry, 25, 29, 168, 217
migration, 9, 80, 83, 87, 121, 125, 131, 133, 162
Ministry of Education and Science of the Russian Federation, 167, 170, 221, 231
Ministry of Europe and Foreign Affairs (France), 219, 222
Ministry of Foreign Affairs of the Russian Federation, 22, 35, 145, 170, 219, 231
minorities, 12, 30, 46, 58, 69, 74, 126, 130, 131, 135
   historical, 203
   national, 30, 62
   rights, 30, 144
   (ethnic) Russian, 11, 12, 14, 69
   Russian-speaking, 85, 223–4
Moldova, (Republic of), 1, 13, 21, 22, 85, 93, 100, 138–56, 171, 205–6, 223
Moldovan *see* Moldovan language
Moldovan language, 98, 100, 103, 113, 138, 154, 155
Mongolia, 165, 171, 224
Montenegro, 194
Moscow, 8, 12, 16, 24, 26, 28, 29, 31, 38, 48, 63, 104, 108, 110–11, 141, 150, 152, 164, 166, 170, 176–7, 179, 180, 189, 224
multilingualism, 7, 8, 52, 92, 97, 187, 191, 196, 201, 204, 207, 229, 234
Muslims, 128, 135
Mykolaiiv, 25, 26, 32

Nationality, 209n.1; *see also* ethnicity
Nazarbaev, Nursultan, 69, 70, 73, 88n.3, 195

'near abroad', 2, 10, 14–16, 27, 168, 216, 224, 230; *see also* former Soviet space
Nikonov, Vyacheslav, 20, 34, 179, 219
nostalgia, 30, 204
Nye, Joseph, 2, 15, 142–3, 215, 235

Oceania, 224, 225
Odesa, 26, 30, 32
Orange revolution *see* colour revolutions
origins
   ethnic, 28, 88, 121–2, 202
Orthodoxy, 6, 7, 12, 29, 38, 93; *see also* Russian Orthodox Church
OSCE High Commissioner on National Minorities, 30, 33

Petropavlovsk, 70
pidgins, 207–8
pluricentrism, 14, 63, 69, 187, 191, 192, 195, 207
Poland, 108, 123, 179, 223
Polish *see* Polish language
Polish language, 99
polyethnicity, 8, 69
Post-Soviet space, 19–22, 73, 85, 123, 139–42, 144, 151, 161–2, 165, 174, 182, 194, 223–5; *see also* former Soviet space
Programme for the Promotion of the Russian Language and Education in Russia, 172
public diplomacy, 1, 4, 13, 139–40, 142–3, 145, 149, 153, 156, 161, 174; *see also* cultural diplomacy, soft power
Putin, Vladimir, 4, 6, 7, 20, 21, 24, 25, 29, 33, 35, 95, 125, 132, 152, 190, 217, 218

rankings, 164, 169–70
regiolects, 188
Rivne, 32
Rogozin, Dmitry, 193
Romania, 171
Romanian *see* Romanian language
Romanian language, 100, 139, 146, 147–5
Rose revolution *see* colour revolutions
Rossotrudnichestvo, 1, 14–5, 22, 24, 47–9, 62, 165, 170–4, 215, 217–18, 220, 221–4, 227–8, 230, 233–4

Russia, 1–4, 6–13, 16, 19–24, 27, 29, 32–5, 38–9, 47–51, 56, 58–61, 70, 72–3, 76, 80, 81–7, 93, 95, 100–1, 103, 104–5, 107, 108, 110, 112–13, 116, 121–3, 125–6, 128, 129–30, 135, 138–42, 144–5, 147, 151–2, 155, 161, 165–6, 168–71, 173–84, 188, 189, 190, 192–3, 194, 195–6, 198, 200, 203, 205, 206, 208, 215, 217, 222–3, 228, 230, 233
  Imperial, 4, 8, 70, 80, 208
  Post-Soviet, 8, 111
Russian *see* Russian language
Russian Centres for Science and Culture, 31–2, 35, 48, 170, 173, 180, 184, 223, 231, 233
Russian Federation *see* Russia
Russian language, 1–3, 7–16, 19, 21–3, 25–6, 30, 31–2, 35–8, 45–8, 52–3, 63, 69–71, 73–5, 80, 81, 87, 88, 95, 98, 100–3, 113, 114, 116, 127, 133, 175, 179, 181, 182–3, 187–8, 190–1, 192, 195, 199, 208, 217, 219, 228, 230
  Belarus, 45–63
  colonial role of, 56
  diasporic, 14, 187–8, 192–6, 205
  Finland, 202–4
  Germany, 120–35
  global, 95, 144, 192, 208
  Ireland, 92–116
  Israel, 204–7
  Kazakhstan, 48–68
  Kyrgyzstan, 82–3
  Latvia, 200–2
  media, 1, 13, 16, 30, 50, 57, 86, 93, 120–1, 124–8, 130, 131, 141, 146, 150, 152, 223, 231
  promotion of, 1, 3, 11, 15, 20, 31, 36, 48, 86, 161–3, 171–4, 180, 183, 218, 227
  Soviet Union, 7, 8, 61, 140, 156, 166
  status of, 8, 15, 30, 37–9, 48, 52, 54, 55–61, 63, 68–9, 72, 75–80, 82, 139–42, 144–5, 149, 155, 162–3, 171–3, 175, 189, 194, 195, 206–7, 235
  teachers, 16, 194, 201–3, 230
  teaching, 172–4, 176–7, 182, 191, 199, 202, 204, 206, 208, 217; 231

  Ukraine, 19–39
  varieties of, 189, 192, 195, 200, 202–3, 209
  world *see* Russian language: global
Russian Orthodox Church, 22, 29, 220; *see also* Orthodoxy
Russian speakers, 2, 9–10, 13, 15–16, 22, 30, 33, 62, 69, 80, 92–116, 120–135, 139, 140–1, 149, 154–5, 169, 171, 173–4, 175, 180–1, 183, 187, 190, 192, 193–203, 206, 222, 228; *see also* Russoglots
Russian World (concept), 2, 4, 11–12, 14–15, 16n.1, 19–24, 27–31, 34–5, 37–9, 49, 57–8, 69, 83–4, 95, 115, 139, 173, 217
Russian World Foundation, 1, 14–5, 16n.1, 21, 24, 29, 30, 31–7, 47–50, 62, 82, 85, 95, 172, 215, 217–24, 227–8, 230–1, 233–4
Russianness, 10, 26, 30, 71, 82, 95, 116, 228
Russification, 8, 24, 36, 70–1, 104, 140; *see also* de-Russification
russkii mir *see Russian world*
Russoglots, 13, 82, 83, 79, 94, 100, 101, 102, 103, 105, 109, 113, 189, 205, 224; *see also* Russian speakers
Russophobia, 37, 49
Russophones *see* Russoglots

St Petersburg, 63, 164, 179, 180, 190, 197
schools, 25, 32, 54, 188, 191
  Belarus, 46, 50, 60
  bilingual, 199, 202
  Germany, 182
  Israel, 205
  Kazakhstan, 74–5, 79, 88n.5
  Russian abroad, 173
  Russian-Finish, 202, 204
separatism
  Donbas, 27, 33, 35, 48, 57
  Georgia, 141
  Moldova, 138; *see also* Transnistria
Sevastopol, 32, 33
Simferopol, 32
Slovenia, 171, 194
social media, 13, 93, 139, 143–7, 150, 152–3, 193, 195; *see also* media

soft power, 1–7, 11, 14–5, 39, 84, 86, 88, 89n.19, 142–3, 151, 155–6, 173, 174, 183, 208, 215, 217, 235–6; *see also* cultural diplomacy, public diplomacy
South Ossetia, 21, 38, 141, 165
Soviet Union, 4, 6, 8–10, 13, 15, 19, 25–6, 45, 46, 60, 72, 86, 105, 109–11, 116, 120, 122–3, 126, 133, 138, 140, 151, 155, 164–5, 166, 188, 190, 208
  disintegration of, 7, 19, 45–6, 53–4, 60, 61, 69, 72, 105, 108, 122, 140, 164, 188, 194, 196, 216
Spanish *see* Spanish language
Spanish language, 170, 227
speech
  children, 199
  colloquial, 60
  community, 94, 99
  dialectal, 60
  hybrid, 99, 198–9, 201, 206
  multilingual, 201
  Sovietisms, 203
  vernacular, 97, 198
Sri Lanka, 171
Standardization, 61, 63, 94–5, 188–9, 208, 235
State Duma, 9, 24
Sukhumi, 141
Syria, 165

Tajikistan, 141, 165
Tatars, 33, 104, 188
Tatarstan, 8
teacher training, 15, 216, 226, 230, 233
teaching material, 192, 231
textbooks, 60, 76, 188, 192, 195, 209, 226, 231–3
Tishkov, Valerii, 20–1
Transnistria, 38, 138–9, 141–2, 151, 224
Trasianka *see* Belarusian-Russian mixed speech
Trump, Donald, 125
Trusau, Aleh, 50, 56–7

Tskhinvali, 141
tuition fees, 162, 168, 176, 178, 181, 183, 232
Turkey, 123, 171, 226
Turkmenistan, 141, 165
Twitter, 145

UK *see* United Kingdom
Ukraine, 1, 4, 6, 9, 10, 11–12, 15, 16, 19–39, 48, 49, 57, 60, 62, 65, 93, 106, 110–11, 123, 130, 138, 141, 142, 144, 165, 194, 203, 205–6, 224
Ukrainian *see* Ukrainian language
Ukrainian conflict *see* Ukrainian Crisis
Ukrainian crisis, 12, 22, 49, 57, 73
Ukrainian language, 12, 25–6, 28, 30, 34, 36–8, 60
Ukrainians, 11, 23, 49–50, 55, 58, 68, 106–7, 113, 196
UN *see* United Nations
Union of Soviet Societies of Friendship and Cultural Relations with Foreign Countries, 216
United Kingdom, 4, 112, 226, 228, 232
United Nations, 76, 228
United States (of America), 2, 4, 83, 128, 142, 147, 163, 164, 166, 171, 193, 206, 223
US(A) *see* United States
USSR *see* Soviet Union
Uzbekistan, 77, 80, 141, 165, 171
Uzbeks, 196

Vietnam, 165, 171, 224
Vinnytsia, 35–6
vk *see* VKontakte
VKontakte, 125, 145

Yanukovich, Viktor, 29, 32, 33, 37, 49
'Year of the Russian Language' 2007, 20
Yeltsin, Boris, 9, 23–4, 218
YouTube, 147, 152
Yushchenko, Viktor, 28–9

Zaporizhzhia, 26, 30, 32

EU representative:
Easy Access System Europe
Mustamäe tee 50, 10621 Tallinn, Estonia
Gpsr.requests@easproject.com